A HUNDRED YEARS OF SOCIOLOGY

A HUNDRED YEARS OF SOCIOLOGY

by

G. DUNCAN MITCHELL
Professor of Sociology, University of Exeter

GERALD DUCKWORTH & CO LTD
3 Henrietta Street, London, W.C.2

First published 1968

SBN 7156 0403 1

PRINTED IN GREAT BRITAIN BY
WESTERN PRINTING SERVICES LTD., BRISTOL

To

Margaret, Jeremy and Catherine

PREFACE

It is said of a Professor of Modern History, who retired not so very long ago, that his course of lectures ended at the sixteenth century. Some historians are more adventurous, even rash. This history might be considered a case of rashness. In self-defence, let me say that there does appear to be a demand for an historical treatment of sociology, and that if one is to write in a Hundred Years Series, then a history of sociology is not a bad thing to write about. Of course, one can trace the origins of the subject, like most other things, back to antiquity. Did not Aristotle make a comparative study of political constitutions? But the fact remains that most of what we call *sociology* is a recent phenomenon, dating largely from the work of Montesquieu, Saint-Simon and Comte, with inspiration from de Tocqueville and Marx. In short, it is a matter of about two hundred and twenty years of history i.e. since the publication of *De l'esprit des lois*. This particular history covers half this period, and the latter half at that; as such it is recent history, always the most difficult to write.

Within the limits set it has not been possible to describe and discuss the founding fathers of sociology. A marginal case is to be seen in the work of Karl Marx. His work, especially his early work which has had an impact recently on some younger sociologists, comes before the time when this history begins. His later work, especially *Capital* published in 1867, had a profound influence on Max Weber, but it is not a sociological treatise, nor strictly can Marx be said to be a sociologist. In any case there are several excellent expositions of his work and accordingly only brief mention is made of it here.

A history is necessarily highly selective and betrays, nay exposes clearly, the historian's prejudices; this history is no exception. The writer's intention has been to trace the various traditions informing the development of an academic discipline; some are very disparate. It may well be the case that the writer has imposed a coherence that is spurious. When considering some of the very recent developments of the subject, especially those in the U.S.A., one may well wonder if there is any connection between the present emphasis on quantified empirical operational research and the reflections of the first occupants of sociology chairs in that country. It may be too early to say what direction the subject will take, but a discipline which does not reflect on its past can easily become narrow, obsessive and trivial. The fundamental problems of sociology are not new. One of the author's prejudices is that too much attention in a history of sociology should not be given to very recent developments. It is difficult to focus on what is very close, and a subject when popular, as sociology is today, is apt to succumb to fashions; and fashions change. Accordingly, little is said about some matters of interest to contemporary sociologists, about the developments in the theory of symbolic interaction, for instance, or about the use of mathematical models in sociology. Indeed, there are many novel products of the contemporary sociologist's imagination some of which, doubtless, will appear in a future history of the subject. For the most part in this book only the most prominent and well known recent developments are mentioned and much that has occurred since the mid-1950s is ignored.

Little has been said about the application of sociology, about criminology for instance, but this subject, like other applications which loom larger and larger as sociology is seen to be more and more useful, requires special treatment. This is especially true when one considers how applications of sociology are usually combined with applications of other social sciences—psychology, social medicine, law and economics. These things deserve separate and special treatment and are not included here. In this book, which has been kept to a reasonable length, I have tried to tell the story of an intellectual adventure that is both distinctive and interesting. I have been helped to accomplish it by the interest of my colleagues, whose brains I have shamelessly picked from time to time; but then this is the privilege of working in a large university department.

Writing a book when one is already engaged in a teaching programme and when one has more than the normal amount of university administration to do does create some strains and stresses. My thanks therefore are extended to my family and my colleagues who have borne with my irritabilities whilst this book was taking shape. I wish to thank especially Dr. Margaret Hewitt, who read Chapter XVII and made helpful comments and suggestions; Miss Pamela Ffooks, who performed a valiant piece of work with a typewriter at short notice and found time also to correct some infelicities in style and expression; and my secretary Miss A. Gosling.

All history is story-telling and the first condition of a good story-teller is to be interesting. I shall withstand with equanimity most other criticisms if I have succeeded in making sociology appear an interesting adventure in ideas and enquiries.

Exeter March 1968

CONTENTS

Contents

ACKNOWLEDGEMENTS

For permission to cite passages from the following books, the author wishes to express his thanks to the authors and publishers:

R. F. Bales, *Interaction Process Analysis* (Addison-Wesley Publishing Co.); F. Thrasher, *The Gang*, and R. E. Park, "The City", *American Journal of Sociology*, 1916 (University of Chicago Press); M. I. Alihan, *Social Ecology* (Cooper Square Publishers); L. L. and J. S. Bernard, *Origins of American Sociology* (T. Y. Crowell Co.); F. Boulard, *An Introduction to Religious Sociology* (Darton, Longman and Todd); W. I. Thomas and F. Znaniecki, *The Polish Peasant in Europe and America* (Dover Publications); R. S. and H. M. Lynd, *Middletown* and *Middletown in Transition* (Harcourt, Brace & World); P. A. Sorokin, *Contemporary Sociological Theories* (Harper & Row, Publishers); M. Abrahams, *Social Survey and Social Action* (Heinemann Educational Books); M. Weber, *Theory of Social and Economic Organisation* (Wm. Hodge & Co. and The Free Press of Glencoe); K. Wolff, *The Sociology of Georg Simmel*, T. Parsons, *The Structure of Social Action* (The Free Press of Glencoe); D. Emmet, *Rules, Roles and Relations* (St. Martin's Press and the Macmillan Company of Canada); M. Mead, *Male and Female* (Victor Gollancz, and William Morrow & Co.); H. V. Dicks, "Personality Traits and National Socialist Ideology", *Human Relations*, 1950 (Plenum Publishing Company); E. Shevsky and W. Bell, *Social Area Analysis* (Stanford University Press); R. Aron, *18 Lectures on Industrial Sociology* (Weidenfeld & Nicolson, and The Free Press of Glencoe).

CHAPTER I

INTRODUCTION

"In the autumn of 1856 it was suggested to Lord Brougham that he should take the lead in founding an association for affording to those engaged in all the various efforts now happily begun for the improvement of the people an opportunity of considering social economics as a great whole. For the ultimate success of such an undertaking, as much reliance was placed on the actual experience of social reformers as on that *a priori* reasoning which would probably strike any thinker on the subject. This reasoning was not, indeed, to be despised. Advancing knowledge has proved an inseparable connection between the various branches of physical science, and disclosed to us, as Newton foreshadowed in his *Principia*, a unity throughout creation, a vast expansion of purpose based on a few simple laws."[1] These words by G. W. Hastings refer to the founding in Great Britain of the National Association for the Promotion of Social Science. This Association, founded in 1857 with Brougham as President and Hastings as Secretary, provides a convenient point to begin the story of the development of sociology during the past century.

Yet it is significant as well as convenient to begin here, for the Introduction to the *Transactions* of the Association goes on to speak of the unity of knowledge which had been secured in the natural sciences. "And is social knowledge, the science of promoting the prosperity, happiness, and welfare of the human race, stamped less with the character of unity? Are the moral laws of the universe promulgated by the same Divine Legislator, less uniform, less simple, and less sure? Are not the whole family of men bound together, not merely by the inheritance of a common lot, but by the tie of a mutual influence? And do not we find that each one of the social problems we have been in any way at pains to unravel strikes its roots into the substance of the nation, ramifying through

[1] *Transactions of the National Association for the Promotion of Social Science*, 1857 (published in London 1858), p. xxi.

a hundred secret crevices into classes apparently the most removed from its influence?"[1]

The presuppositions as well as the conscious direction of thought reflected here are of interest to the historian of sociology, for this was an age when the causes and the connections of things had begun to dominate men's thoughts. Some of the causes were rather fanciful. The same writer declared "The guiltiest city is the most unhealthy. Frames enfeebled and depressed by breathing a vitiated atmosphere must find an artificial stimulus; a dense population, consequently, drinks hard."[2] But it was also an age very conscious that society was undergoing radical and far-reaching social changes. The leisured middle-class and professional gentlemen who supported the Association were confident that by careful work the causes of events could be traced and that by determined application such events might be shaped in a satisfactory manner. These public-spirited people were reformers in the sense that they believed most problems to be administrative and educational in both nature and solution. They were, in fact, practical men and on the whole they were not given to speculative philosophy. "It was their endeavour to obtain aid from all those interested in social improvement, without reference to classes or opinions; sincere help was welcomed from whatever quarter it was offered; and in reply to all enquiries as to the policy of the Association, it was distinctly stated that its object was to elicit truth, not to propound dogmas, and that in every department any argument coming within the limits of the subjects for discussion, and temperately and fairly urged, would be listened to with respect." In short "the aim of the Association is to collect facts, to diffuse knowledge, to stimulate enquiry. . . ."[3]

We have quoted generously from the Secretary's introduction to show the temper of men's minds just over a hundred years ago or, if not all men's, then the minds of enlightened and intelligent middle-class men. In other parts of Europe the situation was different. There is for instance among the members of the National Association no hint of a highly speculative type of enquiry such as that of Auguste Comte who exercised so much influence in France and, indeed, among a few Englishmen such as John

[1] *Ibid.* [2] *Ibid.* [3] *Ibid.*, pp. xxvii–xxviii.

Stuart Mill. Again, the romantic movement in philosophy which we associate with Georg Wilhelm Friedrich Hegel and Gottfried von Herder, and which had already commanded the attention of Karl Marx by this time and helped to shape his thought, has little or no place here. And this fact stands out despite the obsession with the unity of knowledge which nearly all these people shared, and despite the fact that both Comte and Marx were just as much concerned with the task of coping with a changing society and with its reconstruction, as were the members of the National Association. Truly the latter were there "not to propound dogmas", but to produce facts. That they had little sense of direction in their fact-finding was a serious drawback and it probably was a major contributory reason, if not the main one, why the National Association declined in the 1880s after such a notable rise in the 1860s. Indeed, what is important to note is the almost anti-philosophical temper of social science at this time in England in contrast to the earlier interest stemming from the work of Saint-Simon and Comte in France some two decades earlier.

The story of the development of sociology as a distinctive intellectual activity is the story of the increasingly closer relationships formed between speculation and fact-finding; the juxtaposition of philosophical thought and reforming zeal; the puzzlement of the passively inclined theorist and the conscience of the actively inclined citizen. To some extent there has been a national philosophical division of labour so that British empiricism stands in contrast to French rationalism and German idealism. Indeed, there has been a diversity of sympathies so that wholesale changes have been advocated by some whilst others have urged merely piecemeal alterations in the fabric of social life. Sometimes one tradition has predominated, sometimes another. Sociology has been forged very largely in the heat of the conflict between these apparently incompatible traditions.

It is impossible to describe the speculative tradition in sociology without reference to Auguste Comte (1798–1857), that child of the French Enlightenment and the reaction to the Revolution who first used the word *sociology* in the fourth volume of his *Cours de philosophie positive*, published in 1839. Comte's survey of the history of the world as far as it was then known had led him to elaborate a theory of change. The famous Law of the Three Stages, first, of intellectual development, and second, of social development, showed the passage from theological thought to metaphysical and finally positive and scientific thought, and social change from a militaristic to a legalistic type of society finally leading to modern industrialism. It had an immense influence on men's minds, and the influence extended not only from France to England, but also to America.

Some of Comte's ideas about the study of society first made their appearance in England in the work of J. S. Mill (1806–1873) where they appeared in his *System of Logic* (1843), but Comte's major work was published in an English translation by Harriet Martineau in 1853.[1] It is clear that whilst this blue-print for a reconstructed society suited the tastes of few (the ideal society for Comte seems to resemble a well run prison), nevertheless his vision of a social science based on observation and induction was shared by many thoughtful people. Mill himself was initially taken with Comte's ideas about scientific method, although he revolted against the social philosophy implicit in his utopia. In England, Mill may be said to be the most respectable of the speculative minded social scientists, whose chief characteristic is the systematic nature of his thought. He welded together into a comprehensive and fairly consistent system much of the thought of Bentham and the philosophical radicals, the ideas of the classical economists such as Adam Smith and David Ricardo, but he also entertained some of the notions of the early socialist Saint-Simon and, as we have seen, of Comte. There is more than a little sociological thought in Mill's work, but if he was speculative he was also precise in his ideas. There were others, no less speculative but much less scholarly, yet as influential. Such an author was H. T. Buckle (1821–62) who between 1857 and 1861 brought out the two volumes of his *History of Civilization in England*, a popular work, translated into many languages; it even had a vogue in Russia. Here again we see the speculative mind at work, somewhat undisciplined to be sure, but bold in generalisation and rhetorical in style. It was an attempt to work out by inductive

[1] *The Positive Philosophy of Auguste Comte*, translated by Harriet Martineau, London (1853). This is a fairly free and condensed translation.

reasoning the physical, moral and intellectual laws which the author thought to underlie the history of mankind. The attempt was a failure, but the speculative tradition which Comte had initiated and which Buckle inherited from him continued. If Buckle's sociological history was too ambitious and premature it did not discourage Spencer and Hobhouse, to mention only two who followed.

The most outstanding speculative writer in Europe in the mid-nineteenth century, and ultimately one of the most influential in sociology, is clearly Karl Marx. Much of his historico-political writing belongs before our period, but *Das Kapital* was first published in 1867. There are two aspects of his work that should concern us. First, like Buckle, he provided an interpretation of history; his being an economic or, as some would have it, a materialistic interpretation. Second, he provided a discussion of social change in which class structure features prominently. What links these two together is a common subject, the rise and fall of capitalism. What is of sociological significance is his belief that there is a logic of development operating independently of human will which inevitably results in changes in the structure of society, its origins lying in the relationship of man to the means of production (i.e. factories, mills and machinery), whilst behind this there are the fundamental limitations set by a dominant mode of production (i.e. manual labour or steam power). For Marx, the history of mankind is the history of class struggles, with progression to a simplified antagonism between bourgeoisie and proletariat. The story is clearly etched and the prophecies boldly stated in the *Communist Manifesto* published in 1848. The effects of Marx's thought on his contemporaries in America and Britain were slight. In Germany later in the century these were more marked and scholars took his work seriously; today, among economic historians and sociologists his influence is not inconsiderable.

The two broad traditions of sociological thought and enquiry we have been discussing proceeded in separate directions largely because they appeared to be irrelevant to each other. The speculative writers were too general and broad in their approach; frequently they were more concerned with the past than the present, and above all, with the exception of Marx, they were insensitive to the predicament of those caught up in the tide of industrialisation, and they had no eye for the limited practical human problems that could only be satisfactorily dealt with in terms of municipal health and welfare. The members of the National Association for the Promotion of Social Science were on the whole aware of these speculative theories of human society, and at annual conferences speakers from time to time referred to them in passing, but it is clear that they were essentially regarded as irrelevant. The problems facing the Association required a more limited approach, more diligence in sifting evidence and collecting facts. The Association was an informing as well as a reforming body; collection of data occupied their time and attention preparatory to the piecemeal reconstruction of social life. The irrelevancy of the two traditions at that point in time is obvious.

In America, Comte's work was also influential. There we see a speculative tradition flourishing alongside a fact-finding one. As regards the former, there are both the sober and meticulous, and the ebullient and fanciful examples, for we may find similar contrasts to Mill and Buckle. Thus in 1858 H. C. Carey, the economist, who had published his *Principles of Political Economy* twenty years earlier, now produced *The Principles of Social Science* in three volumes. To be sure this is largely still on economics, but it is a much broader treatment. Carey tried to formulate a fundamental law demonstrating the identity of physical and social laws. This he states as follows: "Social science treats of man in his efforts for the maintenance and improvement of his condition, and may now be defined to be *the science of the laws which govern man in his efforts to secure for himself the highest individuality, and the greatest power of association with his fellow-men*" (his itals.).[1] We shall have occasion to look at associationism again, but for the present let us note that Carey's work rests on an attempt to discern social laws. Much of what he wrote is about population growth and distribution, the production and consumption of goods, the advantages of concentration and centralisation and so forth. There are variable amounts of sociological discussion as distinct

[1] H.C. Carey, *The Principles of Social Science*, 3 vols. (1958).

from economic argument. Thus he discussed relations between the sexes, slavery as an institution, family relationships and other similar topics, although he often discussed them in an economic context. He was in fact an economist interested for the most part in the ideas of Adam Smith and David Ricardo, but relating this more theoretical and abstract social science to the history and structure of Europe and America of his day and in so doing examining social institutions. His work is careful, sensible and scholarly.

Much less so is the work of Robert S. Hamilton, who, under the pseudonym of L. A. Webster, wrote a book entitled *Philosophy of Society* (1866); also speculative, but much less rigorous. Hamilton also sought to discern social laws, for the aim of social philosophy, he avers, and its contemporary science, sociology, is: "First, to ascertain what are the causes or laws which determine the social condition of mankind; secondly, to ascertain how far, and by what means, can those causes or laws be controlled or modified by human agency—by human intention or effort, purposively and designedly to that end."[1] His discussion of French and English social philosophers is highly opinionated, but he culled his ideas from many sources: from the ancients—Solon and Confucius; from the French Enlightenment—De Maistre and Comte; from English contemporaries—Buckle and Spencer; and from compatriots like Calhoun. He enunciated and endeavoured to defend a number of propositions, among which, for instance, is the view that people make their institutions rather than the reverse; or again, he argued that it is the collective will of society, or any given class of it, that determines its condition; that the natural environment of man has great bearing on character formation and consequently on political institutions, that the course of human progress is "towards the eventual triumph of the individual over society".[2] It is an apologia for the *laissez-faire* individualistic society of liberal America. He cannot have expected his book to have a large sale, for he avowedly wrote it for the "one in a million" who thinks.

In the United States, however, a connected phenomenon appears which apart from New Lanark is absent from Britain, for in the

[1] L. A. Webster, *Philosophy of Society* (1866), p. 18. [2] *Ibid.*

early part of the nineteenth century some groups of people holding radical and utopian ideas were able to act on them, and thus numerous, strange and novel communities developed, many being short-lived, but these, too, may be said to have contributed in their way to the development of the study of society, or what L. L. and J. Bernard call the "Social Science Movement",[1] and of these we shall have more to say in Chapter II.

Thus the beginning of the second half of the nineteenth century displayed a variety of intellectual and social movements. It is perhaps difficult to see how such diversity could produce a coherent social science. Yet the fact remains that sociology was born of these two parental traditions, one speculative and the other fact finding. The process of development continues, and is uneven largely because of their disparateness. Detached speculation in the grand manner is unreal to the philanthropic reformer with his practical turn of mind, even as the latter seems to the thinker to possess the non-academic propensity to act first and reflect afterwards, to prefer to tinker with what is, rather than plan afresh on the basis of a broad study. But there are also differences in outlook and intention even among those who are content merely to understand or interpret society, for some writers sketch on a broad canvas the panorama of human life, usually impressionistically, although some have an eye for detail, whilst others draw with more precision some particular part, draughtsmanship being preferred to inspiration. The development of sociology has required not only both these for its speculative and fact finding traditions, but contributions from people possessing very different outlooks and talents.

Sociology is still both philosophical and practical, both concerned with society in general and with particular parts or aspects of human social life; it is both encyclopaedic and piecemeal in its approaches, borrowing from other sciences, sometimes with mistaken enthusiasm. Yet over the past century there has been built up an effective way of thinking about human social life, a formulation of the principal questions, which define the discipline, and a drawing together, in an increasingly imposing organisation,

[1] L. L. & J. Bernard, *Origins of American Sociology: The Social Science Movement in the United States* (1943).

of the many diverse strands of knowledge about society. It is this story that is narrated here.

All history is selective. In this book we have not included an account of every contribution to the subject; to do so would have been to produce a work of inordinate length and prolixity. But the principal contributions are here described and of the others a selection has been made by way of illustration. Textbooks with many references and which attempt to cover all aspects of the subject in great detail do exist, but this is not one of them.[1] *A Hundred Years of Sociology* is less a work of reference than a narrative, more an historical guide to the subject than a definitive work or an encyclopaedia of sociology.

[1] Other histories of special significance may be mentioned: H. E. Barnes, *An Introduction to the History of Sociology* (1948); P. A. Sorokin, *Contemporary Sociological Theories* (1928); and *Sociological Theories of Today* (1966); H. Becker and H. E. Barnes, *Social Thought from Lore to Science* (1938), (3 vols.); N. S. Timasheff, *Sociological Theory: Its Nature and Growth* (1955; 3rd edn., 1967).

CHAPTER II

EARLY SOCIAL SCIENCE IN AMERICA, BRITAIN AND FRANCE

The middle decades of the nineteenth century are notable for a variety of ideas, both speculative and practical, which directly and indirectly contributed to the development of sociology. Broadly speaking, these ideas may be divided into three categories: utopian ideas and the movements they gave rise to; philosophical thought about society as a whole; and attempts to carry out scientific social studies. Largely, they originated in France and Britain, but they exerted powerful influences on American thought and social life, often more so than in the countries of origin.

The Utopians

In America the utopian notions of Fourier gained ground in the 1840s. F. C. M. Fourier, one of the early French socialists, had come to believe that a social order based on unbridled individualism and competition was both imperfect and immoral, and that co-operative social life must replace it. His psychological outlook was naturalistic in that he held that the way to both virtue and happiness lay in the unrestrained indulgence of the passions, for he argued that the passions, if unrestrained, interact according to a principle of harmony. His scheme for social reconstruction provided for the grouping of people, 1,620 persons to each group or *phalange*; each phalange to occupy a set of buildings called a *phalanstère.* They were to work on a portion of land of approximately 5,000 acres in area.

Fourier's views, known to Americans as *associationism*, were propagated, not without some success, by Albert Brisbane (1809–1890), who, whilst on his travels in Europe, met Fourier and was much influenced by his ideas. On his return to America in 1834 Brisbane wrote a book, *The Social Destiny of Man*, in support of Fourierist ideas. By 1850 there were about forty-one phalanxes, the most famous being Brook Farm phalanx (West Roxbury Community) founded by George Ripley. Of the others, eight were founded in Ohio, six in New York State, another six in Pennsylvania, and several in each of Massachusetts, Illinois, New Jersey and Michigan. One was even founded in Texas by Victor Considerant.

Owenite ideas too were popular in America at this time. Robert Owen (1771–1858) was a Manchester businessman who set up model mills in New Lanark, Scotland, and in connection with them started a utopian community. His social experiment became famous, if controversial. Disgusted at the lack of support for reforming the Poor Law, for which he made proposals, Owen left for America, and in 1825 established there the community of New Harmony. This eventually disappointed him and in 1829 he returned home. Nevertheless, his ideas remained to influence others. Owen had advocated the development of what he called "villages of co-operation", the most famous being Harmony Hall, or Queenswood, in Hampshire, begun in 1839, and which remained a co-operative community until 1845, after which time it continued as a school until 1858. Above all, Owen believed that the social environment conditioned character and determined human behaviour. Hence his concern for fashioning the entire network of relationships in the community.

What is remarkable about those who took up Fourierist or Owenite ideas is that they conceived society as a whole. They were social engineers, but not piecemeal engineers. They tried to develop a consistent set of beliefs and practices for total social reorganisation. They were joined in this endeavour by the followers of Claud-Henri, Comte de Saint-Simon (1760–1825). Saint-Simonians were also trying to find an intellectual and spiritual basis for social reconstruction to replace the discredited theology of medieval society, a society that had been destroyed in France and was obviously irrelevant to a new country like America or an industrialising one like Britain. Many ideas of the Saint-Simonians were fantastic and their attempts at social reconstruction were often misplaced, but they did try to see human society as a whole and they did possess both imagination and energy. Neither Fourier, Saint-Simon nor Owen achieved much in their own countries, but America was ripe for social innovations, and the thought of these men persisted longer in America than elsewhere as well as having more immediate effect.

Consider for instance the influence they had on Albert Brisbane, a typical utopian and speculative thinker of this early period in the history of social thought in America. *The Social Destiny of Man* presented a philosophy of history as well as a theory of human nature. He saw history in evolutionary terms. Four types of human society had emerged—the savage, the patriarchal, the barbarian and the civilised. He looked towards the emergence of a fifth type. These ideas of Brisbane were not original, nor was his psychological theory which has its roots in Scottish moral philosophy. But he put them forward in a fairly sensible manner and with some effect. Thus he argued that each type of human society has stages of development. Civilisation itself has four phases, those of infancy, maturity, decline and decrepitude. Such social phases possess their own distinctive principles and each produces a complex of institutions, laws and customs reflecting them. In infancy a civilisation establishes principles like monogamy and feudalism. Society is governed by barons with the ideological aid of the illusion of chivalry (for each phase has its characteristic illusion providing a moral sanction). The period of growth to maturity displays the rise of free towns and cities, the cultivation of the arts and sciences; it manifests the principle of enfranchisement for serfs and the labouring classes. Government is nominally through representation sanctioned by the illusion of liberty and democracy. The period of decline occurs under a commercial type of regime, when a fiscal spirit reigns. Here the ruling principle is a maritime monopoly, or imperialism; the ruling power is anarchical commerce, and the sanctioning illusion is financial prosperity. The final phase of decrepitude is seen in the advent of agricultural loaning companies, for this reflects the decline of individual farm ownership. The reigning principle is industrial and commercial control, oligopoly of capital, and the sanctioning illusion in this case is that the people enjoy a true form of human association.

Besides these ideas and the book which incorporated them, Brisbane wrote newspaper articles for the *New York Tribune* and so reached a wider readership. Then in 1876 he published his

General Introduction to Social Science, in which he discussed the theories of Saint-Simon, Comte, Fourier and Owen, and also included references to the work of Herbert Spencer. Brisbane's influence declined rapidly and when he died in 1890 associationism was forgotten. Yet in his lifetime he exerted considerable influence on distinguished Americans—writers like Nathaniel Hawthorne, journalist-politicians like Horace Greeley and on other people of note such as the famous conversationalist Margaret Fuller.

Brisbane was not alone among American utopians. Another was Lewis Masquerier who wrote a book in 1877 with the title *Sociology*. The sub-title of this work is lengthy but explanatory for it reads: "Or, the Reconstruction of Society, Government, and Property, upon the Principles of Equality, the Perpetuity, and the Individuality of the Private Ownership of Life, Person, Government, Homestead and the Whole Product of Labor, by Organizing all Nations into Townships of Self-Governed Homestead Democracies—Self-Employed in Farming and Mechanism, Giving All the Liberty and Happiness to Be Found on Earth". Masquerier wanted to allocate the land in ten acre plots to each family, to abolish cities and leave only warehouses and foundries. He aimed at securing a pure democracy; the influence of Robert Owen may be partly detected here.

L. L. and J. Bernard, in their excellent discussion of these writers,[1] say that the utopian nature of early American sociology did not disappear after the Civil War, but merely became more conservative. The emphasis on reconstruction blinded them to the nature of the situation. "The Associationists sought to achieve administrative reforms mainly through the organisation of phalansteries, and the Post-Associationists also leaned heavily upon communal colonies, ideal communities and co-operative communities." And speaking about a late attempt at this they go on to say: "The group of co-operators led by Albert Kimsey Owen sought to establish a new type of colony but the conditions for its success on an isolated bay on the faraway coast of Mexico, were by no means favourable. This modern co-operative colony therefore fared but little better than the communistic colonies of Robert Owen and other Utopian idealists founded more than

[1] *Op. cit.*

half a century earlier. The land reform advocates could make little progress in a country where land speculation was one of the chief 'get rich quick' grafts available to the professional real estate gamblers. They found it practically impossible to secure the serious attention of legislators. They had an opportunity to learn that land reform is popular only where land is scarce and difficult to obtain. Other related economic reforms had for various reasons as little legislative and administrative success; or even popular acceptance, as far as that is concerned."[1]

The Speculative Sociologists

Brisbane was clearly a speculative sociologist as well as a utopian; so also was Masquerier. There were others, less obviously utopian, but no less speculative. Calvin Blanchard, for example, in *Essence of Science, or The Catechism of Positive Sociology and Physical Mentality*, published in 1859, spread Comtean views but with anarchist overtones, and was avowedly anti-religious. James O'Connel's *Vestiges of Civilization*, published in 1851, is a philosophy of history somewhat similar to Comte's. George Frederick Holmes in *The Science of Society*, published in 1883, whilst partly critical of Comte's sociology, is often appreciative of it. Then Robert Hamilton, writing under the pseudonym of L. A. Webster, already mentioned earlier, may be added to the list. His *Present Status of the Philosophy of Society* (1866) was republished in abbreviated form in 1873 as the *Present Status of Social Science.*

Hamilton's endeavour to discern the scientific basis of sociology led him to look for "the fundamental causes which determine the social condition of mankind—first, of the depressing causes—secondly, of the countervailing causes . . . " He decided that these laws had the same nature as physical laws—centripetal and centrifugal forces operate in the social sciences as in astronomy, he declared. Thus, he concluded, "man is the true centre of the social universe, and around him revolves all his social destiny". And again, there are "the causes, or laws, which determine the social condition of mankind, and . . . the causes which determine the social destiny of an individual and a nation—of the humblest

[1] *Ibid.*, p. 390.

individual in the human family and of the most exalted". These two laws are universal and identical, he argued. Hamilton, we can see, is no utopian, nor is he a reformer primarily, for he held that reform must wait upon a sound knowledge of social laws. "So . . . men do study—imperfectly and superficially enough hitherto, to be sure—the laws of social health and disease, and the possibilities of controlling them to some extent, not only with reference to the purely scientific end of understanding those laws, hitherto shamefully neglected, but with a view furthermore to the great practical and efficient end of actually controlling them, to which latter end indeed attention has been hitherto almost exclusively directed, by a sort of blind *empiricism* in social philosophy—by a sort of shameful *quackery*, indeed, which undertakes to treat social disease without any adequate consideration of its true Diagnosis—almost without any regard whatever to the great and vitally important sciences—hitherto almost wholly uncultivated—of social physiology and social pathology."[1]

It will be seen that the work of speculative sociologists of this period in America varied greatly in quality. R. J. Wright, for instance, was a somewhat cranky writer. His *Principia, or Basis of Social Science,* which appeared in 1875, is an odd mixture of numerology, metaphysics and sociology. His was an avowed attempt to integrate religion and social science: "Social science and Christianity run parellel to each other, most of their length: Social science doing for Society, in most things, what Christianity is doing for the individual."[2] He too was interested in social laws and in progress. Like others, he attempted a fundamental classification; his six fundamental units in human life being: (i) individual, (ii) family, (iii) social circle, (iv) precinct, (v) nation, (vi) mankind. But like many of his kind his work tends to be vague and normative.

Scientific Social Studies

Speculative sociological writers such as those mentioned above all claimed to be scientific. They saw themselves discovering the

[1] Quoted by the Bernards, *ibid.*, p. 271.
[2] *Principia or Basis of Social Science,* p. 21.

laws of society or human behaviour, and yet in fact their methods were often far from scientific. Nevertheless, serious attempts were made to study human life according to the canons of scientific enquiry. In France a writer appeared who not only laid claim to being scientific, but who succeeded in some measure in the attempt. He too exercised an influence both on American and British students of social life, but, although a cautious reformer, he was neither speculative nor utopian.

Frédéric Le Play, a consultant mining engineer, whilst travelling round Europe advising governments on mining matters had opportunity to study the conditions of life of the working classes in different milieux. His main work, *Les ouvriers européens*, was published in 1855. It represented the results of many years of careful observation and recording. It was an immensely influential book, not least because a year after publication Le Play founded the International Society for Practical Studies in Social Economics, a society which had branches in several countries and in effect propagated Le Play's ideas and methods. The significance of the use of the term "social economics" in the Introduction to the Proceedings of the National Association for the Promotion of Social Science referred to earlier (p. 1) lies in the early influence exerted by Le Play and his Society. Indeed, Le Play's work was to become even more influential in England with the founding toward the end of the century of the Sociology Society, later still to be domiciled in Le Play House, London.

Le Play and his followers determined to study social problems by the methods of natural science. These they took to be observation and recording on the one hand and quantification on the other. Thus they studied the structure of family life and made analyses of family budgets. Le Play himself was conservative by temperament, yet keen to effect reforms which would improve the lot of industrial labourers. His followers carried on the tradition he started by contributing to a periodical entitled *La réforme sociale*, first published in 1881; it may be regarded in many ways as the counterpart in France of the *Transactions* of the N.A.P.S.S. in Britain.

Human society for Le Play constituted a system of relationships, but the basic unit of the social system appeared to him to be the family. Indeed, the family seemed to him to be a rudimentary society, the simplest form of social grouping. However, the family was not something to be studied in isolation, he decided; on the contrary it is set in an environment which determines its form and behaviour. Chiefly, of course, the family must adapt to its environment and hence it is always associated with some form of economic activity. Le Play and those who followed in his steps framed their observations in terms of the broad categories of *Place, Work, People*, and by *People* they meant families. The interdependencies of these three categories are fundamental to their analyses.

The scientific inspiration of the work of this school led its members to measure and for this purpose family budgets provided a convenient quantitative element, for it was assumed that the quality of social life of a family was reflected in its expenditure. Thus expenditure on medical attention might reflect the occupational hazards members of the family were prone to endure, or heavy expenditure on clothes the inclement weather conditions that prevailed. The method of study was modified as time passed for Le Play himself had largely restricted his attention to the family and its geographical environment. His scheme did not easily permit the description of major social institutions, nor the analysis of the points of articulation of family structure and other institutional structures. In fact the chief defect of Le Play's work lay in the haziness of the definition of the social system of which the family was the unit, a defect which was only partially remedied by his followers.

Le Play distinguished various kinds of social environments each with its corresponding type of economy and family structure. Thus, for instance, a coastal area like that of Norway compels people to live in small settlements, the fiord type of environment places a restraint on the growth of communities. People in such an environment obtain a living from small-scale fishing and this involves ownership of capital by the fisherman, who thus mans his own craft, although sometimes with the help of his fellows. There is a strong sense of community even if the settlement is small. Such people develop what Le Play called strong "stem-families" (*la famille souche*), that is to say families which bind one married child to the parental household whilst giving other independent members dowries. It is a type of family given to hard work, frugal living, family patriotism and attachment to individual property. The stem-family is by no means to be thought of as restricted to fishing communities, for it is found in many places, in Catalonia, in rural England and Ireland as well as in central Europe. By contrast, on the plains of eastern Europe the terrain is suitable for grazing sheep; it is also highly suitable for the domestic horse, so that the kind of shepherding found there makes much use of this domestic animal. The pattern of family life is nomadic, and furthermore the structure of the family is patriarchal and extended; many kinsfolk are united under one patriarchal leader. To look quickly at these two instances is to recognise immediately that the means of getting a living are different in the fiords from the steppeland of Russia because of the physical environment. Place and work are interrelated and, the family life being different in each case, the characteristics of the people differ. This kind of structural analysis and comparative study, here but briefly indicated, cannot be too highly praised. For its time, it represented a major contribution to sociology, and it is hardly surprising that it gained popularity in Le Play's lifetime, and for years after his death. Napoleon III strongly encouraged Le Play's studies and under imperial insistence he published a three-volume work *La réforme social en France* in 1864 outlining his ideas on social institutions like property and religion, but mainly in the context of his study of the family. His work is by no means above criticism, as we have seen. Indeed, whilst we may applaud his careful observation and systematic recording in terms of defined categories, his scientific urge was slightly misplaced in his emphasis on family budgets, which whilst giving quantitative data, can yet be misleading, for not every aspect of family life is capable of being discussed in terms of cash or income and outlay, and thus in his work some functions of the family, e.g. socialisation and education, tend to be neglected.

We shall return to the Le Play school later. For the present let us note that at about the time of the establishment of the N.A.P.S.S. Le Play was publishing his second great work, and that his earlier study of European working-men had already made an impact both on the members of the Association in Britain and on those who were to found a similar one in America. The speculative and the scientific beginnings of sociology did come together. The utopian tradition was by-passed, and except in a Marxian form did not much influence sociology again.

The American and British Social Science Associations

In the middle of the nineteenth century organisations for the study of aspects of modern society developed both in Europe and America. In Britain the National Association for the Promotion of Social Science held its first Congress in Birmingham, and then annually in the principal cities of the British Isles until the 1880s. The papers published in the first set of *Transactions* in 1858 were divided into five groups. It is interesting to see the foci of attention.

Thus one section deals with "Jurisprudence and Amendment of the Law" and includes an introduction by Lord John Russell, the former Prime Minister. The second section is entitled "Education" and has an introduction by Sir John Pakington. The third section is on "Punishment and Reformation". The fourth section is entitled "Public Health", and the fifth section is called "Social Economy". The papers published cover a great variety of topics from "Adulteration of Food" to "Workhouses", from the laws referring to "Bankruptcy" to "Vaccination". "Education" was often a topic, "Crime" was another popular subject, but so also were "Employment", "Endowed Charities", "Reformatories", "Sewers" and "Ragged Schools".

In 1864 the Association merged with the Law Amendment Society, which itself had had a life of twenty years, and at its silver jubilee in 1882 the secretary issued a Manual for the Congress listing some of the Association's achievements, what he called "Practical Results of the Labours of the Association". They include the Endowed Charities Act of 1860 and the Reform of the Bankruptcy Laws of 1861, the Property of Married Women Act of 1882, legislation on copyright and patents, reforms in prison discipline and the end of transportation, and many others. The Association had taken an interest in the Endowed Schools Bill of 1856, the Public Health Acts of 1858–9, and the Education Act of 1870, and it had received information and advice about hospital construction from no less a person than Florence Nightingale, a selection of her papers having been published and circulated to all hospitals in the United Kingdom. It had discussed baby-farming, registration of nurses, inspection of lodging houses and hostels, compulsory notification of infectious diseases, smoke-abatement and habitual drunkards, social conditions among Irish labourers and among merchant seamen.

The success of the N.A.P.S.S. led to others being formed: such was the case with the Society for Promoting the Industrial Employment of Women, the Ladies' Sanitary Society, the Workhouse Visiting Society, and the Women's Educational Union which later produced the Girls' Public Day School Company. Its influence also extended overseas, both to America and the Continent of Europe.

The American Social Science Association was founded in 1862 in New York. The Association published the *Social Science Review*, which began as a quarterly journal of economics and social statistics; but it foundered in 1866 because it covered too many diverse topics. Later a social science association sprang up in Boston and in 1865 the American Association for the Promotion of Social Science was founded with a constitution similar to its British counterpart, i.e. with four departments: Education, Public Health, Social Economy and Jurisprudence. However, the membership was not a national one but was mainly drawn from New England. The N.A.P.S.S. was also influential abroad in encouraging the founding in 1862 of L'Association Internationale pour le progrès des Sciences Sociales, the first Congress of which was held in Brussels.

The Bernards argue that the members of the American Association saw themselves as applying natural law to social control. Once the "natural" laws of education, public health and social economy had been discerned, they were to be formulated by the jurisprudence department so as to become the laws of the land. This idea, which probably originated in Montesquieu's *L'esprit des lois*, of the formulation of specific laws under the guidance of science for social control was, they say, an inevitable next step in the development of a secular theory of social control.[1]

The American Association split up later, the sociologists forming the American Sociological Society in 1905, and those who were more interested in reform joining the National Conference of Charities and Correction. In England the National Association regrettably came to an end ignominiously with a petty scandal. Yet other formal groups took its place—the Fabians on the reform side and the Sociological Society on the academic side. But before discussing these social movements we must examine some of the main intellectual traditions of the nineteenth century which informed sociological thought, and chief of these is the idea of social evolution.

[1] *Op. cit.*, p. 544.

CHAPTER III

EVOLUTIONARY SOCIOLOGY

The origins of developmental sociology mainly lie embedded in the thought of the French Enlightenment, for writers of those times were preoccupied with both social change and the possibility of discerning a lawful order governing it. Of course it is possible to point to writers of an earlier period, to Bossuet's *Discours sur l'histoire universelle,* published in 1681, but effectively it was the work of R. J. Turgot who, following in Bossuet's steps, produced the thesis that human society has passed through stages; from a hunting to a pastoral stage and thence to an agricultural stage of development. This notion appeared in his *Plan de deux discours sur l'histoire universelle* (1750). And of course there was also the influence in France of the writings of the Scottish philosopher David Hume who in 1742 produced a work entitled *Of the Rise and Progress of the Arts and Sciences.* All these encouraged thinkers to focus attention on social change. Later still there was the influential work of Montesquieu whose *De l'esprit des lois* (1784) emphasised the desirability of discerning natural laws as well as determining sound public laws, but who tended to confuse the two. And there was also Condorcet's small but powerful essay written during the Terror whilst he was in hiding, *Tableau historique des progrès de l'esprit humain* (1794).

All these writings were effective in forming the ideas of Saint-Simon and Comte and, through them, provided strong incentives for building up a social science based on a theory of social change of an evolutionary character. Condorcet and Comte in particular displayed a propensity, shared by many others, to describe the development of human society from earliest times according to some simple principle such as the progress of human reason or morals, or both, or else the advancement of the human intellect and hence of social organisation.

To be sure the fillip given to biology by Charles Darwin and A. R. Wallace in 1859 in turn had its effect on social thought, but the idea of social evolution predates this. Indeed, the most notable exponent of social evolution, Herbert Spencer, had outlined his views in some detail five or six years before.

HERBERT SPENCER (1820–1903)

For Spencer, sociology was the study of social evolution in its most complex form, and the purpose of such a study was to enable men to understand human behaviour and also know what kinds of ideas are appropriate for a society at a given stage in its evolution, for it would be useless to try to foist other and inappropriate ideas on its members. Indeed, Spencer had a lively understanding of the connection between the nature of a social structure and the prevalent ideas and values of the members of that society.[1] But the fact remains that the kind of society he wanted was a static one, enjoying a state of perfect equilibrium, and this society was only to be obtained by the climination of all restrictions and interferences on human association, most particularly those imposed by governments. This was the burden of his early work *Social Statics* (1850). That he saw the existing order of both nature and society as the product of a gradual progress is clear from *Progress, its Law and Cause* (1857). And on this subject his political outlook remained the same, for his *The Study of Sociology* (1873) restates his *laissez-faire* individualist philosophy in all its clarity and its extremity.

Social change for Spencer was a superorganic process analogous to the organic process of evolution. Sociology was thus rooted in biology—an exaggeration of Comte's views. Although he gave an account that purports to be a comprehensive and consistent philosophy, it was his sociological writings rather than his total philosophy which brought him fame, and in particular his *Principles of Sociology* (1877–96). Here the notion is entertained that evolutionary change applies to human society as an integrated whole, but the book also shows how the evolution of different aspects of human society, religious, industrial, military and professional, has taken place.

[1] See *The Study of Sociology* (12th edn. 1895), pp. 390 ff.

Spencer's Organic Analogy

The essentials of Spencer's theory of evolution may be stated quite simply. Firstly, he held there to be a very close analogy between the biological organism and human society; thus what is true for biological phenomena is true for sociological phenomena. Secondly, he argued that the history of both organic and superorganic (social) life is a process of development and that this development involves an increase in both quantity and complexity. Thus, just as earliest forms of organic life were unicellular and simple in structure, so early mankind lived in a few simple isolated groups or hordes; and just as later forms of organic life display differentiation and multiplicity in both structure and function, so do more recent forms of social life. Hence the human organism, being a later instance of the organic evolutionary process, provides the analogy for the modern industrial society, a later instance of the superorganic evolutionary process. Indeed, he went to great lengths to adumbrate the similarities and account for apparent dissimilarities as may be seen in Part II of the *Principles of Sociology*. Examples will illustrate his argument:

> The lowest type of animal is all stomach, all respiratory surface, all limb. Development of a type having appendages by which to move about or lay hold of food, can take place only if these appendages, losing power to absorb nutriment directly from surrounding bodies, are supplied with nutriment by parts which retain the power of absorption. A respiratory surface to which the circulating fluids are brought to be aerated, can be formed only on condition that the concomitant loss of ability to supply itself with materials for repair and growth, is made good by the development of a structure bringing these materials. Similarly in a society. What we call with perfect propriety its organization, necessarily implies traits of the same kind. While rudimentary, a society is all warrior, all hunter, all hut-builder, all tool-maker: every part fulfils for itself all needs. Progress to a stage characterized by a permanent army, can go on only as there arise arrangements for supplying that army with food, clothes, and munitions of war by the rest. If here the population occupies itself solely with agriculture and there with mining—if these manufacture goods while those distribute them, it must be on condition that in exchange for a special kind of service rendered

by each part to other parts, these other parts severally give due proportions of their services."[1]

Or again, when he points to a further structural analogy; this time describing a primary way in which a social organ is formed:

> In animals of low types, bile is secreted, not by a liver, but by separate cells imbedded in the wall of the intestine at one part. These cells individually perform their function of separating certain matters from the blood, and individually pour out what they separate. No organ, strictly so-called, exists; but only a number of units not yet aggregated into an organ. This is analogous to the incipient form of an industrial structure in a society. At first each worker carries on his occupation alone, and himself disposes of the product to consumers. The arrangement still extant in our villages, where the cobbler at his own fireside makes and sells boots, and where the blacksmith single-handed does what ironwork is needed by his neighbours, exemplifies the primitive type of every producing structure.[2]

The analogy is pursued with considerable thoroughness as he turns from general descriptions of growth to detailed ones of structure and function, and then on to an examination of what he calls the sustaining, distributory and regulatory systems, or in superorganic terms economic and governmental aspects of society.

Incorporated in his evolutionary scheme are ideas of natural selection and survival of the fittest, but, unlike Darwin, Spencer held firmly to the view that adaptation is purposive. He does not appear to have questioned this, whereas Darwin's theory that accidental variations which suited the environment were perpetuated and hence tended to survive was sustained.

Spencer was not a consistent thinker. His ideas shift from one view to its contrary. This is particularly the case in his use of the term *social organism*, for just what he believed is by no means clear and the obvious explanation is that he changed his mind whilst developing his ideas about evolution. At one time he speaks as if society *is* an organism but almost at the same time says it is analogous to an organism, and that the analogy is not perfect or complete. At the back of his difficulty we may detect an uncertainty

[1] *Principles of Sociology* (3rd edn. 1893), pp. 439–40. [2] *Ibid.*, p. 467.

as to whether society is essentially a unity or not. In so far as he thought it to be a unity he emphasised the notion of the social organism. However, as W. Stark[1] has pointed out, Spencer in *The Man Versus the State* (1884) seems to place an emphasis on the multiplicity of society, i.e. that it is so many individuals. This presents the problem of accounting for social order, and led Spencer to a contract theory of society, which argues that in the pursuit of individual selfish interests men come together and interact with one another to their mutual advantage. Indeed Spencer says that society is no more than "the mutual limitation of (individual) activities".[2] The truth is that Spencer tried to bend his sociological interpretation to suit his ultilitarianism but he was also confused not only about the essential nature of society, but with the evolutionary process it was his chief purpose to describe. Thus in *Principles of Sociology* he gives two quite distinct evolutionary schemes, each having its own social morphology.

Two Social Morphologies

The first scheme argues a social development from simple to compound societies. A simple society is "one which forms a single working whole unsubjected to any other, and of which the parts cooperate, with or without a regulating centre, for certain public ends".[3] These simple societies are differentiated according to the type and degree of social control and the extent to which they are territorially settled. The following is his scheme showing the social evolution of simple societies with his examples. (See Diagram 1.)

The compound type of society, which is an advance on the simple society, is itself differentiated along similar lines as is seen below. (See Diagram 2.)

In addition to simple and compound societies Spencer identified what he called Doubly and Trebly Compound Societies. His scheme for Doubly Compound Societies is set out below. (See Diagram 3.)

[1] *American Sociological Review*, Vol. 26, No. 4, 1961.
[2] *Loc. cit.*, p. 518.
[3] *Loc. cit.*, p. 539.

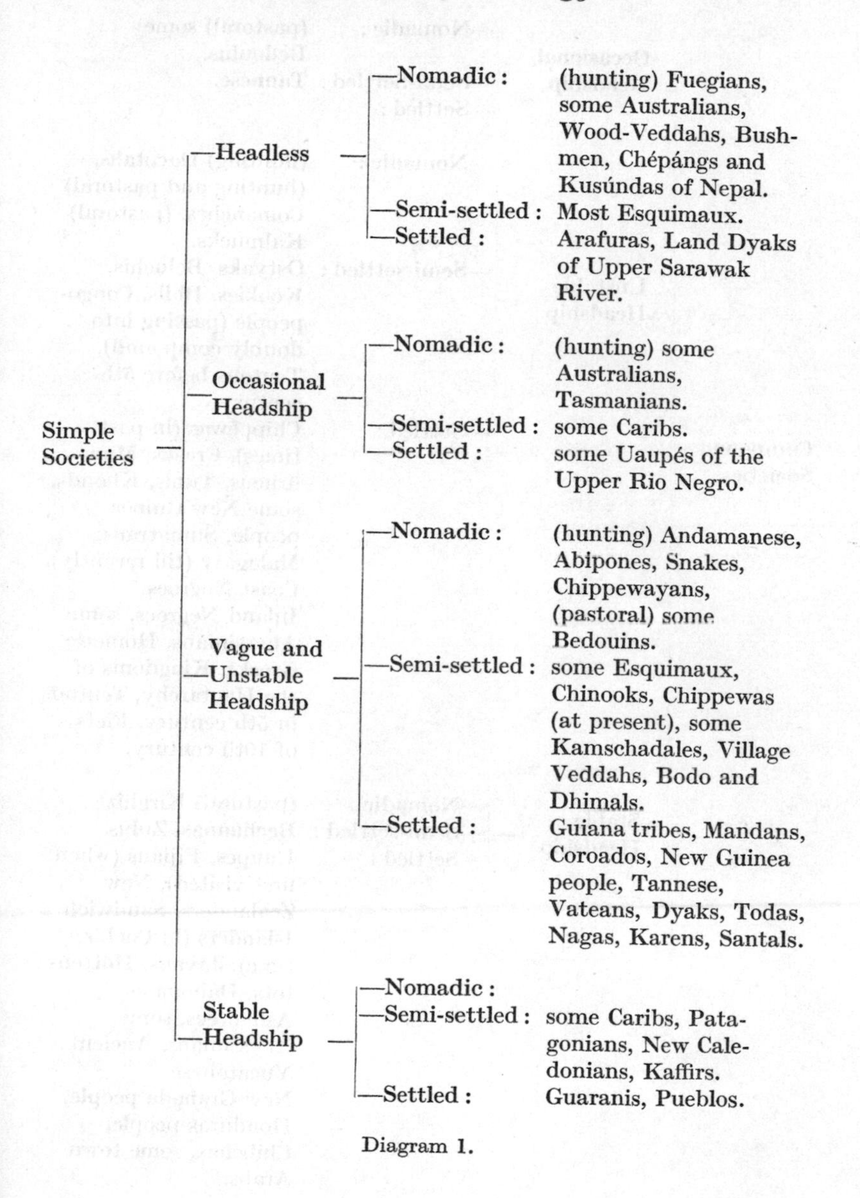
Simple Societies
Headless
Nomadic: (hunting) Fuegians, some Australians, Wood-Veddahs, Bushmen, Chépángs and Kusúndas of Nepal.
Semi-settled: Most Esquimaux.
Settled: Arafuras, Land Dyaks of Upper Sarawak River.
Occasional Headship
Nomadic: (hunting) some Australians, Tasmanians.
Semi-settled: some Caribs.
Settled: some Uaupés of the Upper Rio Negro.
Vague and Unstable Headship
Nomadic: (hunting) Andamanese, Abipones, Snakes, Chippewayans, (pastoral) some Bedouins.
Semi-settled: some Esquimaux, Chinooks, Chippewas (at present), some Kamschadales, Village Veddahs, Bodo and Dhimals.
Settled: Guiana tribes, Mandans, Coroados, New Guinea people, Tannese, Vateans, Dyaks, Todas, Nagas, Karens, Santals.
Stable Headship
Nomadic:
Semi-settled: some Caribs, Patagonians, New Caledonians, Kaffirs.
Settled: Guaranis, Pueblos.

Diagram 1.

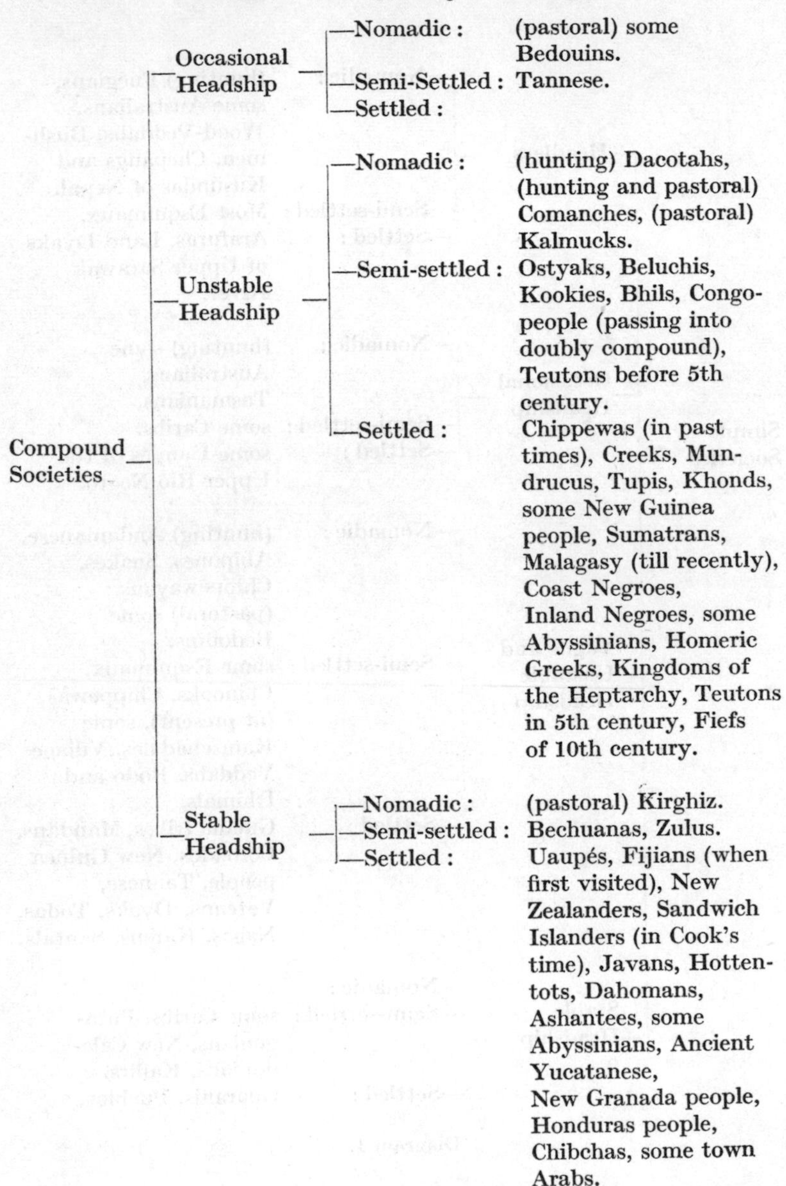
Compound Societies
Occasional Headship
—Nomadic : (pastoral) some Bedouins.
—Semi-Settled : Tannese.
—Settled :
Unstable Headship
—Nomadic : (hunting) Dacotahs, (hunting and pastoral) Comanches, (pastoral) Kalmucks.
—Semi-settled : Ostyaks, Beluchis, Kookies, Bhils, Congo-people (passing into doubly compound), Teutons before 5th century.
—Settled : Chippewas (in past times), Creeks, Mundrucus, Tupis, Khonds, some New Guinea people, Sumatrans, Malagasy (till recently), Coast Negroes, Inland Negroes, some Abyssinians, Homeric Greeks, Kingdoms of the Heptarchy, Teutons in 5th century, Fiefs of 10th century.
Stable Headship
—Nomadic : (pastoral) Kirghiz.
—Semi-settled : Bechuanas, Zulus.
—Settled : Uaupés, Fijians (when first visited), New Zealanders, Sandwich Islanders (in Cook's time), Javans, Hottentots, Dahomans, Ashantees, some Abyssinians, Ancient Yucatanese, New Granada people, Honduras people, Chibchas, some town Arabs.

Diagram 2.

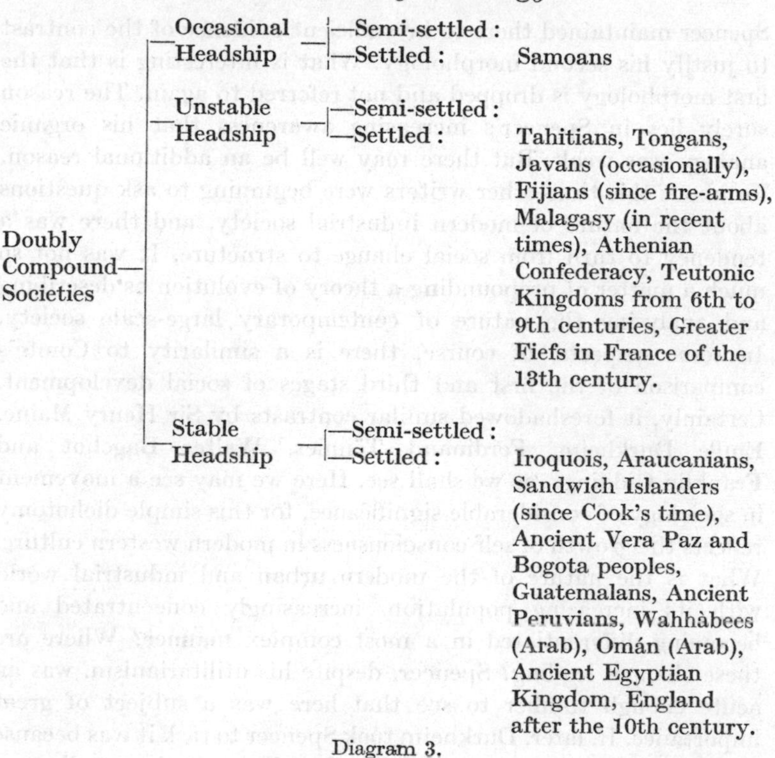

Diagram 3.

The Trebly Compound Societies are the great civilisations of the world: "Ancient Mexico, the Assyrian Empire, the Egyptian Empire, the Roman Empire, Great Britain, France, Germany, Italy, Russia, may severally be regarded as having reached this stage of composition, or perhaps in some cases, a still higher stage."[1]

It will be seen that this is a fairly elaborate morphological scheme. Yet in Part V, which he published some six years later, although subsequently incorporated in the same work, he produced another and much simpler one. This is the division of societies into two principal types: a military type and an industrial type. To be sure there are societies which are not clearly of one or the other but partake of both and there are transitional cases, but

[1] *Ibid.*, pp. 539–42.

Spencer maintained there to be sufficient evidence of the contrast to justify his second morphology. What is interesting is that the first morphology is dropped and not referred to again. The reason surely lies in Spencer's increasing awareness that his organic analogy was weak. But there may well be an additional reason, for about this time other writers were beginning to ask questions about the nature of modern industrial society, and there was a tendency to turn from social change to structure. It was not so much a matter of propounding a theory of evolution as describing and analysing the nature of contemporary large-scale society. In some respects, of course, there is a similarity to Comte's comparison of the first and third stages of social development. Certainly, it foreshadowed similar contrasts by Sir Henry Maine, Emile Durkheim, Ferdinand Tönnies, Walter Bagehot and Franklin Giddings, as we shall see. Here we may see a movement in sociology of considerable significance, for this simple dichotomy reflects the growth of self-consciousness in modern western culture. What is the nature of the modern urban and industrial world with its increasing population, increasingly concentrated and becoming differentiated in a most complex manner? Where are these changes leading? Spencer, despite his utilitarianism, was an acute enough thinker to see that here was a subject of great importance. If, later, Durkheim took Spencer to task it was because he saw with even greater clarity the shape of the intellectual discipline that was required to answer these questions. However, let us examine Spencer's second morphology.

Briefly, his criteria for distinguishing the two types are as follows. They are fundamentally unlike each other in political organisation, for the military type, as the term suggests, is organised for war, the individual is subjected to a centralised government, he is bound by a strict discipline to a life of obedience under pain of repressive penalties, both temporal and spiritual, and thus both government and religion play a prominent part in social life; public life in fact tends to exclude private life, industry is subordinate to the state, and men are graded by rank. The industrial type of society is described largely in terms of the opposite characteristics for it is organised for peace, government is decentralised, subjected to popular control and minimised in its extent; there is private choice and a variety of beliefs and outlook, for religion has a diminished influence and private life is emphasised, and with it the rights of the individual; industry is extensive and free from state control, the state merely providing the conditions for industrial development such as the enforcement of contracts; there is a diminution in the importance of social ranking, for status gives way to contract as a basis for determining social relationships.

Spencer's Contribution to Sociology

In assessing his contribution to sociology two aspects of his thought stand out for consideration. One is his organicism, the other is his study of structure and function. The first social morphology designed to demonstrate social evolution partly depends on an organic analogy. We may overlook his occasional lapses in definitely identifying society as an organism, but even the more moderate approach is unconvincing. One gains the impression that quantity of illustration in the absence of quality is required if there is to be any plausibility in his argument. At some points Spencer is clearly on weak ground as when, for example, he tries to cope with the difficulty raised by his observation that the organism is a concrete entity, whilst society is discrete, i.e. the cells of the organism are all fixed in position relative to each other, whereas individual members of human society may be mobile. He argues in fact that society is less discrete and the organism less concrete than is usually supposed, but it is a poor argument. In the end, of course, he acknowledged the poverty of the analogy. Thus at the end of Part II he categorically asserts: "The social organism, discrete instead of concrete, asymmetrical instead of symmetrical, sensitive in all its units instead of having a single sensitive centre, is not comparable to any particular type of individual organism, animal or vegetal."[1]

Does this criticism of the organic analogy mean that Spencer made no useful contribution to sociological knowledge? To answer this we should not only pay attention to the immense amount of information about human societies all over the world which he

[1] *Ibid.*, p. 580.

collected, but also examine what he has to say at the end of Part II, for there he writes, ". . . there exist no analogies between the body politic and a living body, save those necessitated by that mutual dependence of parts which they display in common".[1] In other words, human society, like organic life, displays systematic qualities. Hence a society may be described as a structure of interdependent parts and the nature of these parts may be described and analysed. Here we have the beginning of a structural-functional analysis, an analysis that was to be developed in the next century in both Britain and America. In Spencer's work this development was hindered, as well as helped, by his overriding biological bias and even more hindered by his individualist *laissez-faire* philosophy. The general evolutionary thesis is not in question, except in so far as Spencer's interpretation is unilinear. Without doubt this aspect of his work influenced many other writers. However, only when the emphasis on biology diminished and individualistic philosophy declined was sociology able to develop further its own distinctive methods of thought. Today, as Crane Brinton wittily put it, "we have evolved beyond Spencer", but nevertheless he was a great figure in the history of the subject and there are many insights into the nature of modern society in his writings.

EVOLUTIONARY SOCIAL THOUGHT IN EUROPE

At first, independently of Spencer's work, although later much influenced by it, a number of European writers took up both the evolutionary theory of social change and the organic analogy that seemed essential to it.

P. E. von Lilienfeld-Toailles (1829–1903), a Russian of Swedish extraction, assumed society to be a "real organism". His principal work, originally written in Russian, was in the German translation entitled *Gedanken über die Sozialwissenschaft der Zukunft*, a book fairly widely read at the time. He was an extreme organicist, too much so to exert a lasting influence. From 1897–98 he was President of the Institut Internationale de Sociologie and took part in its third Congress. He also wrote *La Pathologie Sociale* (1896).

[1] *Ibid.*

Rather more prominent at this time was Alfred Espinas (1844–1922), a French scholar who taught at the University of Bordeaux during the time when Émile Durkheim was on the staff. In 1877 Espinas published *Des sociétés animales*, a book that was both anti-individualist and anti-socialist in sentiment. Like Lilienfeld-Toailles he held that society is a living body—"a living entity subject to such natural laws as those of co-operation, division of labour, delegation of function". In even stronger terms than Spencer's he maintained that his synthesis of organicism and evolutionary thought provided the only possible basis for a scicnce of society. In this connection he wrote an influential article "Être ou ne pas être, ou du postulat de la sociologie."[1]

A younger writer and organiser of sociological discussion and debate was Rene Worms (1869–1926). He was clearly under the influence of both Spencer and Lilienfeld-Toailles when he wrote *Organisme et Société* (1896). Worms also saw a close analogy between organism and society. Both are subject to natural laws, he said, but he added that society being on a higher evolutionary level than the biological organism, social processes necessarily must be more complex. For him the highest evolutionary development was the national group, for he argued that the parts are held together by consciousness, and in its highest manifestation this is national sentiment. Worms wrote several books, among them being *Philosophie des sciences sociales* in three volumes (1903–7) and *Les principes biologiques de l'évolution sociale* (1910), but he is more notable for founding the *Revue internationale de sociologie* in 1892 and the Institut Internationale de Sociologie in the following year together with an International Library of Sociology. In 1895 he founded the Société de Sociologie de Paris.

Rather different from the foregoing was A. J. E. Fouillée (1838–1912), in that he was rather less enamoured with the organic analogy and rather more interested in the contractual theory of society. His treatment of social evolution was highly individualistic, for he believed that the final stage of evolution was a complete union of individuality and sociality under the most advanced form of social contract. Ideas, he argued, are

[1] *Revue Philosophique*, Vol. 51, 1901.

forces which bind the members of a society together. This idealist view is found in his *L'évolutionisme des idées-forces* (1890).

One other writer deserves brief mention, a German, A. E. F. Schäffle (1831–1903). In a four-volume work *Bau und Leben des Sozialen Körpers* (1875–8) he made a bold attempt to develop a philosophical system unifying the natural and social sciences. His attempt, like Spencer's, involved him in a thoroughgoing use of the organic analogy, and he too gives many such descriptions. However, Schäffle was not so materialist in his outlook as Spencer and he introduced into his account of evolution idealist modifications derived from his Hegelian philosophy. He was not an individualist and rather looked forward to a transformation of capitalist society, one of the main features of which would be the development of occupational estates; an idea Durkheim was to take up in modified form in the next century.

Social Darwinism and Racial Theories

All these writers came to be known by the sobriquet "Social Darwinists" which only loosely indicates that they held in common a theory of social evolution allied to ideas about natural selection. They saw sociological thought as requiring the use of biological concepts, a view which suited the temper of the times, for popular thought in the latter half of the nineteenth century was dominated by Darwinian notions. They achieved a measure of success on the Continent, especially when a few of them, logically pursuing their thought without giving up their biological assumptions, became interested in race and racial differences. Thus J. A. de Gobineau (1816–82) wrote a famous four-volume work: *Essai sur l'inégalité des races humaines* (1853–5)—a book which was both anti-democratic in sentiment and pro-German in interest. His views about racial purity and his advice to encourage the cult of ancestors as a means of preserving it appealed to the racist Houston Stewart Chamberlain, whose influential writings owed much to Gobineau. Briefly, Gobineau argued that lack of initiative and courage followed upon racial interbreeding and that this in turn accounted for the decline of a nation or a civilisation. Moreover, he asserted that races are unequal; some being capable of progress, others being quite incapable of becoming civilised. To support this view he pointed to the persistently low state of development of primitive societies where for centuries no progress occurred. That geographical or environmental factors can have no bearing on this is clear, he blandly asserted, when one considers that colonial powers have been able to make rapid progress in such territories.

Gobineau's theory was developed in different fashion by Sir Francis Galton, a cousin of Darwin, and by his follower Karl Pearson. Both men were social statisticians who helped to develop the ideas of Quételet about the Gaussian curve (the normal curve of error) and its relevance to the physical characteristics of man. Galton established a laboratory in London to study physical and psychological data. He held that individuals are unequal in physical and psychological characteristics and that in any society they are distributed in accordance with the Gaussian curve. Such differences are largely the result of heredity. From this point he went on to outline the "science" of eugenics in order to apply his knowledge for the benefit of future generations. His writings include *Hereditary Genius* (1869) and *Natural Inheritance* (1889). Both Galton and Pearson played a part in the Sociology Society of London.

Another writer of this period was G. V. de Lapouge (1854–1936) who published two works that enjoyed some success: *Les sélections sociales* (1896) and *Race et milieu social* (1909). Lapouge discussed Darwinism in relation to social development declaring that there are no pure races, but that sufficient differences exist between races to enable the student to account for differences in achievements. The Nordic or Aryan race, he held, was superior to others. He introduced an argument based on the theory of natural selection to account for the decline in power and influence of some peoples, the unfit races going to the wall. Selection takes place, he averred, in many fields—by warfare, by political struggle, by economic competition, but also as a result of a normative order such as a religion which insisted on celibacy for a numerous priesthood, or polygyny which disturbed the sex ratio in a society, and so forth. Similar to Lapouge's work was that of Otto Ammon (1842–1916), who later collaborated with him. Ammon was a rather more scholarly writer who endeavoured to establish laws relating physical (racial) characteristics to social behaviour. Indeed, he and Lapouge propounded a set of "laws", a typical example being: the restriction of social mobility favours the production of men of ability in the upper classes, for the latter are more thoroughly bred.

Ludwig Gumplowicz (1838–1909), a Polish writer who held a professorship at Graz, was perhaps the most reasonable and the least extreme of this group of writers. Unlike the others, who were mainly amateurs with aristocratic conservative views, Gumplowicz was a professional sociologist. Evolution, he held, was not linear, it was discontinuous and also it arose from social conflicts. Although he discussed race differences he placed less weight on them; races, he argued, cannot be said to have orginated in the same source, but from a variety of sources and therefore there is no necessary blood-tie between them. The conflict which acts as a selection process seemed to him to be mainly economic. Firstly, it is to be seen in primitive societies where conflict operates on a tribal level; secondly, we may see it in advanced societies where it is a class-struggle. His *Grundriss der Soziologie* (1885) displays a modified Social Darwinism. Like other writers in this tradition he drew political lessons from his analysis. In fact he seemed to have conceived of sociology as an applied discipline aiding politics; this is especially noticeable in his *Soziologische Staatsidee* (1892). One notable book was written by a group of Belgians: in 1894 Jean Demoor, Jean Massart and Emile Vandervelde tried to forge a link between biology and sociology in their *Evolution by Atrophy in Biology and Sociology.* This was an attempt to discuss the similarity in natural selection among organisms and social institutions and human groups.

Racial theories continued to be produced and later they infected, with disastrous results, the political and social life of Europe by being sponsored by the National Socialist German Workers Party and acted upon by the forces under the Hitler regime, but sociologists gradually abandoned them long before that attempt to destroy the Jews in Europe and subdue the Slavonic peoples, for the reason that this line of thought proved intellectually unfruitful. After all, the argument was mainly circular: the fittest people or races were those that survived. How do we know they were the fittest? Because they survived. A modern account of this departure in sociological thought may be found in M. Banton's *Darwinism and the Study of Society* (1961), and in Richard Hofstadter's *Social Darwinism in American Thought* (2nd edn. 1955). Moreover, the fascination with biology slowly declined as other ideas inspired sociological thought. But before we turn to this we must examine one other product of this tradition of evolutionary sociology, a product that was much more valuable, namely, the comparative study of social institutions.

CHAPTER IV

THE ANALYTICAL AND COMPARATIVE STUDY OF SOCIAL INSTITUTIONS

The study of social institutions has origins deeply rooted in history. Thus historians have asked themselves questions about a regular form of behaviour, e.g. parliamentary government, or feudal kingship, by examining not only the manner of its development over a period of years but by examining its antecedents. To be sure, the particular forms of behaviour have been limited, for historians have tended to concentrate on political and diplomatic behaviour. The evolutionary sociologists cast their net wider. Spencer collected a vast and varied amount of data about human behaviour in different societies, most of them very primitive and of little or no interest to the historian, but Spencer was too speculative and correspondingly careless of the quality of his evidence to gain the historians' respect or interest. Yet from time to time a writer emerged who examined a society as a whole and attempted to explain its processes, not only by asking the question how did this come about? but asking the equally important question: why did it persist so long? The first question takes a scholar to the genesis of phenomena, the second makes him look at a phenomenon in relation to other phenomena. This second activity is both analytical and comparative. Thus, for example, in a given society the persistence of a social institution may be explained by discerning a relationship between that institution and another; a type of economy and a type of government, or a form of land tenure and a method of agriculture.

The comparative method has, however, been employed in another way. Thus the analysis of a social institution may take the form of comparing that institution as it occurs in a number of societies differing significantly in some respect, or the comparison of diverse examples of the same institution within a society or in several societies. Such an investigation may well yield an explanation by pointing to some structural principle governing diverse forms of the same institution; such a principle may show a relationship between two systems of law, or two kinds of kinship arrangements. In these intellectual activities we have what is probably the most important contribution to knowledge that sociology can make. It is interesting to note that such contributions were being made a hundred years ago and more, and at the same time as the more speculative and less satisfactory excursions of evolutionary sociology. However, to give an account of all this valuable work would occupy many pages, and it is therefore necessary to be selective. What follows is merely illustrative. For this reason we shall examine the work of three authors who wrote during the first quarter of our period; they are chosen both because of the quality of their work and because of their lasting influence in sociology. They are N. D. Fustel de Coulanges, L. H. Morgan, and Sir Henry Maine. It must not be supposed that what follows is a summary of their work; it is but a selection from that part which may truly be said to have informed the development of sociology.

Religion in Ancient Greece and Rome

N. D. Fustel de Coulanges (1830–89) was a French historian and classicist, remarkable for a book published in 1864 entitled *La Cité Antique*. The book was immediately successful and nine years later was translated into English. The abiding value of this work is the discernment of a relationship between the beliefs of a people and the structure of their inter-personal relationships. The people he wrote about were part of the ancient world of early Greece and Rome, and in writing about them he showed the role played by one social institution, religion, in binding a people together in groups of ever increasing size and complexity; he examined what now we would call the social function of religion. How did it happen, he asked himself, that institutions so very different from anything we are familiar with today could, in the first place, become established, and, in the second place, persist for so long a time? In other words, he wrote both history and sociology at the same time; indeed, this may be regarded as one of the finest of the early attempts to write historical sociology. Here is his thesis:

> A comparison of beliefs and laws shows that a primitive religion constituted the Greek and Roman family, established their marriage and paternal authority, fixed the order of relationship, and consecrated the right of property, and the right of inheritance. This same religion, after having enlarged and extended the family, formed a still larger association, the city, and reigned in that as it had reigned in the family. From it came all the institutions, as well as all the private law, of the ancients. It was from this that the city received all its principles, its rules, its usages, and its magistracies. But, in the course of time, this ancient religion became modified or effaced, and private law and political institutions were modified with it.[1]

By an examination of classical literature and such inscriptions as survive, Fustel de Coulanges was able to build up a picture of the social institutions of that primitive rural society. To him it seemed that the body of custom, and later of laws, had their origins in religious beliefs, and that such beliefs determining normal behaviour also conditioned the structure of family life. It was in their peculiar ideas about death and sepulture that he found the beginnings he sought. For if the dead were not given a proper burial, it was thought they would be unhappy and consequently they could and would be a disturbance to the living. Burial was important, and that it be done in a proper or standardised manner was considered paramount. Such an emphasis, he argued, led eventually not merely to reverence for the dead, but to worship of them. It was not merely a matter of giving them a decent burial, but of subsequent periodical attention being paid them, usually in the form of libations being poured on their graves and gifts of food left for them. All this led to a set of family obligations towards deceased members.

> If the funeral repast ceased to be offered to the dead, they immediately left their tombs, and became wandering shades, that were heard in the silence of the night. They reproached the living with their negligence; or they sought to punish them by afflicting them with diseases, or cursing their soil with sterility. In a word, they left the living no rest till the funeral feasts were re-established.[2]

[1] *The Ancient City: A Study on the Religion, Laws, and Institutions of Greece and Rome*, p. 13 (Doubleday Anchor Books). [2] *Loc. cit.*, p. 23.

If death was the first mystery of the ancient world, raising a man's thoughts from the visible to the invisible, from the transitory to the eternal, from the human to the divine, then fire was the second, for fire was sacred. In eloquent words the author describes the religious awe and supplication associated with the altar blaze in the home, for the fire always kept in the hearth was the centre of the home. In later time the common noun denoting the altar fire became a proper name, the personified deity being known as Vesta. That a close relationship existed between the fire in the hearth and the dead in their graves struck the author as significant for the explanation of other phenomena. Thus he writes:

> We may suppose, therefore, that the domestic fire was in the beginning only the symbol of the worship of the dead; that under the stone of the hearth an ancestor reposed; that the fire was lighted there to honor him, and that this fire seemed to preserve life in him, or represented his soul as always vigilant.
>
> This is merely a conjecture, and we have no proof of it. Still it is certain that the oldest generations of the race from which the Greeks and Romans sprang worshipped both the dead and the hearth-fire—an ancient religion that did not find its gods in physical nature, but in man himself, and that has for its object the adoration of the invisible being which is in us, the moral and thinking power which animates and governs our bodies.[1]

The religion which placed a value on sepultural rites and fire worship was essentially a domestic religion. The nearest relative to the dead performed the funeral obsequies and it was therefore imperative for a man to have an heir, in fact a male heir, to perform the task. Two consequences followed, for, in the first place, the senior male member of the family officiated as priest to the family and, in the second place, absence of a male heir led to the practice of adopting an heir. The implications of these beliefs and rites for the structure of marriage can easily be traced, for a daughter left her household gods on marriage to worship at the hearth of her husband and hence to worship his ancestors. This was a serious step for a woman to take and therefore this changing of religion added to the solemnity of the occasion of getting married. It increased the profundity of the experience, not as an individual

[1] *Ibid.*, p. 33

act and experience but in its implications, for marriage was a means of securing an heir and ultimately the felicity of both the dead and the living.

> Marriage, then, was obligatory. Its aim was not pleasure; its principal object was not the union of two beings who were pleased with each other, and who wished to go united through the pleasures and trials of life. The effect of marriage, in the eyes of religion and of the laws, was the union of two beings in the same domestic worship, in order to produce from them a third who would be qualified to continue the worship.[1]

This discussion led Fustel de Coulanges to the point where he was able to describe the kinship system of the ancient world and to define its boundaries. Thus he recalls the words of ancient authorities:

> Plato* says that kinship is the community of the same domestic gods. When Demosthenes wishes to prove that two men are relatives, he shows that they practise the same religious rites, and offer the funeral repast at the same tomb. Indeed, it was the domestic religion that constituted relationship. Two men could call themselves relatives when they had the same gods, the same sacred fire, and the same funeral repast.
>
> Now, we have already observed that the right to offer sacrifices to the sacred fire was transmitted only from male to male, and that the worship of the dead was addressed to the ascendants in the male line only. It followed from this rule that one could not be related through females. In the opinion of those ancient generations, a female transmitted neither being nor worship. The son owed all to the father.[2]
>
> (*Plato, *Laws*, Book V.)

The foundation of the kin relationship was not birth but worship, but the system resulted in kinship being patrilineal in descent. In Roman law two consanguineous brothers were regarded as agnates, whereas two uterine brothers were not. Relationship entirely depended on having a common religious rite. Similar situations, he says, may be traced in India, for this system was not unique. To be sure, new forms came into being as time passed and relationships altered, for when religion declined the tie of common worship gave way to a blood-tie and a kinship relationship by birth was recognised in law.

[1] *Ibid.*, p. 51. [2] *Ibid.*, pp. 56–7.

Another social institution, property, is described and its links with both religion and kinship disclosed. Thus the gods take possession of the soil, but the gods are the dead who belong to a particular family, which alone has the right to invoke them. Indeed, the gods live under the ground. Fustel de Coulanges goes on:

> The soil where the dead rested was inalienable and imprescriptible. The Roman law required that, if a family sold the field where the tomb was situated, it should still retain the ownership of this tomb, and should always preserve the right to cross the field, in order to perform the ceremonies of its worship.
>
> The ancient usage was to inter the dead, not in cemeteries or by the road-side, but in the field belonging to the family. This custom of ancient times is attested by a law of Solon, and by several passages in Plutarch.[1]

Thus religion and not laws first guaranteed property rights. It was, of course, difficult, if not impossible, to dispose of land, and when property was sold, a ritual act always accompanied the sale. Moreover, inheritance was by the son and not the daughter. This was not because of any intended harshness toward women, but because a daughter could not sacrifice on her deceased father's grave and indeed if married she had forsaken his hearth anyway, and hence his gods, for those of her husband; but a daughter might be endowed by her father or by her brothers. The case was similar where a man died childless and intestate.

> A man died without children; to know who the heir of his estate was, we have only to learn who was qualified to continue his worship.
>
> Now the domestic religion was transmitted by blood from male to male. The descent in the male line alone established between two men the religious relation which permitted one to continue the worship of the other. . . . One was a relative because he had the same worship, the same original sacred fire, the same ancestors. But one was not a relative because he had the same mother; religion did not admit of kinship through women. The children of two sisters, or of a sister and a brother, had no bond of kinship between them, and belonged neither to the same domestic religion nor the same family.
>
> These principles regulated the order of succession. . . . In default of descendants, . . . (a man) had as an heir his brother,

[1] *Ibid.*, p. 65.

not his sister, the son of his brother, not the son of his sister. In default of brothers and nephews, it was necessary to go up in the series of ascendants of the deceased, always in the male line, until a branch of the family was found that was detached through a male; then to re-descend in this branch from male to male, until a living man was found; that was the heir.[1]

In this ancient world of Greece and Rome the authority of the family was paramount. Here was a society where religion, family and property were intimately connected, but where religion was the dominant institution. However, it was a rural not an urban phenomenon in the first place. When cities were built this normative order was extended to them, although with some modifications. The ancient culture of Greece and Rome developed with the growth in importance of the *gens*, which was a group of families related to each other, but related in terms of common worship; the members practising the same rite. This development of the gens represented the growth of new loyalties, but by the same token there was the growth of new forms of social control, for the gens acted as a governing unit. Its common religious basis was the deification of a common ancestor. The gens, says Fustel de Coulanges, appears to be the earliest form of social grouping other than the immediate family. However, other forms of social grouping also developed, such as the *phratry* (or the *curia* as it was known in Rome). These were larger collections of families owning a common ancestor, who was deified and made the object of worship. Each phratry possessed an altar and sacred fire as well as liturgical ritual, and worship was presided over by a phratriarch or curion as the case might be. This group was again a self-governing unit, adjudicating among its members and exercising discipline. In time several such groups would come together to form a tribe, and thus was ancient tribal society formed. It is along these lines that Fustel de Coulanges proceeds to account for the rise of the Greek cities: families associate to form gens, gens associate to form phratries and phratries associate to form tribal societies, but all on the basis of respect for religion. When two tribes coalesced on this basis a city was born, and again the common bond was a common rite.

Thus does Fustel de Coulanges come to the main subject of

[1] *Ibid.*, pp. 77–8.

his book, the analysis of the Greek city state and its conquest by Rome, the development of political institutions, the growth of law, and the changes in ideas and beliefs that took place. It is not possible to pursue the story here any further. What has been recounted, however, shows the method he employed and the conceptual notions he brought to the task. Much of his work has been superseded. Thus, whereas he discerned a causal connection between religious beliefs and practices on the one hand, and social and political institutions on the other, we today would prefer to note the interdependency of social institutions, the consistency of religion with other institutional forms, rather than see the latter as the effects and the former as cause. The significant feature of his work for the history of sociology is that he saw ancient society as a whole, and a whole that was a social system of interrelated parts. To be sure he did not possess a great amount of evidence, but such as was available he used with great felicity. For him a society was not a haphazard collection of people, but neither was it an organism; it was a phenomenon of a peculiar kind resting on values, beliefs, rules and laws; it was systematic and coherent; and it represented a cohesion not only of people but of social forms, of institutions. It was subject to change, but change in one part or aspect meant change in another, and this led him to trace changes which resulted in the emergence of a society quite different from the original. As modern Greece is different from the Greece of Demosthenes, so the Greece of his time was different from the ancient Greece that Fustel de Coulanges described in the early part of *La Cité Antique*. As he put it himself:

> We have written the history of a belief. It was established, and human society was constituted. It was modified, and society underwent a series of revolutions. It disappeared, and society changed its character. Such was the law of ancient times.[1]

Kinship, Ancient and Modern

We turn now to one of the most influential sociologists of the nineteenth century, Lewis H. Morgan (1818–81), an American lawyer who turned his attention to the North American Indian

[1] *Ibid.*, p. 396.

peoples and wrote a careful and scholarly book about them entitled *The League of the Iroquois* (1857). Its success prompted him to make a very detailed and technical analysis of kinship terminology, based largely on his own work on the Indians of his continent. This resulted in *Systems of Consanguinity and Affinity of the Human Family* (1870) (a lengthy essay which he published in the *Smithsonian Contributions to Knowledge*, Vol. XVII in 1871). This was followed by *Ancient Society, or Researches in the Lines of Human Progress from Savagery through Barbarism to Civilization* (1877).

Like Fustel de Coulanges, Morgan was interested in the ancient world, but whilst writing about the Greek gentes he also made a comparison with the clan structures of North American Indians. In fact, Morgan's work is much more comparative and, what is more interesting, the focus of his attention is rather different. Whereas the former writer was chiefly concerned with religion, Morgan concentrated his attention on kinship and the family. Indeed, his contributions to our understanding of the nature of kinship are outstanding, to say the least, and stimulated some of the best work that has been carried out in the study of social institutions; it is this interest in kinship that we shall be discussing here.

Early European writers, being educated largely in the classical writings of Greece and Rome, were apt to assume that the origins of human kinship were of the patrilineal and patriarchal kind that we have been referring to. However, about the middle of the nineteenth century several investigators, notably J. J. Bachhofen[1] and J. G. McLennan,[2] pointed to the fact that some primitive peoples did not count descent in the male line, but in the female line. Moreover, McLennan showed that the practice of forbidding marriage inside the kinship group was often extensive, so that many people only very distantly related to each other were forbidden to marry each other. This led Morgan to investigate, more carefully than they had done, the nomenclature of kinship and the terms used by kinsfolk in addressing each other. He

[1] *Das Mutterrecht: Eine Untersuchung über die Gynaikokratie der alten Welt nach ihrer religiosen und rechtlichen Natur* (1861).

[2] *Primitive Marriage*, 1865.

discovered, for instance, that in many parts of the world there is little discrimination amongst the grades of kinship relationships; that grades of kin are merged and a general category term is used to denote them: this he called the "Malayan System" (later the "Hawaiian System"), and deemed it to have been general in Polynesia. In this instance a limited number of kinship terms are employed to cover a large number of kin; terms such as grandparent, parent, brother, sister, child and grandchild, and that no other blood-relationships but these are recognised. That is to say there are no terms like uncle, aunt, nephew, niece, cousin. In addition he discovered a system which obtained in North America, parts of India and Africa, and in a rudimentary form in Australia, which he called the "Turanian System", where a male person will speak of his nephew and niece (in the male line of descent), as his "son" and "daughter" respectively; thus making no apparent distinction between his own and his brother's children. Similarly, he will call his grand-nephew and grand-niece, in the male line only, "grandson" and "granddaughter". This happens in both systems but, unlike the Malayan System, in the Turanian System when a male addresses kin in the female line he calls them "nephew" and "niece" and they respond by using the term "uncle". Again, in the Malayan System nephews and nieces, in both the male and female lines of descent (i.e. a man's brother's and sister's children) are alike named children of the uncle. If the person speaking is female, instead of male, then there is a reversal so that she speaks accordingly to her sister's sons and daughters, calling them "son" and "daughter", and her brother's children "nephew" and "niece", and their children in turn as "grandson" and "granddaughter". These differences, so widespread on the earth, called for explanation. But the most significant contribution to sociology Morgan made was not his particular explanation, which no scholar can accept today, but the fact that he made the distinction and perceived it to be important. However, let us examine his explanation because he was guided in making it by the prevalent interest in social evolution. As the sub-title to *Ancient Society* indicates, Morgan sought to explain human society by tracing its passage through time from Savagery, to Barbarism, to Civilisation. In doing this he was concerned with family and kinship organisation, tribal society and nationhood. But chiefly his interest was in kinship. Thus at the end of *Ancient Society* (in Part III) he presents an argument in evolutionary terms accounting for the observed differences in kinship nomenclature. His discussion opens as follows:

> We have been accustomed to regard the monogamian family as the form which has always existed; but interrupted in exceptional areas by the patriarchal. Instead of this, the idea of the family has been a growth through successive stages of development, the monogamian being the last in its series of forms. It will be my object to show that it was preceded by more ancient forms which prevailed universally throughout the period of savagery, through the Older and into the Middle Period of barbarism; and that neither the monogamian nor the patriarchal can be traced back of the Later Period of barbarism. They were essentially modern. Moreover, they were impossible in ancient society, until an anterior experience under earlier forms in every race of mankind had prepared the way for their introduction.

Five different and successive forms may now be distinguished, each having an institution of marriage peculiar to itself. They are the following:

I. *The Consanguine Family*
It was founded upon the intermarriage of brothers and sisters, own and collateral, in a group.

II. *The Punaluan Family*
It was founded upon the intermarriage of several sisters, own and collateral, with each other's husbands, in a group; the joint husbands not being necessarily kinsmen of each other. Also, on the intermarriage of several brothers, own and collateral, with each other's wives, in a group; these wives not being necessarily of kin to each other, although often the case in both instances. In each case the group of men were conjointly married to the group of women.

III. *The Syndyasmian or Pairing Family*
It was founded upon marriage between single pairs, but without an exclusive cohabitation. The marriage continued during the pleasure of the parties.

IV. *The Patriarchal Family*
It was founded upon the marriage of one man with several wives; followed, in general, by the seclusion of the wives.

V. *The Monogamian Family*
It was founded upon marriage between single pairs, with an exclusive cohabitation.[1]

Morgan then went on to point out that the most primitive form of family, i.e. the "Consanguine Family", has a Malayan type of structure. Actually there are no living examples and the type is inferred; this he admits, but he asserted that the Polynesians had this structure before it altered to become Punaluan. Yet this is an explanation in terms of an assumption for which no evidence is available. "In course of time", he wrote, "a second great system of consanguinity, the Turanian, supervened upon the first, and spread over a large part of the earth's surface."[2] What Morgan wanted to do in this argument was to show how family structure evolved from intermarriage among brothers and sisters through various forms of group marriage to the monogamous state known today in Europe and North America. He imagined that variations in kinship terminology explained these different usages. The practice of a group of brothers speaking to each other's children as "sons" and "daughters" indicated, he thought, that they at one time had practised group marriage. All this is highly speculative and not very important. What is important is the recognition that kinship systems vary, and broadly speaking he pointed to two main types.

> These systems resolve themselves into two ultimate forms, fundamentally distinct. One of these is *classificatory*, and the other *descriptive*. Under the first, consanguinei are never described, but are classified into categories, irrespective of their nearness or remoteness in degree to *Ego*; and the same term of relationship is applied to all the persons in the same category.[3]

The recognition of different types of kinship systems was a development that later led to continued work in social anthropology as we shall see, for it laid the basis for the study of small and simple societies. It was perceived that in simple societies the forms of

[1] *Loc. cit.*, pp. 393–4. [2] *Ibid.*, p. 396 [3] *Ibid.*, p. 403.

organisation are centred much more around kinship than any other kind of relationship. The numbers of kinsfolk that a member of such a society had relationships with is immense, and some method of classifying male and female relatives is important. Kinship nomenclature indicates social position, and the terms of address suggest the nature of the relationship and hence the type of behaviour that it is appropriate to display toward a relative. For example, a man has a relationship to his son which is social as well as consanguinal, similarly he has the same kind of *social* relationship to his brother's son, and this is reflected in his use of the term "son" in addressing his brother's child; the same principle may be extended to much more distant kin and frequently is. In other words, analysis and comparison of kinship systems leads us to an understanding of social organisation and behaviour; this is the consequence of Morgan's work, for his influence was great not only because of his evolutionary account, which indeed made its impact on Frederick Engels[1] and through him on Marxism,[2] but in spite of his evolutionism on others such as A. R. Radcliffe-Brown.[3] This subject, however, we must leave for the present in order to turn to another institutional aspect of society, namely law.

Law, Ancient and Modern

For this purpose we shall look at the work of the English jurist, Sir Henry James Sumner Maine (1822–88), who having been employed by the government in India was able successfully to make comparative studies of Indian native law and Roman and English law of considerable significance not only for the history of legal studies, but for sociological investigation.

Maine's thought, like that of these other writers, was also conditioned by the prevailing interest in social evolution. To understand the nature of variations in an institution, it was necessary to see what the antecedents were and to trace the

[1] *The Conditions of the Working Class in England in 1844* (publ. in German 1845, in English 1885).

[2] *The Communist Manifesto* (publ. in German 1848, in English 1850).

[3] "The Study of Kinship Systems", *J. Royal Anthropological Inst.* LXXI, 1941.

development of the institution from its earliest form up until the present. Thus his interest in law, especially as it is related to property, led him to trace the evolution of property in land from the archaic collectivism of the most primitive condition of man through various stages, where the notion of contract had been vaguely entertained, through forms of feudalism and similar arrangements, until the final stage was reached displayed in the individualistic attitude defining the institution of private property. Yet his pursuit of this end was unusual, for he saw the development of this kind of law in the new light shed on the subject by his various comparative studies not only of conditions in India, but of those among the southern Slavonic peoples, and medieval Celts and Teutons. To be sure he abandoned the chronological limitations that had restricted the vision of other students of law, but he oddly held fast to ethnic limitations, thus confining his studies to people of the same race, i.e. the Aryan race. Indeed, he explicitly disavowed the validity of extending generalisations drawn from studies of the life of non-Aryan tribes which some of his contemporaries wanted to make.

Maine's most famous work is *Ancient Law* (1861), but other works of note are *Village Communities in the East and the West* (1871), *Early Law and Custom* (1883), and *Lectures on the Early History of Institutions* (1874). Briefly; his argument is that law developed as society developed. In the earliest forms of social life there was no law:

> It is certain that, in the infancy of mankind, no sort of legislature, nor even a distinct author of law, is contemplated or conceived of. Law has scarcely reached the footing of custom; it is rather a habit.[1]

Habit thus brought about a body of rules which were part of the oral tradition of a people; this may be called *customary law*, unwritten but guarded by an élite:

> The epoch of Customary Law, and of its custody by a privileged order, is a very remarkable one. The condition of jurisprudence which it implies has left traces which may still be detected in legal and popular phraseology. The law, thus known exclusively to a privileged minority, whether a caste, an aristocracy, a priestly tribe, or a sacerdotal college, is true unwritten law.[2]

[1] *Ancient Law* (1906), p. 7. [2] *Loc. cit.*, p. 11.

Customary Law in turn gave way to Codes of Law, such as those of the Twelve Tables, of Hammurabi and of Moses, but these represent less the results of legislation than the pronouncements of judges. Moreover, he says, they follow upon the invention of writing. When primitive law has thus been embodied in a code there is an end of what may be called spontaneous development. At this point the growth of law takes on a new character, changing *pari passu* with the development of society; in fact from relative stasis society enters a dynamic phase. This dynamic factor is connected with man's newly "conscious desire of improvement", or at all events of man's ability to compass objects other than those which are aimed at in primitive times.[1] However, when the codes were compiled there was no conception of law as distinct from religion or philosophy. Indeed, there is not only little sense of order in the rules, but clearly they were not all observed, or not all were regarded as requiring to be observed at any one time. We may observe in passing that although he adhered to an evolutionary explanation of social institutions, Maine was no linear evolutionist:

> It should be noted that the growth of institutions is much too complicated, even if we confine our attention to one society, to be represented as a simple series in order of time. We constantly speak of one rule or custom as belonging to a more advanced stage of ideas than another; but this does not mean that in every society where it is found it must have been preceded in fact by a less advanced institution belonging to the next lower grade of culture. Imitation of neighbours or conquerors, or peculiar local conditions, may materially shorten a given stage in the normal development, or even cut it out altogether. What we do mean is that the order is not found reversed.[2]

His argument outlining the growth of legal institutions rests then on a theory of the development of human society. This theory encompassed the belief that "consanguinity or kinship" provided the main tie binding men in communities in earliest times. Thus primitive society consisted of a collection, not of individuals but of families. Moreover, as part of this theory he persistently held, despite criticisms from McLennan and Morgan, that the primeval

[1] *Ibid.*, p. 26. [2] *Ibid.*, p. 22.

condition of the human family was "patriarchal". His evidence was largely drawn from the first books of the Old Testament, but in his later work on *Early Law and Custom* he appealed also to the writers of antiquity:

> The Patriarchal theory of society is, as I have said, the theory of its origin in separate families, held together by the authority and protection of the eldest valid male ascendant. It is unnecessary to add that this theory is of considerable antiquity. So far as we can judge, it first occurred to the great Greek observers and philosophical thinkers of the fourth century before Christ.[1]

His assumption about the nature of the primitive family led him to the view that communities began to exist wherever a family held together, instead of separating, on the occasion of the death of its patriarchal chieftain. Such communities grew larger and larger and an ascending series of groups formed, based first on the family, then on the gens, and finally on the tribe. When considering kinship a number of problems presented themselves. Thus he was aware of the part played by adoption, and he also perceived the significance of patrilineal descent and its exclusively agnatic character. What, he asks, is the reason for this arbitrary inclusion and exclusion. "Why should a conception of kinship so elastic as to include strangers brought into the family by adoption, be nevertheless so narrow as to shut out the descendants of a female member?"[2] These problems are resolvable, he argued, if we examine the powers of the father. For the foundation of marriage, he asserted, is not the marriage of a father and a mother, but the authority of the father. If the defining quality of the family for Fustel de Coulanges was Worship, for Maine it was *Patria Potestas*. "Where the Potestas begins, Kinship begins; and therefore adopted relatives are among the kindred. Where Potestas ends, Kinship ends; so that a son emancipated by his father loses all rights of Agnation."[3] He went on to draw the conclusion that if a woman dies she could have no legitimate descendants. If she married, her children came under the *Patria Potestas*, or rule, not of *her* father, but of her husband, *their* father, and were thus to this extent lost to her family. It would be utterly confusing,

[1] *Loc. cit.*, p. 196. [2] *Ancient Law*, p. 154. [3] *Ibid.*, p. 155.

he observed, for descent through families to be recognised, for a man could not inherit two potestas, his father's and his mother's father's. It is regrettable that Maine ignored the evidence that descent through females is widely practised on the Earth, and that bilateral descent systems are not uncommon.

All this essay into prehistory was for Maine the preparation for his discussion of the movement from customary rules of corporate morality to the idea of individual obligation and the legal concepts of modern times. His account is best given in his own words:

> The movement of the progressive societies has been uniform in one respect. Through all its course it has been distinguished by the gradual dissolution of family dependency, and the growth of individual obligation in its place. The Individual is steadily substituted for the Family, as the unit of which civil laws take account. The advance has been accomplished at varying rates of celerity, and there are societies not absolutely stationary in which the collapse of the ancient organisation can only be perceived by careful study of the phenomena they present. But, whatever its pace, the change has not been subject to reaction or recoil, and apparent retardations will be found to have been occasioned through the absorption of archaic ideas and customs from some entirely foreign source. Nor is it difficult to see what is the tie between man and man which replaces by degrees those forms of reciprocity in rights and duties which have their origin in the Family. It is Contract.[1]

In the ancient society relationships were understood in terms of a person's status *vis-à-vis* another's status, but in modern society relationships are contractual. Thus social evolution, says Maine, has witnessed the change in the status of the female originally under tutelage, of the son in a father's power, and of the slave in a man's possession; so that today a woman is bound by a contractual tie, civil obligation is the bond uniting a parent and an adult child, and slavery is abolished; only the contractual relationship of master and servant remains. Hence the great change is from *status* to *contract*, and this is seen largely in terms of the institution of property and the laws pertaining to it. Whatever we may think of his arguments and his selection of evidence (and both his evolutionary theory and his analysis of

[1] *Ibid.*, p. 172.

legal development are open to serious criticism), there is much merit in his general method of analysis and comparison, in relating social institutions to each other, especially kinship and descent, succession and law, and his contribution to that tradition of sociology we call the comparative study of social institutions which developed so strongly in the last half of the nineteenth century.

CHAPTER V

THE LATER EVOLUTIONARY TRADITION OF SOCIOLOGY

The last quarter of the nineteenth century was marked by the publication in America and Britain of a number of sociological books, all of which were, in varying degrees, inspired by the evolutionary approach to the subject. Some of them stand in the sociological tradition of modern historicism, that is to say the tradition of Comte, Spencer, and Marx, and are concerned with the future of modern Western Civilisation; others more properly belong to the tradition of anthropology and focus attention on primitive man and his culture. Indeed, about the end of the century in Britain and America we may see a division of labour taking place along these lines, representing a growing divergence of the traditions, and not until comparatively recently did they converge again. Here we shall look briefly at the thought of some of these writers and consider their contributions to sociology.

BENJAMIN KIDD (1858–1919)

For Kidd evolution was inevitable but progressive, not however that progress is intentional, for he saw no conscious purpose at work in primitive society. Progress, he argued, takes place in conditions of stress and conflict. In this he was partly influenced by Karl Marx's theory of dialectical struggle. Yet unlike Marx he believed, as did Sir Henry Maine, that the movement of progressive societies is uniform in respect of growth of individual obligation, and with it the development of what we would today call individualistic attitudes. This development emerged from conflict, he said, for the advance of science made the "interests of the social organism and of the individual . . . antagonistic, and the former must always be predominant, there can never be found any sanction in individual reason for conduct in societies where the conditions of progress prevail".[1]

[1] *Social Evolution* (1894), p. 80.

Progress cannot take place without a submission of the reason of the individual. This is necessary because if man's reason were not checked in some manner it would reverse the conditions producing progress. The rational self-assertiveness of the individual serves narrow interests, whilst progressive society must entertain processes serving wider interests. The factor bringing about this latter end is religion. All religions, says Kidd, appear to involve an instinct having one invariable characteristic, namely the application of sanctions controlling individual desires. Speaking of this instinct he says: "Moved by it, man would appear to be always possessed by the desire to set up sanctions for his individual conduct, which would appear to be *super*-natural against those which were natural, sanctions which would appear to be *ultra*-rational against those which were simply rational."[1]

The function of religious beliefs for the evolution of society is to provide an ultra-rational sanction for social conduct in the individual. In most of his discussion of social evolution, religion as the primary social institution plays a big part. Following Spencer he perceived that the development of Western Civilisation depended on the breakdown of the military type of social organisation which both he and Spencer associated with oriental despotism and medieval kingship, and coterminously the enfranchisement of large sections of the population. Free labour, as far removed as possible from slavery and serfdom, was an essential. Yet, he pointed out, all this cannot be attributed to an increase in intelligence, or to enlightenment. To be sure there is a growth in altruistic feelings and this is a cause, but it is an intermediate one, for the source is religion, or at least a religious system which can deepen and soften the characters of people; for Kidd there is no doubt that this is the peculiar quality of Christianity. Indeed, he states categorically that the conclusion that "Darwinian science" must eventually establish is that: "The evolution which is slowly proceeding in human society is not primarily intellectual but religious in character."[2] And yet religious qualities cannot be divorced from others, and there is consequently a constellation of factors which combine to enable progress to take place: "great mental energy, resolution, enterprise, powers of prolonged and

[1] *Ibid.*, p. 92. [2] *Ibid.*, p. 245.

concentrated application, and a sense of simple-minded and single-minded devotion to conceptions of duty".[1] At this point Kidd in rudimentary fashion is aware of the set of religious and secular attitudes that prevailed in the period of early industrialisation and which Max Weber later was to describe at length but much more perceptively.

LESTER F. WARD (1841–1913)

The interest in social evolution in America took a new turn as a result of the work of two men, both of whom only in later life became academic sociologists—L. F. Ward and F. H. Giddings. Ward was for most of his life a research scientist employed by the government, but he published a number of large books including *Dynamic Sociology* (two volumes—1883), and *Outline of Sociology* (1898), followed by *Pure Sociology* (1903) and *Applied Sociology* (1906). There is much repetition in these works, but his ideas did develop throughout his life; here a brief résumé of his mature thought will be given.

Ward had no doubt about the fact of progress, but he held that an evolutionary theory which argued the case for a self-determining system, which happened to bring beneficial results to mankind independently of human will, was neither possible nor satisfactory for human dignity. Thus, whilst he was much influenced by Comte and Spencer he tried to restate the theory of social evolution allowing for human consciousness. Accordingly, his work has been described as psychological evolutionism; a term descriptive of Giddings' work too.

Ward's fundamental starting point is the belief that a sociological system must account for human achievement. It is what men do rather than what they are that matters. He saw a great difference between organic and social evolution precisely because the latter shows human purposiveness. As he put it: "the environment transforms the animal, while man transforms the environment".[2] Whilst progress depends mainly on material developments this cannot be regarded as the limit of progress, for the results are very far from being merely material. What he was trying to say was

[1] *Ibid.*, p. 287. [2] *Pure Sociology* (1903), p. 16.

that progress is a cultural phenomenon, using the word in its contemporary meaning to include material artefacts but also custom, law, morals, ideas, philosophies and other beliefs. Progress is a subject for the sociologist because it is a collective phenomenon. It is insufficient for the sociologist to restrict himself to the study of social structures as static entities, for structures alter in type. If this were not so there could be no progress. Hence, he concluded, social dynamics is the heart of the subject.

Although he was more abstract than Spencer in his treatment of social evolution, Ward, in a manner which bears some similarity, examined the parallels in both organic and social evolutionary processes. Unlike Spencer, however, he did perceive some dissimilarities, indeed some radical differences of potential, some societies being structurally better placed than others for change, although he made allowances for what we now would call culture contact. Secondly, both conscious (telic) and unconscious (genetic) factors influence the development of innovations making for progress. Thirdly, there is social energy operating to provide creative syntheses. Ward's psychological arguments are by no means always clear and his categories appear at times to be confused. To some extent this is attributable to the then current confusion about the relationship of the individual to society, but it also arises from his almost purely speculative treatment of the subject, for empirical evidence is conspicuously absent, and concepts not rooted in empirical referents are apt to be loosely used.

FRANKLIN H. GIDDINGS (1858–1931)

The intellectual temper of America in the last quarter of the nineteenth century would scarcely permit any theoretical development in sociology that was not able to do justice to robust purposive intention. Ward's work was largely ignored at first; not so that of Franklin Giddings, whose *Principles of Sociology: An Analysis of the Phenomena of Association and of Social Organisation* was published in 1896. In this work Giddings says he decided that sociology could only proceed by first answering the question: what are the fundamental social phenomena? Other writers had attempted answers, suggestions being: conflict, contract, imitation, external constraint on the individual, and so forth. His own reflections led him to consider man's consciousness. He wrote: "A sufficient account of the purpose and scientific character of sociology, originally and at the present time, has now been presented. It is a science that tries to conceive of society in its unity, and attempts to explain it in terms of some fact of consciousness or motive and an objective interpretation in terms of cosmic cause and law. To accomplish such explanation it must work out a subjective interpretation in terms of a physical process. These two interpretations must be consistent, each with the other, and must be correlated. The subjective process and the objective process must be shown to be inseparable, each being at all times conditioned by the other."[1] And he later continues: "Since contract and alliance are phenomena obviously more special than association or society, and imitation and impression are phenomena obviously more general, we must look for the psychic datum, motive, or principle of society in the one phenomenon that is intermediate. Accordingly, the sociological postulate can be no other than this, namely: The original and elementary subjective fact in society is *the consciousness of kind.*"[2]

This term "consciousness of kind", Giddings said, is applicable to any creature which recognises another as of the same kind as itself; it distinguishes inanimate from animate things. It is, among mankind, the only thing distinguishing social conduct from purely economic, political, or religious conduct. It is also a determining principle, for around it "all other motives organise themselves in the evolution of social choice, social volition, or social policy. Therefore, to trace the operation of the consciousness of kind through all its social manifestations is to work out a complete subjective interpretation of society."[3]

The evolution of human society, he thought, had proceeded along the following lines. Firstly, social aggregations were formed by external conditions, e.g. food supply, temperature; the units being homogeneous and the process physical. Then, within the aggregation a consciousness of kind appears among similar individuals developing into association. This in turn reacts

[1] *Principles of Sociology,* chap. I. [2] *Ibid.,* chap. II. [3] *Ibid.*

favourably on the pleasures and life-chances of individuals, who become more aware of this and begin to will association, deliberately seeking to extend and perfect their social relations. In all this process, he claimed, association, social choice, and social will are determined by consciousness of kind.

It is at this point, he argued, that the physical process reappears, for choices have differing consequences. Taking the welfare of the community as a criterion some choices are sound, others foolish, and hence there is plenty of scope for natural selection: "In the struggle for existence, choices, no less than individuals, may not survive. The choices and the resulting activities and relations that, on the whole, are baneful are terminated, perhaps through the subordination or the extinction of individuals, perhaps through the disappearance of whole societies."[1]

The cycle of social causation begins and ends with the physical process, and natural selection is just so much more complicated in the social sphere. This led Giddings to identify the sociologist's task. There are three main quests, he says: "First, he must try to discover the conditions that determine mere aggregation and concourse. Secondly, he must try to discover the law that governs social choices, the law, that is, of the subjective process. Thirdly, he must try to discover also the law that governs the natural selection and the survival of choices, the law, that is, of the objective process."[2]

The advanced forms of society are the result of the pressures brought about by conflict and competition which compel mankind to develop organisation. To a large extent, he claimed, this depends on the leadership that élites provide. Departing from Spencer's view of society as an organism, Giddings says "society is more than an organism . . . it is an organisation, partly the product of unconscious evolution, partly . . . a result of conscious planning".[3] An organisation may have a function, and this he saw to be the development of conscious life and the creation of human personality, for conscious association of men together is what develops moral character. The highest manifestation of the evolutionary process is the development of personality. It follows, says Giddings, that the sociological task is twofold: firstly, to learn how social

[1] *Ibid.* [2] *Ibid.* [3] *Ibid.*, chap. IV.

relations are evolved, and then to see how they react on the development of personality.

His work has a tighter argument than Ward's and it is illuminated by great erudition and a high sense of purpose. He was probably the greatest expositor of social evolution America had produced, and his psychological slant on sociology may be seen to have had lasting effects on many of his successors.

SIR EDWARD BURNETT TYLOR (1832–1917)

In passing on to examine the thought of E. B. Tylor we are in fact retracing our steps, for his main work entitled *Primitive Culture* was published in 1871. The sub-title of this work indicates its contents, for they are his "researches into the Development of Mythology, Philosophy, Religion, Language, Art and Custom". It was in many ways a continuation of his earlier *Researches into the Early History of Mankind and the Development of Civilisation* (1865).

"Culture or Civilization, taken in its wide ethnographic sense, is that complex whole which includes knowledge, belief, art, morals, law, custom, and any other capabilities and habits acquired by man as a member of society."[1] His argument was that the uniformity of civilisation may largely be ascribed to "the uniform action of uniform causes". He also argued that various grades of culture may be regarded as stages of *development* or *evolution* (he preferred the former word to the latter), each grade "being the outcome of previous history, and about to do its proper part in shaping the history of the future".[2] Tylor accepted the current view that the history of mankind was to be described as a progress from savagery through barbarism to civilisation; a view that Morgan made even more popular a few years later. Civilisation, he said, represented "the general improvement of mankind by higher organisation of the individual and of society, to the end of promoting at once man's goodness, power, and happiness". He readily appreciated that as far as material and intellectual culture went, this was definitely the case, but he was rather less sure that other aspects of the proposition were as clear. He was

[1] *Primitive Culture* (1873), p. 1. [2] *Ibid.*

aware of "developments of science and art which tend directly against culture".

It is Tylor's detachment and reasonableness that appeals so strongly to the reader of his books, for he sifted and weighed evidence carefully and he possessed a critical acumen, not common in his day, which enabled him to avoid most of the grosser errors of the evolutionists; moreover, he was less prejudiced than many of his contemporaries. Although he was not primarily a field-worker but a speculative writer, his anthropological writings are judicious scholarly works. As R. H. Lowie puts it: "It is impossible to exaggerate Tylor's services in separating the dross from the gold of early chronicles and thus rescuing a substantial body of authentic fact on every phase and period of civilization."[1] He was caught up in contemporary discussions of evolution with respect to the origins of cultural items. The two main positions were those of independent evolution and historical contact, known respectively as *parallelism* and *diffusion*. It was argued in the one case that customs and practices developed in broadly similar fashion in different areas of the world independently, and that the same mentality produces like results under like conditions. In the second case it was argued that the ubiquity of usages is the result of contacts between people and the transmission of culture from society to society. Tylor tended to favour the first of these views, but by no means exclusively. Indeed, if his parallelism was an advance on that of others, through his abandonment of vague psychologising which he replaced by a discernment of specific social factors contributing to cultural developments, he also argued on many occasions that historical factors were also important in accounting for developments and, moreover, instances of these he set out clearly and in detail on several occasions.

His discussion of cultural survivals was assisted by persistent attempts to establish criteria for making judgments. In this he was influenced by Adolphe Quételet's early contributions to statistical method, but his application was not always sound. He was apt to assume that a correlation provided evidence of a time sequence, for cultural survivals associated with one usage, like patrilineal descent, which were not found associated with an

[1] *The History of Ethnological Theory*, p. 71.

incompatible usage like matrilineal descent, showed, he thought, that the latter was prior in time. Similarly, like Spencer, he tended to assume that classificatory differences had chronological meaning. However, his detailed and erudite accounts of myths and his comparative studies of religious and magical phenomena were a great contribution to his subject. His definition of religion, a minimal one, as *animism*, i.e. the belief in spiritual beings, did much to bring order into the discussions of belief systems, and he helped to dispel much fantastic nonsense about primitive peoples, for he showed that "animism characterizes tribes very low in the scale of humanity, and thence ascends, deeply modified in its transmission, but from first to last preserving an unbroken continuity, into the midst of high modern culture".[1] Animism includes belief in souls and in a future state, in controlling deities and subordinate spirits; doctrines which practically result in some sort of worship. His comparative studies in animism constitute about half of his book *Primitive Culture.* His discernment of parallels to primitive customs in pre-industrial Europe and his discussion of survivals of such customs did much to induce less prejudiced attitudes toward non-literate peoples.

WILLIAM GRAHAM SUMNER (1840–1910)

After being educated in America, Switzerland, Germany and England, Sumner, who was a Presbyterian Minister, eventually became Professor of Political and Social Science at Yale University. He was a somewhat careless and inaccurate writer, who, whilst ranging freely over a wide variety of facts, displayed little ability to formulate coherent theories. Instead he marshalled his data in loose categories. Although he was manifestly influenced by Spencer, he was ignorant of the work of many of his contemporaries. His evolutionary outlook was extreme, crude, dogmatic and uncritical. He is worthy, nevertheless, of mention. Some contemporaries welcomed his social darwinism, but his importance today lies in his contributions to the sociologist's vocabulary and his attempts at sociological analysis. He was fortunate to have a devoted pupil and successor in A. G. Keller, who advanced his

[1] *Op. cit.*, vol. I, p. 426.

fame by writing and editing the large three-volume work *The Science of Society* published under both their names in 1927.

Although Sumner's ideas about social evolution are crude and over-simple, his discussion of what he called *folkways* is important. His intention was to show the regulative nature of folkways, which become habitual for individuals and customary for societies. He hoped that it would be possible to show how they change and thus, by identifying the forces bringing about these changes, to shed further light on social evolution. His theoretical equipment was not strong enough for this task and in the event he found he could not account for such changes. His book largely consists of social usages classified in *ad hoc* institutional categories. Folkways are the rules, unconsciously derived from the past, which govern man's behaviour. Some folkways may be distinguished as *mores*; being of more importance to society, having greater power to control behaviour, containing in themselves their own justification, presenting themselves as final and immutable. In our modern society table manners and greetings are examples of folkways, the standards of marital fidelity and ideas of neighbourly conduct are examples of mores. Mores themselves may be transmuted into either institutions or laws. An institution he defined as a concept and a structure, by which he meant that an idea, doctrine or interest is connected to an apparatus, or just a number of functionaries, so as to provide a means whereby social life may be carried on. "Property, marriage, and religion are the most primary institutions. They began as folkways. They became customs. They developed into mores by the addition of some philosophy of welfare, however crude. Then they were made more definite and specific as regards the rules, the prescribed acts, and the apparatus to be employed. This produced a structure and the institution was complete."[1] Acts of legislation also emerged from mores. When mores become laws and institutions, however, they change their character, for mores primarily reflect sentiment and faith, whereas institutions and laws have a rational and practical nature. Thus did he describe the different kinds of norms and their relationships to each other.

Sumner's analysis of folkways and mores was intended to

[1] *Folkways* (1959), p. 54.

provide a way of distinguishing the "group character" of a people. This group character he called the *ethos*. It consists of "the totality of characteristic traits by which a group is individualized and differentiated from others".[1] In this concept we may see the beginnings of the idea of studies of national character and total cultures, which was a feature of later American anthropology. Sumner introduced the terms "in-group" and "out-group" into sociological discussion to describe the ways in which sentiments are produced to enhance the differences between groups by promoting loyalty to the one and contempt for the other. In this connection he coined the word *ethnocentrism* which denotes an outlook "in which one's own group is the centre of everything, and all others are scaled and rated with reference to it".[2] His chief claim to our attention therefore lies more in the concepts he used and the data he compiled to illustrate their use, rather than in his critical acuity, which was slight. His focusing of sociological attention on social norms of various kinds gave direction to the subject, making the analytical examination of data a valuable undertaking and thus contributing, albeit modestly, to the development of a more analytical outlook in the subject. A lesser scholar than Tylor, an inferior theorist to Giddings, he nevertheless performed a similar function in Yale to that of Tylor in Oxford, and like the latter exerted more influence in his day by his lectures than by his writings; together with Albion Small he helped to establish the teaching of sociology in American universities.

EDWARD A. WESTERMARCK (1862–1939)

Edward Westermarck was a Swedish-Finnish scholar who spent part of the year teaching philosophy at the Academy of Abô in Helsinki and the other part teaching sociology in the University of London. In addition he found time to make a number of visits to North Africa in order to undertake studies of the inhabitants of Morocco.

His chief aim was to discover something of the origins of moral ideas and he regarded his large two-volume work entitled *The*

[1] *Ibid.*, p. 70. [2] *Ibid.*, p. 13.

Origin and Development of the Moral Ideas, published in 1906, as his *magnum opus*. Today, regrettable though it be, it is less for this book than for his earlier works that he is known, for his discussions of the institution of marriage were detailed and polemical. They began with his book *The Origin of Human Marriage* (1889), and *The History of Human Marriage* (1891), a fifth edition of which appeared in 1921 to be followed in 1926 by the famous and more popular work *A Short History of Marriage*.

Westermarck made some trenchant criticisms of the cruder sort of evolutionary sociology and in particular took to task Lewis Morgan and others who believed that originally mankind was sexually promiscuous and that marriage and the family emerged in the course of social evolution by stages through a kind of group marriage to a stage of polygyny with a matrilineal form of descent and so to the bilateral kinship system with monogamous family structure of modern times. In attacking this older theory he also tendered explanations of the rules of exogamy, and these too aroused keen interest. Later he extended his criticisms of the early social evolutionists by his attack on the theory of primitive communism, showing that whilst there is some evidence obtainable from simple societies of communally held property, nevertheless there is ample evidence also of privately held property. To be sure he was not the first to voice these criticisms, but his was an effective attack because on their appearance his works made a notable impact on intellectual opinion.

It is instructive to note the roots of Westermarck's criticism of evolutionary sociology, for whilst he was sceptical as to the possibility of tracing stages of development he did not abandon it although he eschewed the unilinear view. Yet on the other hand we must observe his keen interest in biological theory. Indeed, it must be said that he tried to offer a biological explanation of social institutions. Thus he argued that marriage is caused by the fact of human needs. For sheer survival humanity had to be protected in infancy; both the mother and her child required prolonged protection by the man, and thus, he said, natural selection ensured that paternal as well as maternal instincts developed to combine with sexual instincts to keep the parties together. The beginnings of family organisation are thus delineated.

Habit received the support of custom and the origins of marriage are similarly made clear. Westermarck shared with other writers of his day this view of explanation, finding the roots of institutions in human needs, and appealing to the biological predelictions of his age to account for specific kinds of development. He appealed frequently to the theory of natural selection as an explanatory device. His work was an extension of evolutionary sociology in that he did not abandon explanations in terms of origins but in addition he endeavoured to determine the nature of the conditions of human life and argued from the basis of survival needs.

Frequently, he selected examples to illustrate his arguments and sometimes he did this uncritically, tearing them from their context. He has been criticised by Sorokin[1] for his attempt to prove by illustration, and by Lowie[2] for his total lack of interest in cultures as wholes. Both criticisms are to the point, for Westermarck was not primarily a sociologist but a philosopher who turned to sociological studies for illustrations for his philosophical views. In this he was like most of his sociological contemporaries in Britain and America. His contributions were in the nature of solvents of the cruder evolutionary hypotheses. Yet he failed to free comparative sociology from its biological shackles. We must now turn to another figure in this general tradition, a greater man who may fairly be said to be its last and best example.

LEONARD TRELAWNY HOBHOUSE (1864–1929)

Most of the sociologists of the social evolutionary tradition were encyclopaedic in their view of the subject. Of none is this more true than Leonard Trelawny Hobhouse. His view of social evolution was that it represented the liberation of human personality, that through corporate life, through the growth of social organisation and the development of social institutions the latent powers of human personality were made manifest and realised. To Hobhouse all developing social structures are instrumental for the growth and enlargement of the human mind.

Hobhouse was in some ways a liberal minded latter-day Comte, for he also correlated stages of human thought with stages of

[1] *Contemporary Sociological Theories* (1928), p. 176. [2] *Op. cit.*, p. 97.

social development. There appeared to him to be four stages of intellectual development: an early stage where articulate thought is barely discernible, a second stage where common-sense notions are developed, a dialectical stage where conceptualisation takes place and critical abilities receive some encouragement, and finally a stage of experiential reconstruction, where the concepts of human thought are referred to the facts of experience; a critical and constructive stage. His sensible empirical approach is seen here to be linked to a discussion of values, and indeed it should be said that the greater part of his work is concerned with values. Thus his major sociological treatise is a study of comparative morals and social institutions designed to show that in history we may see a progressive development in moral and ethical ideas, not unconnected with development of religion, but not necessarily entirely bound up with it. Hobhouse viewed development both as an historical fact and as an ethical evaluation. His sociological problem was to correlate the factual aspects of social change, whilst his philosophical problem was to establish an ethical theory and then find a way to apply his ethical criteria to social development to see if the ethical and the social coincided. Sociology, treated comparatively, should, he thought, be able to show if progress was real. "We can take any phase of civilization, and going back over its ancestry . . . we can ask what growth 'amounts to'. We can inquire into the direction and distance of the social movement which we find . . . When we have discovered this movement we can go on to ask whether it is a movement of progress or not, i.e. whether it is one which tends to the realisation of ends on which we can reasonably set a value. But first of all we want to know what the movement actually has been. We want to determine the orbit, if orbit there be, of human social evolution. This I take to be the prime object of sociology, and the method by which it is to be approached is a social morphology."[1] Hobhouse was aware that the evolutionary tradition was not as firmly based as some of its proponents had thought. Thus in the preface to *Morals in Evolution* he argues that a hypothesis of social evolution is not essential to his task, which is purely a matter of distinguishing and classifying forms of ethical ideas. Nevertheless, "the results

[1] *Social Evolution and Political Theory* (1922), pp. 117–18.

of such a classification when seen in the light of evolutionary theory acquire a wholly new significance and value. They furnish us with a conception of the trend of human development based not on any assumption as to the underlying causes at work, but on a matter-of-fact comparison of the achievements reached at different stages of the process itself."[1]

Morals in Evolution was intended to complete the work begun in *Mind in Evolution* (1915), for Hobhouse held that "the function of mind in social life is the central problem of sociology". By means of the comparative method his attempt to study the rules of conduct and human ideas was intended to establish a morphology of ethics. By using the data of ancient history and anthropology he traced the development of the *good* through custom and law to ideas concerning the fundamentals of morality, for he argued that if the rules of conduct and a theory of conduct develop coterminously then it may be asserted that there is a line of ethical development which is the result of the growth of mind. The first half of *Morals in Evolution* accordingly discusses rules of conduct as expressed in forms of social organisation, the nature of justice, the status of women, the relationships between human communities, between social classes and economic relationships. In all of these Hobhouse discerned growth, but to him this growth was a growth in the reconciliation of personality development with social obligation. This he traced from earliest times, supporting his argument by references to the origins of the intelligent direction of behaviour in animals and its development in human conceptual thought. Self-consciousness is paralleled by ethical consciousness.

In his last major work of a sociological nature entitled *Social Development*, published in 1924, he set out the criteria, which he claimed were not ethical in themselves, in terms of which an estimate of growth might be made. They are: growing efficiency in control and direction, extension in the scale of social organisation, the increasing degree of co-operation oriented to the satisfaction of mutual needs, and increasing scope for personal fulfilment. His own inspection of the facts did assure him that in the light of his theory of the *rational good* a substantial degree of progress had been achieved, but it has been achieved, he said,

[1] *Op. cit.*, p.v.

not automatically but as a result of human purpose and thought.

We may be sceptical about his empirical evidence, especially that adduced in support of his psychological statements relating to mental development, but also it has to be said that much of his anthropological data was taken out of context; a mistake, it seems, easily made by comparative sociologists. Hugh Carter in his appraisal of Hobhouse's work lists these criticisms baldly: "The comparative method unless used with caution takes facts out of the setting in which they exist. The statistical treatment of ethnological material finds it difficult to establish a satisfactory unit of measurement; it minimises the significant factor of diffusion; it tends to overlook various qualifying factors such as differences in the density of population."[1] Hobhouse's attempt, however, must be recognised as a great one, even if the achievement is uneven in its contemporary usefulness. He was the last of the sociological system builders, more scholarly than most but destined to mark an end rather than a beginning in the history of sociology.

[1] *The Social Theories of L. T. Hobhouse* (1927), p. 121.

CHAPTER VI

THE DEVELOPMENT OF SOCIOLOGICAL THEORY

I: ÉMILE DURKHEIM (1858–1917)

The importance of Durkheim's work for the development of sociology cannot be over-estimated, but it is necessary to be quite clear wherein his importance lies. Durkheim did not abandon evolutionary sociology; on the contrary it was his original aim to establish the laws of social evolution. Yet he failed to do this and the example of his failure in part led to a new orientation. But what is more important, his well-trained philosophical mind turned to a series of perennial problems some of which loom large in any consideration of Durkheim's work; these too have helped to reorient sociological thought. The questions he raised included the problem of how societies cohere, precisely what initiates great social changes, just wherein lies the social element in human life, and whether it is possible to establish a science of society. These problems were not new ones, but they were freshly examined by Durkheim and every sociologist since his time has had to pay attention to them and to his thoughts about them. For this reason we may assert that Durkheim stands at a critical point in the history of sociology. We cannot say that he solved all his problems; indeed, at his death most of them still remained unresolved, but without the benefit of his powerful intellect sociology would have been immeasurably poorer today; indeed it may be asserted that his influence has probably been greater than any other single person in the history of sociology. Certainly this is true of sociology in France, it is true of social anthropology in Britain as a result of the bearing Durkheim's work had on A. R. Radcliffe-Brown, but it is also true of anthropology in the U.S.A. to some extent and latterly to a great extent on sociology in both America and Britain through the work of Talcott Parsons.

Émile Durkheim, the son of a Jewish Rabbi, was born in

Epinal in the province of Lorraine, and both his family background and his place of origin may well have had something to do with his interests, for the two gave him a vantage point from which to view and review the institutions of France. He was a boy of twelve when the Second Empire suffered ignominious defeat at the hands of Prussia at Sedan, and thirteen years of age when the Commune was bloodily suppressed in Paris. As a child he could not have experienced much anti-semitism, for France then was singularly free of it, but in the 1890s there was a sharp outbreak of anti-semitism centred round the Dreyfus case. Again, as a young man he lived through the political upheavals in which Republicanism, Royalism and Bonapartism contended for the future of France. The sources of his ideas on social order, the moral nature of society and educational policy may be traced in these events to be sure, but they are also to be found in his philosophical training, for Durkheim was a critical philosopher and it was the flaws in current philosophical ideas which started him off on his sociological quests, although it was his educational and political opinions which channelled his interests.

The Positivist Background

Initially, Durkheim followed Comte in accepting positivism as the basis for sociological investigation, for it seemed to him that sociology must be a natural science if it was to be anything. Although it might contribute to philosophical thought, in itself it could not be based on any philosophy nor derive its method from philosophy. Positivism was the basis of science and the philosophy which put an end to idle speculation. Only observable facts and general propositions about them mattered and it is with these that sociology must be exclusively concerned. This was the basis of his early work and it was expressly avowed in his book *Les règles de la méthode sociologique* (1895). His later work in its nature betrayed positivism and showed how inadequate a basis it was, although Durkheim does not seem anywhere to have explicitly rejected his early positivistic beliefs.

Yet positivism was not his essential sociological concern, rather it was a recognition that modern industrial society is a new type of social species. He was familiar with Spencer's second morphological analysis of the military and industrial types of societies, and he was aware of Ferdinand Tönnies' distinction between two kinds of social order described in his study entitled *Gemeinschaft und Gesellschaft* (1887), a book he reviewed in *Revue Philosophique* in 1889. Reflection on these distinctions led Durkheim to consider afresh the nature of the social order and the basis of social solidarity. It was here that he questioned the prevailing individualist and utilitarian philosophy, associated so closely with the name of Herbert Spencer.

Durkheim's first major work was *De la division du travail social* (1893), a book whose title is misleading, for whilst it is true he was writing about the division of labour and trying to offer an explanation for it, his main interest was in accounting for social solidarity in modern society. Briefly, Durkheim argued that in primitive societies there is a sameness that is striking. Men are like each other in ideas and outlook. The common body of values and experiences renders them of one mind and heart and thus social solidarity is maintained; it is a mechanical kind of solidarity. This, he asserts, is obviously not so with modern industrial societies; these are rather to be distinguished for the differences between the members by virtue of variety of experience, upbringing and training; in short, by the division of labour. If this is so, how is it that the modern industrial kind of society coheres? Why is there not more social disruption, more social disorganisation, more fundamental disparity of interest leading to a breakdown of relationships and hence of social order? The purpose of Durkheim in this work is to argue that it is the very function of the division of labour to provide this cohesive factor.

Durkheim's Typology

Like Spencer, he declared there to be two main types of society; those whose solidarity is *mechanical* and those whose solidarity is *organic*. The former have certain characteristics in common. They are societies where law and customary law are repressive, where an offence against the community is met with collective reaction of a punitive and repressive kind. The latter are societies where there is a greater preponderance of restitutive law, law which endeavours, after a breach, to restore the *status quo ante*, law which is also differentiated, so that, for example, some of it, applies to merchants only, other parts to innkeepers, other parts to employers, to professional men and so forth. To be sure, he points out, there is also repressive law, yet it is but a small part of the total and, moreover, is much more consciously repressive, less unthinkingly reactionary, rather something which is resorted to after other measures have failed. Durkheim pursues this analysis of legal sanctions pointing out that in the primitive society most offences are public whilst in modern societies they are private, civil rather than criminal, calling for adjustments rather than strong and violent reactions.

What is the purpose of this long and interesting contrast of the two types of society? Ostensibly it was Durkheim's aim to write a dissertation on the division of labour, but in fact he was interested to discern what, in the *Rules*, he calls the "social factor". What led him to undertake this quest was his criticism of the prevailing individualist and utilitarian philosophy which argued that society is composed of individuals who act in such a manner as to satisfy their individual wants, and that in so doing they enter into contractual relationships which thus form the basis of social order. Durkheim set out to destroy this false view of human society. To do so, the true science of sociology had to be established, for sociology must be able, he thought, to account for the social factor. If it could not do this then there was no point in a separate science of society, and Durkheim was convinced that other sciences could not answer the question posed. The chief contender amongst the new sciences was psychology. Gabriel Tarde, for instance, had attempted to explain social phenomena in terms of the characteristics of individuals as when he emphasised the psychological process of imitation.[1] Durkheim rejected this kind of explanation because it failed to account precisely for the social factor. His alternative approach was to look for social phenomena that were exterior to the individual, that could not be attributed to internal psychic states, but which instead stood over the individual in some compelling way. For Durkheim

[1] *Les lois de l'imitation* (1895).

these were law and custom and the whole range of obligations which morally compel the individual, and which exercise constraint on him. These he called *social facts* and he declared it was the task of sociology to study these social facts and that herein lay the peculiar subject matter of this social science, for this, he said, is the study of society; society is a moral order.

The concept of the *social fact* receives lengthy treatment in the *Rules of Sociological Method*, which was written after the *Division of Labour* and which constitutes his reflections on the nature of sociology raised by this book. The use of the term *social fact* is specific, for it does not mean any fact having a social connotation, but rather it refers to facts which, in the first place, are "general throughout the extent of a given society" and, Durkheim added, at a given stage in the evolution of that society.[1] In other words the incidence of the social phenomenon is general in a society of a given type. Thus in every industrial society there is a certain amount of crime; this is a social fact. The same is true as regards divorce, drunkenness, suicide and so forth; these have a certain incidence in all industrial societies. But Durkheim also asserted that a social fact is a manner of acting which exercises exterior constraint over the individual. If individuals are constrained by external social facts like laws, they are also constrained by some social facts which are not so clearly perceived and identified, and here Durkheim argued that the sociologist must discover statistical rates which reflect these social facts; it is the rate of crime, the suicide rate, the birth rate, the divorce rate and the incidence of drunkenness which provide the empirical referents for an analysis of social currents and trends. This he amply showed in his famous study *Le Suicide* (1897).[2]

The Study of Suicide

Although this is one of the earliest essays utilising social statistics, and follows hard on the pioneer work in that field by Adolph Quételet,[3] and although as a result of it being an early development

[1] *Rules of Sociological Method* (translated by S. A. Solovay and J. H. Mueller, and edited by G. Catlin, 1938), p. 13.

[2] *Suicide* (translated 1951).

[3] L. A. J. Quételet, *Sur l'Homme et le développement de ses facultés, ou essai de physique sociale* (1835).

much of its methodology necessarily is crude and unsatisfactory by modern standards, it remains a classical model of sociological research. At the outset Durkheim points out that whilst there may be many explanations given to account for suicide, those mostly offered are cast in terms of individualist psychology. In other words, suicide is usually explained in terms of depressed psychic states, financial loss, sudden bereavement, or even perhaps unrequited love; but none of these explanations will suffice to account for changes in the *rate* of suicide, or the differences in the rates between one society and another. All this means that he was again trying to find the social factor but this time by an examination of suicide rates. Yet he could quite as well have taken crime rates or some other similar kind of statistical rate, perhaps the incidence of industrial strike action or the rate of drug addiction.

The interesting feature of this work by Durkheim on suicide lies in the sociological classifications he employed to shed light on the subject. He argued that the classification of suicides must be sociological, just as in the *Division of Labour* where the classification of law into repressive and restitutive law was sociological because the classification is in terms of sanctions applied by law. Here the classification is primarily in terms of group attachment and detachment. Some suicides are *egoistic* in the sense that they occur in cases of people who have a loose group attachment. Durkheim presented statistical evidence to show that there is a higher suicide rate among married people without children than among those who are married and have children; and that it is higher among single, divorced and widowed people than among married people. On the other hand there are *altruistic* suicides, that is to say there are suicides which are socially enjoined, as when a man dies by his own hand to avoid dishonour, or an elderly person in a nomadic tribe ends his life to avoid being a burden on the group and is regarded highly for this altruistic act, or as used to happen in the case of a Hindu widow who, practising *suttee*, immolated herself on the funeral pyre of her husband, or in ancient times when servants and followers of a great king ended their lives on the occasion of his death to be entombed with him. Quite clearly there is a social factor in the latter altruistic case, but also, says Durkheim, in the former egoistic one. Moreover, he also detected another type of suicide which he called *anomic*, for he noticed that whilst in time of severe economic depression and dislocation the suicide rate rose, it also rose when there was a sudden flush of prosperity. The two phenomena he considered might be related to a single causal factor. This he saw in the disruption of people's expectations. His theory was that human well-being and happiness depend upon there being limitation and regularity in human expectations. When expectations are suddenly unfulfilled either in terms of sudden and marked deprivation or equally sudden indulgence, personal equilibrium is upset, and in a proportion of the cases affected the stresses are so acute as to result in suicide.

Durkheim's classification of suicides is interesting and ingenious, but it is unsatisfactory. His own evidence could have shown him this, but he was too far committed to a sociologistic outlook to perceive it. In an interesting comparison of suicide rates among Protestants and Catholics in European states he shows that the rate is much higher in predominantly Protestant countries than in Catholic ones, even when national and linguistic factors are allowed for, as a study of suicide rates in the various cantons of Switzerland provides. His own explanation is that the Protestant is less closely tied to his group than the Catholic, for the Catholic is more closely directed in his personal life than the Protestant. This matter of the degree of group attachment of an individual is unsatisfactory. Talcott Parsons,[1] in his penetrating study of Durkheim's methodology, points out that there is no very sound evidence with respect to Protestants and Catholics supporting the theory that one is more attached to his group than another, but rather he points out that there *is* a difference between the Protestant and the Catholic, in that whilst both are forbidden to commit suicide, it being a mortal sin in each case, nevertheless in the case of the Protestant there are religious ideas obliging him to "work out his own salvation in fear and trembling" rather than rely, as the Catholic is permitted to do, on the authority of religious specialists; and that in the former instance strains and stresses may be set up which are so severe that in a proportion of the

[1] *The Structure of Social Action: A Study in Social Theory with special reference to a Group of Recent European Writers* (1937), pp. 332 ff.

cases suicide results. It is not a matter of the degree of group attachment, but rather the content of the attitudes a devotee is obliged to acquire and manifest that is significant. As Parsons puts it, the Protestant is forced to be free in a way the Catholic is not. The implications for sociological analysis are considerable, for it suggests that what is important is the content of a value system and its effects on the believer and devotee rather than group-attachment.

Indeed, the classification needs to be revised. There is a category of cases of suicide where the society enjoins it as a duty explicitly; and there is a category where it exceptionally follows as a result of adherence to social values, the structure of relationships and the peculiar character of the social order; however there is also a category where the social order breaks down and the values of the society no longer appear to be relevant to the human condition, where there is indeed *anomie* or a state of normlessness. At this point we return to the basic problem of social solidarity in the *Division of Labour*, for we are able to answer Durkheim's question about the source of order in modern industrial societies. It is the same as that accounting for order in the primitive society; that is to say, it is to be located in the adherence to a set of common values, not in the fact of the division of labour. To be sure the common body of values in a modern industrial society differs sharply from that in a primitive society, but in both there is the basis for social solidarity. The rate of anomic suicide is an index of the degree of solidarity in a society just as the rate of altruistic suicide might provide an index of solidarity in a group, of a given type. These empirical insights of Durkheim have thus enabled us to locate the social factor that he was looking for. Today sociologists have a much better idea of the relation of the individual to his society than Durkheim had, but he it was, we should remember, who helped to point to this as an important topic of sociological investigation.

One concept of some importance in Durkheim's thought in connection with what has just been said remains to be explicitly mentioned. This is the term *conscience collective* and it refers to the totality of beliefs and sentiments common to average citizens of the same society. It is, says Durkheim, a determinate system having a life of its own.[1] The collective conscience is prominent in primitive society and Durkheim made much of the concept in his early discussions of social order in that type of society, but he returned to it again, albeit in slightly different guise, in his later work, when his attention was focused on the values that are prevalent in the modern urban industrial society. However, what interested him when considering his own society is not so much the sameness of values, i.e. that which makes them common in the *conscience collective*, which he emphasised when discussing primitive society, but the fact that values are commonly held and form a hierarchy. Thus Durkheim spoke of "collective representations" and in a celebrated essay distinguished them from "individual representations".[2] In this essay Durkheim again expressed his anti-reductionist view, for he argued that there is a hierarchy of values in a society which cannot be reduced to the values of individuals; it is in a sense independent of individual members of society. In another essay, "Value Judgments and Judgments of Reality",[3] he distinguished between personal preferences, i.e. statements about reality e.g. "I prefer beer to wine", and general statements e.g. "this picture has great aesthetic value" or "this jewel is worth so much", which are statements of value but value independent of the individual's estimation; something which exists independently of individuals and their subjective states, and which reflect an objective reality. Furthermore, these valuations can only be estimated in relation to some conception of the ideal. The question arises: what is the source of such ideals? Clearly, this is an important question, for it will be seen that Durkheim's conception of human society has developed into that of a moral order; his theory of social life is a transcendental theory.

[1] *The Division of Labor in Society* (translated by G. Simpson, 1947), p. 79.
[2] "Individual and Collective Representations", originally published in *Revue de Métaphysique et de Morale,* May 1898 (translated and published in *Sociology and Philosophy* by D. F. Pocock, 1953).
[3] "Value Judgments and Judgments of Reality", originally published in *Revue de Métaphysique et de Morale,* July 1911 (translated by D. F. Pocock and published in *Sociology and Philosophy*, 1953).

Sociology of Religion

To answer the question he posed Durkheim embarked on an analysis of religious behaviour. A basic distinction in the analysis of religion is the difference between the sacred and the secular, between what is holy and what is profane. Religion is concerned with sacred or holy things. When a person is conscious of his relationship to the sacred he is, at that moment of time, freed from the bondage of personal wants and sectional interests. The essence of social life is the interaction of people's minds. When there is close relationship between human minds, individual selves are subordinated. Sometimes, indeed, there is a peculiar intensity in the interaction which brings forth new sentiments, sentiments which possess a stronger power than purely individual sentiments possess, for these are group ones and represent a collective ferment of intense social communion out of which something new may emerge, something creative, indeed a new ideal. Thus are values created. Durkheim cites a number of historical instances. The growth of scholasticism in the twelfth and thirteenth centuries in Europe sprang from the meeting and intense interaction of scholars gathered together in Paris. The Renaissance and the Reformation were other instances, the French Revolution in the eighteenth century and the rise of socialist movements in the nineteenth century; all these he argues were cases of creative syntheses. In such times new ideals are born, sectional interests are subdued and forgotten for a while and the ideal becomes real. Of course the occasion passes and life becomes humdrum again, so it comes about that men wish to revive the memory, for faith in the new ideal has to be repeatedly restored, and the experience has to be relived. Hence ceremonies, religious events and feasts, public occasions and speeches, plays and pageantry are utilised; they are "minor versions of the great creative movement". And Durkheim goes on: "Through the very awareness of itself society forces the individual to transcend himself and to participate in a higher form of life. A society cannot be constituted without creating ideals".[1] It is interesting to note in passing how far removed from his original positivism Durkheim is at this point.

[1] Ibid., p. 93.

In his later intellectual period Durkheim developed these ideas further, focusing his interest on religious beliefs and practices. The reason for this is that he saw religion as a social matter. His mind was directed to answering the question: what is the origin of religion? He took for examination what he thought was the most primitive society on Earth, that of the Australian aboriginal. His reason for doing so was that the totemic object among the Aruntas was connected not only with religion but also with clan membership. Thus the Australian aboriginal's clan takes the totem as its emblem, but the totem, being a religious or sacred object, inspires respect and awe, and especially is this true when the otherwise scattered parts of the clan come together periodically on a ceremonial occasion. It is then that an excitement is bred which lifts the individual out of himself. It is a minor case of creative synthesis. The totem is but an object, yet it is symbolic of a reality unseen. Durkheim argued that the reality is in fact the social group itself. This in short is the burden of his famous work *Les Formes élémentaires de la vie religieuse* (1912).[1] Durkheim's conception of society is a spiritual and not a materialist one. If his assumptions about Australian totemic societies were partly mistaken, in that they are not the most primitive in their religious beliefs and practices, or in their clan organisation, or for that matter in their representing an early stage in the evolution of mankind; nevertheless his work is impressive, both as a detailed secondary analysis based on other people's field-work and in the generality of the hypotheses he discusses. Especially interesting is his analysis of the relationship between beliefs and ritual acts and the power exerted by symbolic objects. Of particular importance historically is the fillip he gave to the sociological study of religious behaviour in terms of the social functions of religion. He began by examining values and it was a long journey before he was brought back again to the *conscience collective*—the body of common values which lies at the heart of human social existence, and which for him constituted the essence of society.

To conclude this brief survey of Durkheim's work we must point out that he endeavoured to distinguish sociology from other sciences, to show it possesses a distinctive method, and so to indicate it

[1] *The Elementary Forms of Religious Life* (translated by J. W. Swain, 1915).

has a unique contribution to make to human knowledge. He saw that social evolution is not unilinear but much more complex than had been supposed, and he discovered that primitive societies were more than a single identical social type. He provided useful concepts and pointed to important distinctions, all of which helped later sociologists to advance the subject, and he brought back into sociological discussion the question of how social order is maintained; a question which had for long been overshadowed by the question about the nature of social change. Above all, his work displayed a desirable combination of abilities. As P. Sorokin says: "He fortunately combined the ability of broad, logical, and philosophical thought with the scrupulous and careful method of a scientist. Every hypothesis formed by him is formulated on the basis of patient study of the corresponding facts. After the formulation, he carefully tries to verify it again through an inductive study of the factual data. This has made his works quite superior to the purely speculative philosophizing in social sciences, as well as to the narrow, matter-of-fact descriptions of a definite phenomenon. Hence the eminence of Durkheim."[1]

[1] *Contemporary Sociological Theories* (1928), p. 464.

CHAPTER VII

THE DEVELOPMENT OF SOCIOLOGICAL THEORY

II: MAX WEBER (1864–1920)

The positivist tradition which Durkheim inherited did not prevent him from seeing that simple observation was useless unless criteria could be provided to help in deciding what should be observed. Hence his attention was directed to the definition of social facts. What is more, he also saw that it was necessary that sociology be comparative, and at the close of his *Rules of Sociological Method* he concludes by defining the subject as the comparative study of social institutions.[1] To fulfil this aim sociologists must ensure that the things to be compared are comparable. It was for this reason that Durkheim spoke of social species or types, although it must be confessed that he was not very clear about what types should be determined, and this is probably the greatest weakness in his work. It was a task which Max Weber, that other great sociological scholar of the time, set his mind to. Durkheim's main achievement was to bring sociology and anthropology together and to forge common concepts which helped the two subjects to advance together in an orderly way. Weber's achievement was more far-reaching, for he brought the scientific tradition of sociological thought into relationship with the historical tradition of German scholarship. If Durkheim's main emphasis was on the analysis of social structures, then Weber's contribution was that, having added to it, he augmented it by an analysis of social processes.[2]

Durkheim and Weber were very different kinds of people with quite dissimilar backgrounds. Yet there was a striking similarity in their interests. Both were concerned with methodological problems, both sought to advance sociological thought by an

[1] *Op. cit.*, chapter VI.
[2] Vide H. Stuart Hughes, *Consciousness and Society* (1959), chapter 8.

examination of religious phenomena, both were passionately interested in the fate of their nations, and it may be said of them that they have shown that sociology is not hindered when its proponents have practical political interests, although they both kept these political interests under strict control. In fact they have both demonstrated that far from prejudicing the rigorous development of scientific method and its use in sociology, a practical social interest may both enhance the sense of urgency for, and give direction to, sociological research.

Max Weber was the son of a lawyer who was a member of the Prussian Diet and a National Liberal member of the Reichstag. His mother came from a Westphalian family of scholars and pastors. In his father's house in Berlin as a youth he met men eminent in academic and political life at that time in Germany's fortunes when academic activity was both intense and of a high order. As a student he studied law and economics, but soon his interests shifted in the direction of economic and social history, and thence to sociology. At all times he was involved in both methodological discussion on the one hand and in political disputation on the other. He became editorially jointly responsible in 1903 for one of the great social science journals, the *Archiv für Sozialwissenschaft und Sozialpolitik*, in which many methodological articles appeared. Despite a four-year period of illness with recurrent relapses and despite premature death at the age of fifty-six, his output was prodigious. Much of his writing has been translated by American sociologists and until recently his influence was noticeably greater in the United States than in Britain.

The development of sociological theory has been advanced by Weber's use of the comparative method, for he has contributed more to comparative sociology than almost any other scholar, and in this respect his work is much more consciously methodological than Durkheim's. Partly, this is because Weber was less wedded to the prevailing academic tradition in Germany than Durkheim was to that in France. Thus we see at an early age he had decided that if modern western civilisation was to be the subject for investigation, then there must be a basis from which comparisons may be made with other civilisations, and that such a basis should provide for the comparison of aspects or parts of such civilisations. The basis required he found in the *ideal-type* concept. Before turning to this let us pause to see how he came to see his main task.

The Intellectual Climate of Nineteenth-Century Germany

In Germany the intellectual world was dominated by historical studies. Not only had great developments taken place in historical scholarship but history permeated other cultural disciplines like law and economics. The historical tradition in Prussia stemmed in the main from the days of the Napoleonic conquest and could be said to have started in Berlin University by B. G. Niebuhr, the author of a great work on Roman history; but others followed and among them greater men than Niebuhr. Thus classical history was raised to a new high level by Leopold von Ranke and later still by the great Theodor Mommsen. But there were others like K. R. Eichhorn who founded the historical school of jurisprudence, later to be ably followed by F. C. von Savigny. Yet others had contributed to economic and social history like Otto von Gierke, whose lectures the young Weber attended and whose writing on medieval corporations laid a basis for Weber's early researches. But the study of economics was also historical in its orientation as well as having practical applications and Weber was brought into direct contact with Wilhelm Roscher, who taught him, and Karl Knies, whose chair at Heidelberg Weber later occupied.

Prominent in philosophical discussion in the last quarter of the nineteenth century was the question of the place of science in human studies. The prevailing idealist philosophy denied the validity of scientific method when applied to cultural subjects, for it was said that explanation could only be genetic or historical, that is to say in terms of tracing and interpreting sequences of unique events, and that general categories, of the kind which science utilises, were inappropriate because they distorted the unique facts of human life, and so could not provide true explanations. The kernel of this argument was that social phenomena are unique and are not generalisable. Weber in part rejected this view, for he claimed that scientific categories could be used, but he hastened to add that they must be used with care. On the other hand he accepted the view that in pursuing social studies it is necessary to take a subjective as well as an objective approach; he was sympathetic to the ideas of Wilhelm Dilthey, who asserted that it was necessary to understand the motives and points of view of the historical persons being studied and not just to record positive facts.[1] However, the dominant factor in the intellectual background of German economic and social history was the work of Karl Marx. The historical tradition in Germany obliged scholars to pay attention to this set of radical views and arguments in a way in which it did not in England until after the first world war, and even then only slightly. German historians took Marx's work seriously; its influence may even be seen in Mommsen's famous work *The History of Rome* (1856). Perhaps one reason for this was the Marxist character of the German Social Democratic Party, which differed in this respect from the British Labour Party. The fact is that although he was not a socialist Weber was strongly influenced by Marx's analysis of modern western society. As Albert Salomon put it: "Max Weber became a sociologist in a long and intense dialogue with the ghost of Karl Marx."[2] So it came about that he set himself the task of understanding the nature of modern Capitalist society as known in Western Europe. It was a tremendous undertaking but he did not blink at the fact that he had chosen such a great task, and he proved almost equal to it. If a premature death had not put an end to his labours his achievement might have been even more remarkable than it is, and it is impressive.

The Comparative Method and the Ideal-Type Concept

Weber's belief that scientific method was relevant to social studies encouraged him to establish a set of operational definitions and to construct concepts which could be used. To avoid vagueness he decided to classify by describing types of social phenomena. For, he argued, if the types were rigorously defined and the elements of each type were consistent with each other, then it should be possible to compare existing cases to the type. The

[1] Vide H. A. Hodges, *The Philosophy of Wilhelm Dilthey* (1952).
[2] "German Sociology" in *Twentieth Century Sociology* (1945), edited by G. Gurvitch and W. E. Moore, p. 596.

latter he called an *ideal-type*. It is a concept which is much misunderstood. It was Weber's purpose to select, from the mass and complexity of data which is social reality, those features of a structure that were in some way significant, that indeed defined the structure, and which were worthy of attention by being relevant to his discussion; moreover, they had to be observable and preferably measurable. Although he allowed that historical data were unique, Weber maintained this to be irrelevant to his task, for to do anything other than describe sequences it is necessary to abstract; even the narrative historian must select data. The real question is: how is such abstraction to be effected? Weber argued that the best way is to conceive of a pure type. Let us see how he used the concept.

As his base-line Weber took the concept of *action*, assuming that this was the most fundamental social concept. He conceived action as being normatively oriented, that is to say he did not regard human beings as mechanically responding in set ways to stimuli, but rather as endeavouring in their behaviour to conform to some ideal conception of action. Thus a man performing quite simple social tasks like buying a commodity in a shop or playing a game with a child has some standard by which he measures his behaviour. There is, therefore, an ideal-type of shopping or playing with children, and actual instances approximate to it. It may not be ideal in the sense of being the best conceivable way, but at least the elements are selected in terms of the ends and values of the actors. As he put it, the ideal-type describes "objectively possible action". It may help if we take an example and quote at length from Weber's discussion of his ideal-type concept. He is discussing in this passage the "city-economy": "The ideal-typical concept will help to develop our skill in imputation in *research*: it is no 'hypothesis' but it offers guidance to the construction of hypotheses. It is not a *description* of reality but it aims to give unambiguous means of expression to such a description. It is thus the 'idea' of the *historically* given modern society, based on an exchange economy, which is developed for us by quite the same logical principles as are used in constructing the idea of the medieval 'city-economy' as a 'genetic' concept. When we do this we construct the concept 'city-economy' not as an average of the economic structures actually existing in all the cities observed but as an *ideal-type*. An ideal-type is formed by the one-sided *accentuation* of one or more points of view and by the synthesis of a great many diffuse, discrete, more or less present and occasionally absent *concrete individual* phenomena, which are arranged according to those one sidedly emphasised viewpoints into a unified *analytical* construct (Gedankenbild). In its conceptual purity, this mental construct cannot be found empirically anywhere in reality. It is a *utopia*. Historical research faces the task of determining in each individual case the extent to which this ideal-construct approximates to or diverges from reality, to what extent, for example, the economic structure of a certain city is to be classified as a 'city-economy'.[1]"

Let us move from the concept of *city-economy* to that of *action*. Although he began by constructing ideal-types of action it cannot be said he used them much, nor are these particular types very useful, for as Talcott Parsons points out they are not all types of the same order.[2] Some actions are oriented to past ways of behaving, they are *traditional*; other forms of actions are governed by feelings and are thus *emotional*; yet other action is related to a normative order which may be religious, ethical or even aesthetical, so that action of a particular kind is considered right irrespective of its consequences for the actor in question or for other actors; in this case it is called *value-rational*. Yet other action may be of a fourth kind where the consequences are the prime consideration; such action is practically oriented and may be described as *purposively rational*. It was this last type of action that chiefly interested Weber, for it was the type of action he associated with his other and most important ideal-type concept of modern Western Capitalism.

The Study of Capitalism

Weber asked two kinds of questions about capitalism: firstly, what are the distinguishing features of this socio-economic phenomenon

[1] M. Weber, "Objectivity in Social Science and Social Policy", *Methodology of the Social Sciences* (trans. E. A. Shils 1949), p. 90.

[2] Talcott Parsons, Introduction to M. Weber's *The Theory of Social and Economic Organisation* (1947), pp. 11 ff.

as it is manifested in the West? and secondly, how did it come about? These are sociological and historical questions, and in asking them he did justice to both his interests: the scientific interest which he wanted to introduce into what were called the social sciences (*Kulturwissenschaften*), and the historical interest that was so strong in German intellectual life and which he saw was best served by a sociological orientation.

Primarily he aimed to describe clearly the distinctive features of modern Western Capitalism, initially because he was impressed by the importance of treating it as a unique historical individual. He later saw that it only made sense to do this in terms of it being one variant of a type of socio-economic system, and hence he was led to develop a typology of such systems. He recognised that Capitalism had appeared at various times in the history of the world and in various places. There were different kinds of Capitalism in the Venetian Republic, in the city-port of Antwerp in its heyday, in Elizabethan England, and so forth. But what were the values of the significant variables that rendered the modern western variation unique? In his famous book *Wirtschaft und Gesellschaft* (*Economy and Society*) Weber outlines six types of capitalist activity. They are set out below:

1. Profit-making activity may be oriented to the exploitation of market advantages in a continuous process of purchase and sale on the market where exchange is free; that is, formally not subject to compulsion and materially, at least relatively, free. Or it may be oriented to the maximization of profit in continuous productive enterprises which make use of capital accounting.
2. It may be oriented to opportunities for profit by trade and speculation in money, taking over debts of all sorts, and creating means of payment. A closely related type is the professional extension of credit, either for consumption or for profit-making purposes.
3. It may be oriented to opportunities for acquiring "booty" from corporate political groups or persons connected with politics. This includes the financing of wars or revolutions and the financing of party leaders by loans and supplies.
4. It may be oriented to opportunities for continuous profit by virtue of domination by force or of a position of power guaranteed by the political authority. There are two main sub-types: colonial capitalism operated through plantations

with compulsory payments or compulsory labour and by monopolistic and compulsory trade. On the other hand there is the fiscal type, profit making by farming of taxes and of offices, whether in the home area or in colonies.

5. The orientation to opportunities for profit opened up by unusual transactions with political bodies.
6. The orientation to opportunities for profit of the following types: (a) To purely speculative transactions in standardized commodities or in the securities of an enterprise; (b) by carrying out the continuous financial operations of political bodies; (c) by the promotional financing of new enterprises in the form of sale of securities to investors; (d) by the speculative financing of capitalistic enterprises and of various other types of economic organization with the purpose of a profitable regulation of market situations or of attaining power.

Types (1) and (6) are to a large extent peculiar to the modern Western World. The other types have been common all over the world for thousands of years where the possibilities of exchange, money economy, and money financing have been present.[1]

What is essential to this modern western type is its rational quality. To analyse the source of this quality and its implications Weber had to cover a lot of ground, for he made excursions into law and legal history, he ranged over the field of administrative theory and practice, he surveyed leadership in its various forms, and he journeyed through the jungle of theological debate and dogma of the seventeenth and eighteenth centuries. It was a large and detailed series of enquiries and only brief mention of them can be made here.

Rationality in Law and Administration

The peculiarly rational character of modern Western Capitalism is clearly seen when we contrast the type of administrative organisation associated with it to other types such as that of Feudal England and France, but because he wanted to be precise in his description, Weber described and analysed *types* of law and administration. Fundamentally, he argued, there is always a conception of authority, for in a corporate group some individual member or members give orders and others obey, and moreover

[1] M. Weber, *ibid.*, p. 255 f.

those who give the order expect to be obeyed. The reason for this is that both the order-givers and those who obey commands share certain beliefs about the rightness of the process; in other words authority is held to be legitimate. Yet the bases of this legitimacy may differ from one instance to another. There are, he said, three ideal-types of authority distinguished according to their legitimacy:

1. *Rational legitimacy* reflects belief in the legality of patterns of normative rules and the right of those people designated by the rules to exercise authority to command.
2. *Traditional legitimacy* depends on belief in the sanctity of immemorial traditions and the right of those established in positions of authority to exercise it.
3. *Charismatic legitimacy,* so termed after the Greek word for grace, depends on the devotion by followers to an individual who for them is endowed by exceptional sanctity, heroism or other personal qualities. Such a leader is obeyed because of a belief in whatever normative patterns or order he reveals or ordains.

Weber points out that in the first case obedience is owed to the legally established impersonal order, whereas in the second and third cases it is owed to a person. The significant item in this typology is rational legitimacy; and hence this corresponding type of authority, which is unique for it emerged only in western civilisation. Of course, as he points out, none of these ideal types are to be found in a pure form in any historical instance, but any case can be seen to approximate to one or the other of them.

In the second part of *Wirtschaft und Gesellschaft*[1] Weber engages in a long disquisition on law, the main burden of which is to trace, in various civilisations over the centuries of history, the broad changes in the character of legal systems, picking out especially the relationships between legal and economic systems, and showing how there has been a progressive development in the rationality of law.[2]

[1] Vide *Max Weber on Law in Economy and Society* (1954), edited by Max Rheinstein, where most of Part II of *Wirtschaft und Gesellschaft* is translated.

[2] Max Weber's use of the term *law* is a precise one; "an order will be called *law* when conformity with it is upheld by the probability that deviant action will be met by physical or psychic sanctions aimed to compel conformity or to punish disobedience, and applied by a group of men especially empowered to carry out this function". *The Theory of Social and Economic Organisation* (1947), p. 116.

When he speaks of rationality Weber is referring to two things: *formal* rationality and *substantive* rationality. Whether men are engaged in legislating, or in discovering what the law is, their activities are substantively rational if they consciously follow a set of principles. Such principles may be vastly different in different systems, for they may be religious principles, or ethical ones, or they may be political principles based on what is thought to be the national interest—thus the former State Prosecutor of the U.S.S.R. Andrei Vyshinski argued that "law is an instrument of politics", which itself reflects the Soviet view that law is a means for supporting the Communist ideology. In contrast to this there is irrationality such as in Moslem Kadi justice. Here the Kadi, traditionally sitting in the market place, adjudicates on an *ad hoc* basis freely considering the merits of each case as he sees them. Formal rationality, as distinct from substantive rationality, refers to the processes of legislating and law discerning. In this formally rational instance what is held to be important is the set of formal rules governing procedures. Formal rationality may itself be of one of two kinds; in one case law is *extrinsically* formal as when a contract is held to have been validly entered into on the evidence of it being written down and signed, or sealed, or concluded in some prescribed manner; the other case is where it is *logically* formal, as when the rules employed in drawing up the law or determining it are themselves made up of abstract concepts of a legal nature and are employed systematically. This stands in contrast to procedures based on oracles, or on ordeal, or some other similarly irrational means. What Weber is doing in this analysis of law is to stress the fact that formally rational law is a relatively new phenomenon in the world's history, and that its advent coincided largely with the rise of modern Capitalism. Like modern Capitalism it is a product of modern western civilisation. What then is the link between the two, if there be a link at all? Weber had no doubt there was a connection and he discerned it in the development of what he called bureaucratic administration.

Again, Weber analyses types, types of administrative organisation, but he selects the ideal-type of *bureaucracy* for special attention. It is based on rational-legal authority, which is the source of its legitimacy. As an organisation it is a continuous performance of official functions according to rules. Persons performing these functions have specified spheres of competence and they are endowed with the authority necessary to enable them to fulfil their duties. This authority is differentially distributed so that a hierarchy of official positions is formed, some officials having controlling and supervisory duties with respect to others. Moreover, to exercise authority certain specified qualifications are required. Those performing functions do not own the means of production or of administration, nor may they make use of them for private purposes. Positions that are occupied cannot be appropriated by the occupants. Acts of an administrative kind are recorded in writing; thus providing the chief reason for the continuous nature of the administrative process.

The characteristics of the lives of officials in a bureaucratic type of administration are as follows: they are personally free agents, but they must act impersonally according to rules which define their specific spheres of competence. They are not elected to their positions but are appointed according to their possession of formal qualifications, usually based on examinations. They are paid a salary, although this may be on a scale of salaries, increases being given according to age and experience, and they are pensionable after a fixed number of years of employment and at a given age. They normally have no other employment and at all times officials are subject to rules governing their conduct as it is related to their official duties.

We may contrast this analysis with that of administrative organisation associated with the traditional form of authority. In this case "obedience is not owed to enacted rules, but to the person who occupies a position of authority by tradition", but the tradition may either closely determine the way a chief acts and the content of the commands he issues, or on the other hand it may leave him free to act arbitrarily. In making use of his followers he may recruit from among those who are bound to him by particular traditional ties of loyalty, or he may choose favourites who owe a purely personal loyalty.

Putting his argument in a very cursory fashion, we may say that Weber identified modern Western Capitalism with rationality in law and administration, and that this rationality rested on certain fundamental assumptions, basic beliefs which members of western society held, namely what he called rational-legal legitimacy. But there were other features of Capitalism as known in the West and we must briefly look at them.

The Modern Western Type of Capitalism

It will be recalled that earlier in this chapter we set out Weber's types of profit-making activity together with his indication of which of them were specifically relevant to the socio-economic system of the modern western world. This kind of Capitalism was seen by Weber to represent a complexity of institutionalised forms of behaviour. It was closely founded on the establishment of the joint stock company, or corporation, and on stock exchange machinery. But Weber also saw that other things were involved such as a certain type of currency and means for making currency exchanges; also certain political requirements were necessary; but above all he recognised the necessity for what he called the Spirit (*Geist*) of Capitalism, for what distinguished the kind of economic activity found in the western world was not acquisitiveness, nor a strong desire to engage in economic adventures. To be sure these are present, but then they are ubiquitous and may be discerned in many kinds of economic activity as it has obtained in other ages and other places. What Weber laid his finger on was the set of ethical *desiderata* associated with the modern form, it was a moral outlook, a set of attitudes to life and what man should do with it; this was the Spirit of Capitalism and it was, he concluded, indispensable for the modern western variety.

Weber's attention had been drawn to this at an early stage, in fact when he first considered the rise of modern western society, and it is most fully expressed in the celebrated essay on *The Protestant Ethic and the Spirit of Capitalism*[1] which endeavoured to identify some, if not all, of the origins of Capitalism. By the term *Spirit of Capitalism* Weber meant a set of attitudes including the belief that it is a good thing to spend one's energies earning an income, indeed making money, and to do so even beyond that point where one had provided for the necessities. That is to say,

[1] *The Protestant Ethic and the Spirit of Capitalism* (1930), trans. T. Parsons.

it incorporates a belief in maximising wealth without much consideration of the means as long as the means are efficacious. All this represented a sharp break with traditional attitudes, for not only does this spirit approve of practices like usury, traditionally forbidden by the Church, but a premium is placed upon flexibility and innovation, qualities which are either opposed to traditionalism or inconsistent with it. This Spirit of Capitalism, enjoining it as a duty on the individual to behave accordingly, thus comes to be subjectively perceived as a form of self-fulfilment. Of course people at many times and in many places had entertained such values, but only in isolated cases, and they were often ephemeral; only in the past two centuries in Europe and America had they developed systematically and generally in such a far-reaching manner. In past times, individuals, if they shared such values, had seldom been able to sustain them for long; now it was universal or nearly so. That this spirit was so strong in the West called for explanation. How did this Capitalist Spirit originate?

It is not difficult to see how a well developed capitalist economic and social system can generate such attitudes and so enable them to persist, but how could they develop in the first place out of a situation in which the values of people and their habits were so vastly different? There must, Weber argued, have been some particular factor favourable to the emergence of the Spirit of Capitalism. He discovered it in the rise of the Protestant movement. Of course, it is not the case that Protestant Christianity enjoined these values and attitudes on the part of its adherents, for indeed Protestantism propagated the traditional Christian virtues of selflessness, humility and charity. But there were elements in the Protestant ethic which were congruent with the Capitalist Spirit. Firstly, there was a degree of asceticism which was also a necessary part of the Capitalist Spirit; there was also a this-worldly orientation originally derived from Lutheran teaching, which being critical of the monastic ideal had emphasised salvation in this world of common everyday activity; furthermore, there was the systematic ordering of the Christian's personal life and his relationships, so highly esteemed by the pietistic sects, and allied to this the strange inner tensions of the strict Calvanist arising from the built-in uncertainties incorporated in the doctrine of double-predestination and which, so Weber argued, provided a strong restless driving compulsion to live a life that was well ordered, disciplined, activist and tending to impersonality. Above all, the Protestant ethic was highly individualistic.

In a very brief compass we have expressed Weber's argument, but some warnings are necessary, for this discussion has been much misunderstood. As Talcott Parsons points out "It is *not* Weber's thesis that Protestantism influenced capitalism through religious *approval* of acquisitive activities, expressed by preachers or otherwise, but because the religious *interests* of the believing individual directed his action in that direction."[1] To this we must add another warning. Weber did not argue that Protestantism caused Capitalism, in fact he explicitly denied anything so crude. Nor did he present an idealist interpretation of history to counter Marx's so-called materialistic one. As R. H. Tawney laconically put it: "He hoped—O sancta simplicitas!—to avoid misunderstanding by underlining somewhat heavily the limitations of his theme."[2] Weber's last words in his essay on the subject are: "it is, of course, not my aim to substitute for a one-sided materialistic an equally one-sided spiritualistic causal interpretation of culture and of history".[3]

All this work raised some general questions in Weber's mind about the relationship of religion to other aspects of human social structure, and particularly of course to the economy. Some religious beliefs, or at least some aspects of them, could easily be seen to facilitate economic activity; others laid obstacles in the way of economic development. The position is well known today as attention is drawn to the difficulties in under-developed territories where traditional beliefs, often indirectly but sometimes directly, prevent technological innovations from taking root, and thus hinder a new and more economically viable system of human relationships being established. In Weber's thought there were two aspects of this problem. Firstly, he was concerned with beliefs

[1] Talcott Parsons, *The Structure of Social Action: A Study in Social Theory with Special Reference to a Group of Recent European Writers* (1937), p. 531, FN. 2.

[2] R. H. Tawney, *Religion and the Rise of Capitalism* (first published 1926, 1935 edition p. 23).

[3] *Op. cit.*, 183.

of an ethical and religious kind which bore upon economic values, but secondly he was interested in the way in which beliefs conditioned the growth of social groups and the ways in which these groups facilitated or hindered economic development. This kind of enquiry led him to embark on his studies in the sociology of religion, but they also led him to examine urban development in various parts of the world in various ages. It was thus according to a definite plan that he embarked on what amounted to the comparative study of civilisations.

In a posthumously published work, included in *Wirtschaft und Gesellschaft*, but translated under the title *The City*,[1] and also in his lectures on *General Economic History*,[2] Weber made comparisons of cities of different types, showing how kinship ties weakened in urban areas as compared with rural ones, but especially indicating the manner in which in the cities of Northern Europe kinship ties dissolved as a basis for urban economic organisation with the growth of the Church, for every Christian community was fundamentally a confessional association, whose members were regarded as individuals; the Church was not, as in other urban religions like those of ancient Greek cities, a kinship grouping met to carry out ritual acts. He then went on to trace the development of the urban community into a secular association, whose members enjoyed civic rights and received economic advantages in return for their payment of taxes. Such cities differed in many subtle ways from those in other cultures. In short, he concluded, some urban developments were more suited to the development of Capitalism than others.

In his study of Hinduism[3] there is a reference to the nature of the craft guilds and the merchant's and trader's guilds which existed in India about the time of the emergence of the great

[1] *The City*, trans. (1960).

[2] *General Economic History*, trans. F. H. Knight (1927).

[3] Weber's *Gesammelte Aufsätze zur Religionssoziologie* (1920–1), 3 vols. translated. *The Protestant Ethic and the Spirit of Capitalism* (1930), translated by T. Parsons, "The Protestant Sects and the Spirit of Capitalism", "The Social Psychology of the World Religions" and "Religious Rejections of the World and Their Directions" in *From Max Weber: Essays in Sociology*, trans. H. H. Gerth and C. W. Mills (1947). *The Religion of China*, by H. H. Gerth (1951). *Ancient Judaism*, trans. by H. H. Gerth and D. Martindale (1952). *The Religion of India*, by H. H. Gerth and D. Martindale (1958). *The Sociology of Religion*, trans. E. Fischoff (1965).

salvation religions and which are, of course, associated with the growth of cities. Weber compares these guilds to those in medieval Europe, but he is careful to point out that unlike the latter they did not lead to a growth of autonomy for the city. It was the caste system and not the guild system which became prominent and this, he argued, arose directly out of the emerging religious beliefs. Correspondingly, the caste system possesses a *spirit*, but it is radically different from that of the medieval guilds, even though the occidental merchant and craft guilds cultivated religious interests, and even though matters of etiquette and ranking played a big part in them, as of course they do in castes. In short, whilst questions of etiquette and ranking have been common to both castes and medieval guilds, they never in the latter assumed the religious importance that they did in castes, nor for that matter were the medieval guilds politically and socially so powerful in directing the course of economic affairs.

To take yet another example from his comparative studies of oriental cultures, let us briefly refer to Confucianism in pre-revolutionary China. Here is a religion which is little more than a set of moral precepts embedded in a secular literature, but it was amply supported by the government. Its officials were educated laymen and from their numbers were selected the administrators of the state. There were also guilds in China, but they never acquired much place or power, for a person's primary loyalty was to his family and clan. Instead, the group that emerged as a powerful body was the bureaucracy. Nevertheless, the bureaucratic structure was not a highly organised set of functions as it was in the West, but a system of tax collecting by *literati*. Here again, Weber pointed to the relationships between religion, economic attitudes and the emergence of social groupings. The state religion was explicitly oriented to the maintenance of good order and discipline, and it was therefore conservative, supportive of the feudal society. It also supported the virtues of the small trader and the peasant farmer, and of course this meant it was traditional in the extreme; qualities hardly conducive to the radical reorientation of human lives and that reorganisation of society which the rise of Capitalism represented. The main social groups which emerged in China were the kinship group and the status group of literary gentlemen-officials. Like the caste groups of India, but for different reasons, these did not prove the stuff out of which industrial entrepreneurs are made.

These erudite studies in the sociology of religion, far-reaching in scope, marshalling large quantities of data, rich in their insights, containing many generalisations, albeit qualified again and again, constitute a most impressive achievement. It is largely for these studies of religion and civilisation in India, China and Palestine, all throwing light indirectly on the modern western world, that Weber will be lastingly known. The immense fields he covered do not permit condensation and it would be foolish to attempt it, but the greater part of his work is now translated into English.[1] His work provides a model for sociological investigation as yet unmatched.

The parts of his writings which have been most influential for the growth of sociology, since his death in 1920, are his general ideal-type of bureaucracy, which has stimulated research into organisational problems, and his analysis of social stratification, which distinguished economic classes from status groups and both from political parties; an analysis which facilitates discussion of the distribution of the social values of wealth, prestige and power. Both these themes are treated in Part II of *Wirtschaft und Gesellschaft,*[2] which itself being a large work and originally planned to be larger still, is part of an even greater undertaking that Weber embarked on called *Grundriss der Sozialökonomik.* This *Outline of Social Economics* was edited and published after his death in nine parts and extends to thirteen volumes.

To conclude: what were Weber's main contributions to sociology? They surely include a determined attempt to explain the socio-economic system known as Capitalism and to do so both historically and sociologically, and in the largest possible framework by the use of comparative studies. In doing this he forged many tools of analysis, especially the ideal-type concept which laid the basis for the present use of sociological models, which theoretical economics has also inspired[3]. He introduced rigour into sociological

[1] A summary is given in Max Weber: *An Intellectual Portrait* (1960) by R. Bendix.

[2] *From Max Weber: Essays in Sociology* (1947), chaps. VII and VIII.

[3] D. Martindale, "Sociological Theory and the Ideal-Type" in *Symposium on Sociological Theory,* edit. Ll. Gross (1959), chap. VI.

analysis as well as providing it with such breadth of vision that it must remain an inspiration to social scientists, and he did justice to the humanistic tradition of German historical scholarship, which subsequent sociologists have been relatively insensitive to. Above all, he was intellectually bold, politically committed and thoroughly professional in his outlook and habits. These are qualities indispensable to the growth of sociological studies.

CHAPTER VIII

ANALYTICAL AND FORMAL SOCIOLOGY

Contemporary with Durkheim and Weber were a number of sociologists, mostly German, who were concerned *inter alia* with the conceptual problems of sociology. Among them were Ferdinand Tönnies, Georg Simmel, Alfred Vierkandt and Leopold von Wiese. Their work was analytical and conceptual in character, just as some of Weber's was. However, Tönnies, like Weber, also engaged in empirical research, much of it of a fact-finding nature; but for the most part others remained merely theorists. For the present we shall examine some of the conceptual work of these writers.

The mainspring of the movement which has come to be known as *formal sociology* lay in the recognition that sociology is about social relationships and that it is necessary to distinguish between them. But which social relationships should be distinguished? Some are of great consequence for individuals, like intimate family relationships, others are subjectively of small account as between shopkeeper and customer. If we leave subjective factors on one side we may decide that some relationships are essential for the maintenance of a social group, others less so. If we are analytical then we shall want to distinguish classes of relationships as, for example, Max Weber did when he analysed the constituent elements of the Capitalist system. The question is of fundamental importance to the sociologist, not only in the general sense that it facilitates generalisation and comparison, but in a particular sense in that it sets limits to the area of discourse, defines the problem, and enables the sociologist to develop an orientation. At best, to answer the question is the preparation to meaningful research into a definable problem, at worst it can lead to abstract aridity of a most depressing kind; both are true judgements historically.

The Theoretical Work of Ferdinand Tönnies

Tönnies was born in 1855 in North Germany and spent most of his life there, holding an appointment in Kiel University until deprived of it by the Hitler regime. He died in 1936. His family background was rural and he had an abiding interest in the development of rural social life. Although a proponent of descriptive studies, which he called sociography, and in which he emphasised quantitative data, he is chiefly known as a theorist. This reputation rests on two of his writings. The famous book *Gemeinschaft und Gesellschaft*, first published in 1887, and his essay of the same title published in the *Handwörterbuch der Soziologie* in 1931, five years before his death.[1] The book was a great success, running into many editions. It was, in fact, an early attempt to analyse the nature of social relationships and to make the comparison between two types of social systems characterised respectively by *gemeinschaftlische* relationships or those pertaining to community, and *gesellschaftlische* relationships such as obtain in formal organisation or when people meet in a formal and well defined but restricted context. In making this distinction Tönnies was somewhat influenced by Sir Henry Maine's distinction between *status* and *contract*.

The source of this distinction derives from his examination of the human will, for he argued that in the modern world men pursue their self-interests rationally. This somewhat Spencerian view did account for much that he observed, for men enter into relationships with each other for particular purposes; they need each other but not in any total sense, merely instrumentally. This distinguishes *society* and *association* from *community*. The former are connected with deliberate choice and planning, a specific kind of willing (*Kürwille*); the latter is an expression of traditional behaviour, of behaving in accordance with the consensus of those with whom one is related (*Wesenwille*). Of course there are many other distinctions to be made, such as between types of authority relationships, types of obligations, and so forth, and

[1] First translated into English by C. P. Loomis in the U.S.A. under the title of *Fundamental Concepts of Sociology* (1940). It was later published in England under the title *Community and Association* (1955), together with a translation of the essay from the *Handwörterbuch der Soziologie*.

these cut across his major dichotomy. Yet essentially Tönnies points to two ideal-types to which there are approximations only in reality. On the one hand, *Gemeinschaft* relations are inclusive, as they are in marriage and in the family where persons face each other as ends rather than as means to ends; in such circumstances people share a common fate, be it enjoyment or suffering. On the other hand, *Gesellschaft* relations are specific and limited, exposing only given facets of persons to each other, as in membership of an association for the pursuit of a common interest, such as a hobby or in a commercial enterprise; in such relationships the coherence depends upon agreements and contracts, and the limitations of obligations are specified. In giving examples of these two types some qualifying remarks are in order, for there is no simple relationship between *Gemeinschaft* and *Gesellschaft*. In the first place these types are not antithetical. The existence of a pure *Gesellschaft* type of relationship is inconceivable. At the same time, even in marriage, and certainly in the family, there are *gesellschaftlische* elements present from time to time. As Tönnies pointed out, his theory of *Gemeinschaft* starts out with the assumption of a perfect unity of human wills as an original or natural condition.[1] It is difficult to think of a social group where this holds without qualification.

To some extent the dichotomy lends itself to a discussion of social development. It cannot be denied that coterminous with the large-scale organisation of modern industrial society there has taken place a progressive development of *gesellschaftlische* relationships, nor that in the same process much that exemplified *gemeinschaftlische* relationships has diminished, e.g. decline of village life. This historical treatment was not Tönnies' main purpose, however, nor was he especially concerned to introduce an evaluation into his analysis, although in fact he wrote in a manner that makes it clear he regretted the trends of his time. Rather, his analysis is designed to help the sociologist ask proper questions. The study of paired contrasts, as Kaspar Naegele[2] calls them, such as doctors and patients, priests and confessors,

[1] *Op. cit.* (1955), p. 42.

[2] "The Institutionalization of Action" in *Theories of Society* (edited by Parsons, Shils, Naegele and Pitts, 1961), p. 184.

teachers and pupils, or other than professional ones, like fathers and sons, husbands and wives, employers and employees, is an important undertaking, and to make a sensible analysis some sort of scheme such as this one of Tönnies is required. The question that may be asked, as a result of his work, is what is the nature of the social bond in these various instances. Or again, how far is the relationship personal or impersonal, and in what senses. This kind of analysis preceded the continuing work of Durkheim in France and Weber in Germany. It has had a wide influence on sociological thought everywhere.

Before passing to examine the rest of Tönnies' thought it should be noted that in making his distinction between two types of relations he was by no means clear about their analytical status. That is, he failed to make clear whether *Gemeinschaft* is a sociological or psychological category. At times he regards it as if it were psychological, for he refers to the emotional character of the tie binding people in that kind of relationship. It remained for an otherwise obscure philosopher, Hermann Schmalenbach, in an article written in 1922,[1] to point out that the *Gemeinschaft* relationship did not necessarily possess this emotional content, although it might do so. To clarify the discussion he introduced the concept of *communion* (*Bund*) which denotes those relationships where there is such *rapport* between the persons concerned. Schmalenbach's development of the theme has many interesting implications, for it points to factors which may be common to both *Gemeinschaft* and *Gesellschaft* relations and, moreover, it prevents the error of reification.

Tönnies' social thought was much influenced by his interest in Thomas Hobbes, the seventeenth century English political theorist. It was Hobbes' writing about both social order and natural law that conditioned Tönnies' interest in theoretical sociology. The Hobbesian problem of how order is maintained in human society was also Tönnies' problem, as indeed it was that of his contemporary, Durkheim. From this interest sprang his discussion of types of relations depending on types of will and the nature of the tie

[1] "Uber die Kategorie des Bundes" in Die Dioskuren *Jahrbuch für Geisteswissenschaften* I, 1922, translated freely by Kaspar D. Naegele "The Sociological Category of Communion" in *Theories of Society* edited by Parsons *et alia* (1961), p. 331.

which binds people to one another. Much of his book is concerned with discussions of the nature of the human will and the various ways in which behaviour is institutionalised to constitute social order. This discussion led him to consider law, mores, folkways and religion.[1] Briefly, his definitions and classifications place folkways, morals, religion and concord in the *Gemeinschaft* category, whilst law, and public opinion belong to the *Gesellschaft* category; mores are for him "ideal law" and appear to belong to both categories. Thus did Tönnies elaborate his scheme of thought to provide a means to the understanding of historical development. Strangely, Tönnies hardly used these categories in his own empirical work, but his ideas have influenced several generations of sociologists engaged in community studies both urban and rural, perhaps because his typology is relatively simple, but mainly because of a general predeliction for perceiving social development during the past two hundred years in his terms. His was the first successful attempt in analytical sociology and it prepared the way for the development of the formalists to whom we now turn—Simmel, Vierkandt and von Wiese.

The Insights of Georg Simmel

Simmel, a Jewish scholar of independent means, was born in 1858 and died in 1918. He lectured in the University of Berlin with considerable acceptability. In later life he was called to Strasbourg as Professor Ordinarius, his promotion being delayed largely because of anti-semitism. His fame was the result of his lectures and his articles on formal relationships, some of which appeared in newspapers and popular journals. Although he wrote on various topics in philosophy, economics and history, it is his sociological writings that are of particular and abiding interest. He distinguished three different kinds of sociology: *general sociology*, concerned with a "one-sided abstraction" (i.e. sociological abstraction), even "although it covers almost all human existence", and which is the study of a social phenomenon or problem in developmental terms as a product of a social group; *philosophical*

[1] Further discussion of norms is found in his essay *Die Sitte* translated *Custom: An Essay on Social Codes*, by A. F. Borenstein (1961).

sociology which is a study of what he calls the epistemological and metaphysical aspects of society, in other words the philosophy of the social sciences or general methodology; and lastly *formal sociology*, for which he is best known, and which he describes as the study of societal forms. Society, for Simmel, consisted of the interaction of individuals. The description of the forms of this interaction is the task of formal sociology; the method is to abstract the societal forms. "It proceeds like grammar, which isolates the pure forms of language from their contents through which these forms, nevertheless, come to life. In a comparable manner, social groups which are the most diverse imaginable in purpose and general significance, may nevertheless show incidental forms of behaviour toward one another on the part of their individual members. We find superiority and subordination, competition, division of labour, formation of parties, representation, inner solidarity coupled with exclusiveness toward the outside, and innumerable similar features in the state, in a religious community, in a band of conspirators, in an economic association, in an art school, in the family. However diverse the interests are that give rise to these sociations, the *forms* in which the interests are realised may yet be identical."[1] This quotation introduces us to the terms *sociation* and *forms*. To Simmel society is not merely a collection of individuals, nor is it something metaphysical and apart from the individuals that compose it, but rather it is the individuals and their interactions; and by using the term "interaction" he implies reciprocity in human relationships. From such human interactions, Simmel argues, we should abstract those elements which are common to diverse situations and instances, like competition and subordination.

Some of Simmel's most interesting disquisitions are about these forms. Competition he saw as a special case of conflict about which he wrote a celebrated essay.[2] Super- and sub-ordination are topics he came back to on numerous occasions. His writings on sociology take the form of essays on various social forms or aspects of them. Very often he examines the form of a relationship in groups of

[1] *The Sociology of Georg Simmel*, edited by K. H. Wolff (1950), pp. 22 ff.
[2] "Der Streit", ch. 4 of *Soziologie* (1908), translated "Conflict" in *Conflict. The Web of Group Affiliations*, by K. H. Wolff and R. Bendix (1955).

varying size. Thus, for example, he has some interesting things to say about dyadic and triadic groups, i.e. groups with two or three members respectively. After discussing the properties of dyadic groups, such as their permission of great intimacy, he goes on to show what differences occur when such a group by the addition of one is turned into a triad. "Dyads thus have very specific features. This is shown not only by the fact that the addition of a third person completely changes them, but also, and even more so, by the common observation that the further expansion to four or more by no means correspondingly modifies the group any further. For instance, the marriage with one child has a character which is completely different from that of a childless marriage, but it is not significantly different from a marriage with two or more children. To be sure, the difference resulting from the advent of the second child is again much more considerable than is that which results from the third. But this really follows from the norm mentioned: in many respects, the marriage with one child is a relation consisting of two elements—on the one hand, the parental unit, and on the other, the child. The second child is not only a fourth member of a relation but, sociologically speaking, also a third, with the peculiar effects of the third member. For, as soon as infancy has passed, it is much more often the parents who form a functional unit within the family than it is the totality of the children."[1]

Simmel's sociological thought is of this speculative kind, with frequent reference to examples to illustrate his statements. On the whole, he did not formulate hypotheses in such a way that they could be tested, although many of his observations can be used to formulate hypotheses capable of such treatment and, indeed, his work is a fruitful source for hypotheses, as people interested in small group studies have found.

Essentially, his work is thought-provoking. He frequently associates phenomena of disparate nature, showing interesting parallels and similarities in form , and his examples are drawn from numerous sources. It is easy to see how, despite his rather heavy German style of writing, the presentation of his ideas before an audience aroused so much enthusiasm. His work cannot be described as

[1] *Op. cit.* (1950), pp. 138–9.

systematic sociology. He left no body of disciples to carry on his work, but several people did try to develop his ideas in more systematic fashion. He was, in fact, unusual and inimitable, a shining star in the sociological firmament, and well worth reading for the many different ways in which he looked at social life and the light he shed on it.

Despite his emphasis on form, much of his writing is about the content of social situations. One of his most illuminating essays is about the urban metropolis and the psychology of those who live in it.[1] This essay on social psychology argues that in the modern urban situation there is a heightening of nervous stimulation. As he put it, "the metropolis exacts from man as a discriminating creature a different amount of consciousness than does rural life ... The reaction to metropolitan phenomena is shifted to that organ which is least sensitive and quite remote from the depth of the personality. Intellectuality is thus seen to preserve subjective life against the overwhelming power of metropolitan life, and intellectuality branches out in many directions and is integrated with numerous discrete phenomena."[2] Because the metropolis is the heart of economic activity the role of money is great;[3] it is a means of reducing qualitative factors to quantitative ones, a means of overcoming variety and differences. As a result the key-note is anonymity and matter-of-factness. There is precision in calculation and forecast, but there is also impersonality and the development of a blasé attitude; for this last characteristic of mankind results from constant change, that is to say from constant stimulation from ever changing impressions; here is the source of failure to make discriminations, the origins of the reserved attitudes of the inhabitants to one another, but also the reason for the high degree of personal freedom people enjoy.

Like Durkheim, he saw in the city the mainspring of the division of labour, which implies the one-sided accomplishment of the individual. In his discussion of the effects of this development on the personality, Simmel points to the threat it makes to individuality. "On the one hand, life is made infinitely easy for the

[1] "Die Grossstädte und das Geistesleben" (1902). Translated by K. H. Wolff "The Metropolis and Mental Life", *op. cit.* (1950), ch. 4.

[2] *Ibid.*, pp. 410–11.

[3] A theme which he developed at length in his *Philosophie des Geldes* (1900).

personality in that stimulations, interests, uses of time and consciousness are offered to it from all sides. They carry the person as if in a stream, and one needs hardly to swim for oneself. On the other hand, however, life is composed more and more of these impersonal contents and offerings which tend to displace the genuine personal colorations and incomparabilities. This results in the individual's summoning the utmost in uniqueness and particularization, in order to preserve his most personal core. He has to exaggerate this personal element in order to remain audible even to himself."[1] The metropolis, says Simmel, is the arena in which the demands for liberty and equality are made, but also where men demand to be recognised as unique individuals; in this arena the conflict takes place, and the metropolis thus becomes a great historical event, pregnant with possibility, as within it the roles of man are defined.

It was a cardinal principle in Simmel's view of sociology that it should not be encyclopaedic, but rather be strictly limited in its scope. Hence, he defined it in terms of the study of the forms of interactions. As Sorokin says,[2] he departed from this principle in fact. Indeed, he did this in more ways than Sorokin allows for, as he not infrequently introduces psychological factors into his discussion of such forms. This is clearly apparent in the essay from which we have just quoted, but it is noticeable in others. We should also note that Simmel was much influenced by Marx's writings. Indeed we can see in his work two recurrent elements: a preoccupation with the nature of society, what it in fact is, and a fascination with the conflicts that enter into human relations. For Simmel saw no unity that may be called *society*. In his small book on philosophy of history[3] it is apparent that he regards only the individual as real. To describe society is merely to describe the social interactions of individuals; society only *seems* real. But, moreover, essentially it is in the conflict and interchange in human interaction that social reality is to be found. Inevitably, this led him to refer to the characteristics of individuals, that is to say to personality. This, however, means that he was concerned

[1] *Op. cit.* (1950), p. 422.
[2] *Contemporary Sociological Theories* (1928), ch. 9.
[3] *Die Probleme der Geschichtephilosophie* (1892).

with the *sociability* of mankind. It was this subject that he took for his address to the first congress of the German Sociological Society in 1910.[1]

Other Contributions to Formal Sociology

Both Alfred Vierkandt and Leopold von Wiese made contributions to this development in sociology. Vierkandt in particular was anxious to limit the field of the subject and took an even more restricted view than Simmel himself. Thus, he argued that sociology should be limited to the study of the principal forms of social organisation with special emphasis on power relations, conflict, leadership and so forth. It should be the sociologist's task to set out typologies of such forms and eschew discussions of content, which could well be left to the historian.[2]

The influence of Tönnies may be seen in Vierkandt's work too, for he held that, in the typology of relations, a major division must be between those relations which are intimate and those which are remote. In other words, again we see the dichotomy of *Gemeinschaft* and *Gesellschaft* being regarded as fundamental laws, for he traced a development from "society" to what he called "experience-community" and from this to "life-community". His manner of approach to social data was phenomenological, that is to say he accepted the Husserlian view that we can understand a mental process only by an act of intuition which itself rests upon an awareness of the subjective motive and the object of the action; both the subject and the object are to be considered together. His purpose was to arrive at basic elements of a social kind, and these, he held, are found in such social entities as liking, obeying, submitting, etc. Again, this is incipient in Simmel, explicit in Vierkandt.

The work of von Wiese is much more ambitious but it shows the weakness of the formalistic approach when followed too rigorously. What in Simmel led to interesting and stimulating essays, became in the work of von Wiese an arid and lengthy

[1] "Soziologie der Geselligkeit". Translated "The Sociology of Sociability" in *Theories of Society*, Vol. I, *op. cit.*, pp. 157 ff.

[2] *Gesellschaftslehre* (1923, new edition 1928).

classification, devoid of content except in so far as, in support of the classification, numerous examples are given; it is almost incapable of providing the framework from which hypotheses can be derived and operationally defined. It is in fact an attempt at a systematic sociology.[1]

It is asserted firstly, by von Wiese, that there are two fundamental processes in human society, associative and dissociative. All relations may be divided into one or the other, and if they cannot it is because they belong to a third category sharing both associative and dissociative characteristics. Secondly, individuals are linked to each other or they are detached. These categories are exhaustive. Similarly, not only may individual relationships be so classified but so also may groups and collectivities. The fundamental processes may themselves be divided firstly into principal processes, and secondly into sub-processes; these in turn become separated into single processes subsuming concrete social actions. Thus an associative process may be one of adaption or equalisation, whilst a dissociative process may be one of conflict, opposition, or competition. The method may be used to analyse any social situation; it is logical and has many refinements. It is interesting to note, in passing, that von Wiese carried out a study of the village in Germany, *Das Dorf als soziales Gebilde* (1928) which was an attempt to make use of his formalistic scheme. Other empirical investigations followed, but with less relevance to the theoretical work which is so closely associated with his name.

In 1932, von Wiese, in collaboration with Howard Becker, an American sociologist, brought out in English an enlarged version of the original work entitled *Systematic Sociology*.[2] This work makes reference to other American sociologists who had initially been influenced by aspects of the work of Simmel, Vierkandt, the Belgian sociologist E. Waxweiler[3] of L'Institut de Sociologie Solvay, and whose work in turn had proved to be of interest to von Wiese. Among these Americans are E. A. Ross,[4] E. Bogardus,[5]

[1] *System der Allegemeine Soziologie* (1924).
[2] *Systematic Sociology*: On the Basis of the *Beziehungslehre* and *Gebildelehre* (1932).
[3] *Equisse d'une sociologie* (1906).
[4] *Social Control* (1901). *Principles of Sociology* (rev. edn. 1938).
[5] *Introduction to Sociology* (1913, 1927, 1931, 1949); *Essentials of Social Psychology* (1917, 1923).

and Robert Park and E. W. Burgess.[1] To be sure there had been a determined attempt to introduce formal sociology into the U.S.A., beginning with Albion Small's endeavours when he was editor of the *American Journal of Sociology*, for Small translated several of Simmel's articles and they appeared in 1895 and subsequent years, but we cannot say that his ideas took root easily. It should be noted also that the works of both Tönnies and Simmel were read by Durkheim in France, and whilst partly critical of Simmel's assertion that form and content should be rigorously separated, Durkheim nevertheless secured a contribution from the German for his *L'Année Sociologique*. Clearly some writers outside German academic circles[2] were interested in formal sociology, but soon the aridity of this development and its relatively small bearing on social research at that time was responsible for it being put on one side; analytical sociology eventually took on a different complexion. One thing it did was to fill a gap between evolutionary speculation and empirical sociology. But, it did more, it also introduced a different kind of theorising, and some of the concepts have proved to have an abiding use.

To conclude, the verdict must be that Formal Sociology failed to establish a science of society, although it was a brave attempt to do so. Apart from the talent Simmel displayed, it failed to be interesting and degenerated into the multiplication of many abstract categories. Moreover, categorisation, or the development of typologies, does nothing to advance explanation. In the event, the classifications of these writers, as Sorokin rightly points out, do not discriminate between processes which are permanent and universal (i.e. to be found in all social groups) and those which are particular and temporary, (i.e. found in some groups and in some periods of time). And yet, whilst bearing little immediate fruit, these writers, and Simmel most especially, may have been responsible for preparing the ground for the development of small group studies, the field where there has been a great deal of systematic and analytical sociology in the past two decades. We may possibly see the influence of Simmel in another direction,

[1] *Introduction to the Science of Sociology* (1921).

[2] R. Aron, *La Sociologie Allemande Contemporaire* (1936). Translated *German Sociology* by M. and T. Bottomore (1957).

especially his ideas about conflict in intra-groups relations, in the work of those British social anthropologists, who, whilst immersed in a functionalist framework of thought, have been alive to the necessity of doing justice to opposition and ritual antagonism, and here we must refer, in particular, to the work of Max Gluckman.[1]

[1] *Custom and Conflict in Africa* (1955), *Order and Rebellion in Tribal Africa* (1963), *Politics, Law and Ritual in Tribal Society* (1965).

CHAPTER IX

PARETO'S SYSTEMATIC SOCIOLOGY

It is a curious matter that it is not possible to write the history of sociology without referring to Pareto, for whilst he has been influential, in a limited but powerful way, in the development of sociological theory, and whilst he is still read with interest, it remains true that he failed to conform to his own most explicit principles, that his sociology belongs more to the era of Comte than to Durkheim and Weber, that his knowledge of psychology was slight, although he relied heavily on a theory of sentiments, and that he could have read both Freud and Weber to great advantage, if only he had known German. Whilst placing great emphasis on scientific impartiality he was deeply prejudiced, whilst eschewing metaphysics he supported an extremely conservative view of politics that relied on mystique, and whilst seeking to establish sociology on sure foundations he embarked on a grand scheme of general sociology which inevitably rested on a slender and inadequate basis. We may well ask, therefore, wherein lies his significance? Apart from the mass of examples he used to illustrate his point—examples culled from a variety of sources ancient and modern and which are often very interesting although of uneven reliability—his influence lay in his ideas about systematic sociology on the one hand and his analysis of social and political change on the other, both of which he related.

Vilfredo Federico Damaso Pareto, born in 1848, was an Italian-French bourgeois whose family had been granted a marquisate by Napoleon I. His father was an engineer by profession, and the son, after a general education in both the arts and the sciences, followed him in becoming a consultant railway engineer; later he became a business manager of three iron mines. During this time Pareto developed an interest in Italian politics, but he also entered into scholarly correspondence with economists, wrote papers on economic topics and addressed learned societies and conferences. In 1894 he succeeded Leon Walras in the chair of economics in the University of Lausanne. His early publications were mostly texts on economic theory, but in the years 1902–3 he published a tightly argued criticism of socialist theory, which is political and sociological as well as economic in treatment.[1] In later life he turned more and more to sociological and political subjects, and in 1916 he published his famous *Trattato di Sociologia generale* in two volumes, bringing out a second edition in 1923. It is with this work that we shall be concerned in this chapter. The book was translated into English by A. Bongiorno and Arthur Livingston in four volumes under the title *The Mind and Society* (1935). Pareto attempted to take part in politics but was unsuccessful. However, shortly before his death Benito Mussolini appointed him a Senator, a position he reluctantly accepted and never actively filled; he died in Switzerland in 1923.

Rational and Irrational Behaviour

Under the influence of the positivist tradition of the French Enlightenment, Pareto declared that the fundamental distinction in social life was to be made between the logical and the non-logical forms of social action. There is an intellectual approach to logical acts which needs little elaboration, but an intellectual discipline is also needed which will give an explanation of non-logical or irrational action; this is sociology. What then are the irrational acts which the sociologist must study? There are several kinds: there are futile or useless acts which serve no end either subjectively or objectively; there are acts which the subject thinks are achieving an end but in fact are not doing so, such as magical practices; there are acts which have an aim but this is not consciously held by the subject, such as instinctual acts; and there are acts which achieve an end which differs from that aimed at.

After a relatively brief discussion of rational action and the method of considering it, Pareto devotes nearly all the rest of his treatise to a discussion of non-logical or irrational action. The reason for his practice of calling it *non-logical* rather than using the more familiar term *irrational* was to draw attention to

[1] *Les Systèmes Socialistes*, 2 vols., 1902. A selection from this work is translated by D. Mirfin and edited by S. E. Finer in *Vilfredo Pareto, Sociological Writings* (1966).

the correspondence between forms of irrational thought and forms of rational or logical thought. Thus he argued that there are theories which are irrational and statements and beliefs which correspond to theories, not in the sense that such theories are verifiable, which they are not, but in the sense that they possess a structure similar to verifiable theories. Indeed, he drew a comparison between logical and non-logical acts, for just as logical actions are usually, or in large part, the products of reasoning, so non-logical actions, he says, "originate chiefly in definite psychic states, sentiments, subconscious feelings, and the like". In logical action there is the behaviour or action of the individual which may be observed, and there is also a substantively rational theory and an application to a particular instance. Similarly, in non-logical action there is behaviour, a statement which represents an expression of a sentiment, and there is a psychic state of the individual. The difference lies in the propensity for human beings to try to transform non-logical into logical action, and this is seen in their attempts to perceive their behaviour as stemming directly from their beliefs and sentiments, as if the former were the direct consequence of the latter. Pareto argues, for example, that man has a horror of murder (an act) and he will not commit murder, but he will say that the gods punish murder, and this constitutes a kind of theory. The existence of such a theory reacts upon the psychic state which it reflects, tending to reinforce it. The fact is that the behaviour, the psychic state and the rationalisation are interdependent factors. The way in which Pareto discusses these relationships is highly mechanistic and perhaps somewhat out of temper with the modern approach; yet he is able to point to the importance of analysing irrational actions and seeing them as products of social systems. To this end he devoted the greater part of his treatise, for it is an analysis of sentiments and the way in which sentiments affect thinking; these discussions constitute his analysis of *residues* and *derivations*.

Residues

"Residues correspond to certain instincts in human beings", says Pareto, "and for that reason they are usually wanting in definiteness, in exact delimitation." They are in fact the manifestations of what he calls sentiments or instincts, the ways in which these fundamental psychic drives are concealed or, rather, disguised, and Pareto goes on to say that their very vagueness is a trait which serves to distinguish them from scientific facts or principles, which otherwise may bear some resemblance to them, and adds that these residues often have resulted in scientific principles following attempts to formulate them in a more exact manner. Fundamentally the residues are the unchanging, or relatively unchanging, elements in human life. They are the deep seated prejudices; when the rational or logical matters have been described, what is left is residual, and these residual elements are what he is describing. They can be classified.

Pareto discerned *six* classes of residues. Firstly, he observed that human beings have a propensity to combine things, sometimes these are things which are similar, but sometimes they are different. This set of class I residues he called the *instinct for combinations*. The process of classification is itself a manifestation of this instinct, but it may well take the form of associating things or events with striking happenings, or phenomena which terrorise or inspire awe, or for that matter which are associated with good fortune. Pareto's analysis of class I residues is lengthy as is also that of class II which he calls the *persistence of aggregates*. These group-persistences may be seen in all kinds of human relationships, for example in family ties, relationships with particular places, social classes, the living and the dead and between the dead and objects which were associated with them when living. Sometimes the use of abstractions to denote such persistences leads to belief in the existence of the abstraction as a concrete thing. Class III residues include the need to express sentiments by means of external actions as for instance in religious rituals. Class IV residues are connected with social life and constitute the discipline required of people in so far as they have to live together; this may be seen in ancient colleges and medieval guilds as also in modern trade unions. They are manifested in uniformities and in imitation and are most noticeable in the uniformity of fashions, which are imitated. Other variants of this class of residues are when pity or cruelty is expressed, self-sacrifice for the good of others, e.g. altruistic suicide, sentiments of patronage, and benevolence and sentiments of reverence and fear towards others—e.g. the old, the mighty or the noble. Class V residues include those involving individual integrity. These may, indeed, take the form of maintaining individual property, or the presentation of resistance to changes in the social order. It was in this class of residues that Pareto discerned the source of homeostasis in society whereby the social equilibrium once disturbed brings into play forces which tend toward its restoration. Another instance of this class of residues is the sentiment of equality fostered by a group, often to disguise their own interests in contradistinction to those of others. Yet another instance is the action of those who wish to restore integrity after it has been impaired, e.g. through penance, sacrifice, ritual purification. Still another instance is the sentiment of anger at an abstract or imaginary offender. Class VI has a single residue, the sex residue, for sex is a phenomenon around which sentiments cluster, e.g. legitimacy, adultery, celibacy and many others often associated also with religious beliefs. These, briefly, are the six classes of residues but it was the first two that Pareto seized upon as most significant in his sociological scheme.

Derivations

Pareto lists four classes of derivations. These are the types of justifications that men offer for the sentiments they manifest. The first class is sheer assertion of fact, assertions made in a dogmatic or axiomatic way; many maxims are of this order such as "It is better to receive a wrong than to inflict one" or "Silence is an ornament to all women". Instead of being an assertion of fact, it may be an indirect manner of expressing certain sentiments as when a person reads a poem and exclaims "It's beautiful" rather than more precisely saying "It seems to me to be beautiful." Such an assertion is accepted because of the various sentiments it excites in the hearer. Sometimes assertions of fact and of sentiment are combined.

Class II derivations depend on authority. It may be the authority of one or of a number of individuals in one sphere, but taken by gullible people to be an expert or experts in other spheres. Pareto indulges his sarcastic wit on this theme at the expense of Teddy Roosevelt and Anatole France. The form of authority may be traditional or customary and may be embedded in legends, verbal sayings or in written form; a sacred book like the Bible or the Koran being clear examples. But authority may reside in divine beings or personifications, or even in abstractions like *Progress* or *Science* or *Truth*.

Class III derivations are those justifications arising quite simply from the identification of one's own behaviour with that of one's sentiments, and these are identified with the sentiments of the generality of mankind. Another form taken is in inducing a person to do something he would not do of his own accord, by showing it is in his own interest to do it when in reality it is not, perhaps as a result of pseudo-experimental demonstration. Or a person may justify his individual desires by arguing he wants it for the common weal, e.g. protective tariffs. Or the justification may be made in terms of legal or moral entities; of such a kind were the occasional trials of animals or dead persons in medieval times. Justifications may appeal to metaphysical entities like *Justice* or the *higher good*, or may refer, as Comte did, to humanity as a *Great Being*. Pareto adds Kant's *categorical imperative* to his list. Appeal may also be made, of course, to supernatural entities.

Class IV derivations are verbal proofs. It might be argued that these cover all derivations in so far as use is made of indefinite terms and ones possessing doubtful or equivocal meaning, but Pareto stresses those instances where the verbal character of the derivation is particularly conspicuous. He cites logical sophistries, the middle term of a syllogism which contains an ambiguity, a pun, or which originates in vagueness. Thus it might be said that: "One lives well according to Nature. Nature recognises no private property. Therefore one lives well without private property." The ambiguities and vagueness of "Nature" are overlooked. Again, a justification may selectively use a term or make an analogy to load the argument. Steadfastness in one's religion is *zeal*, in another's, *obstinacy*. Or, as he quotes from Jules Zeller's *Histoire d'Allemagne*: "Gregory VII, successor to St. Peter, and vicar of Jesus Christ on earth, thought himself authorized to chastise the successors of Nimrod, who in his eyes were naught but rebellious angels. Did not the soul prevail over matter, the Church over lay society, and the priesthood over the Empire, as the Sun over the Moon and gold over lead?" Here there is loose use of metaphor: the comparison of papal power to spirit and of lay powers to matter, of papal power to the Sun and lay power to the Moon. Indeed, the last kind of instance of this class is merely vague terms, indefinite and corresponding to nothing concrete like "dynamic" and "Spiritual"; much the same could be said of Algernon Swinburne's poetry, some of which one of the translators quotes.

Having listed and described at great length the residues and derivations, Pareto asserts that two problems arise. How do they function? and What is the bearing of their action on social utility? Here is the beginning of Pareto's functionalism, for he continues with a lengthy discussion of the elements of the social system; in other words with the properties of residues and derivations. Of course there are other elements in the system, and among them there are economic factors, the heterogeneity of human beings and the groups they form, and the social mobility of people and the circulation of *élites*; but whilst this does not exhaust the list, these are the more significant ones and receive fairly full treatment.

The elements of the system are mutually interdependent in a variety of ways. Lopreato sees in Pareto's sociology a highly developed functionalism, for he argues that society is a system tending to a certain state of equilibrium.[1] In the system the various elements contribute in manifest or latent manner to the maintenance of this equilibrium. To be sure the terms *manifest* and *latent* and the concept of *function* are not used; Pareto speaks of *utilities* and this term includes what modern sociologists mean by *function*.

Circulation of Élites

Apart from his analysis of residues and derivations and his theories of economic and sociological systems, Pareto is famous for his discussion of social change. This arises out of his ideas of a system in equilibrium where the elements over time change their

[1] Lopreato, Joseph, "A Functionalist Re-appraisal of Pareto's Sociology", *American Sociological Review*, Vol. LXIX, No. 6, 1964.

values. Change for Pareto is cyclical, not linear, and it is change that maintains the system. The elements whose values alter are the residues and the derivations, but they alter quantitatively. Pareto supposed that society is made up of *élites* and *masses*; only the élites are responsible for change. The élite groups are distinguished accordingly as they are governing or non-governing élites. Within an élite there is a certain distribution of residues, although this distribution may alter over a period of time. An élite strong in those residues he called an *instinct for combinations* is one which, in exercising its power, makes great use of guile and subterfuge, whereas another élite may be strong in those residues he calls *persistence of aggregates*, i.e. class I and class II residues respectively. However, the complexion of an élite may change, and because of the change in personnel over time, one strong in class I residues may become strong in class II residues instead. Indeed, as a governing élite carries out its task of governing it will call upon those individuals skilled in intrigue and possessing cleverness in negotiation; but after a time such an élite becomes discredited and a premium is placed upon qualities like loyalty, strong sentiments of order and discipline, honesty and forthrightness; in other words class II residues. People and groups strong in these will then take over government but, in turn, as a result of the exigencies and difficulties of government the élite will change, class II residues being replaced by class I residues; the cycle is thus repeated. It will be observed that class II residues favour the use of force, and hence Pareto saw a certain degree of force to be normal in politics. He was apt to describe the two types of political animal as the foxes and the lions, a usage reminiscent of Machiavelli's practice and indeed largely a reflection of his political though as well.[1]

Besides the two kinds of persons in the political élite there are two kinds in the economic sphere, not themselves of the political élite but corresponding to it. Thus there are *speculators* who correspond to the foxes, and *rentiers* who correspond to the lions. Among the former, class I predominate; whilst among the latter, class II residues are stronger. The speculator is more inclined to change and is primarily responsible for change in the economic sphere,

[1] *Il Principe* (1513).

whereas the rentier is more inclined to want stability. These distinctions, says Pareto, must not be confused with others. A rentier is not a conservative or a speculator a liberal, for both are conservative on the whole; nor is one a big businessman and the other a small man economically speaking. Indeed, a man who is strong in class I residues may, by his speculative activity, build up a big financial concern, but when it is developed and bringing in a good return he will change and tend to display predominantly class II residues—he is now a *rentier*. These economic kinds of élite influence the political élite; clearly, when the complexion of the political and economic élites alters in a similar way then change is either rapid or a changing situation is halted suddenly as the case may be. "In France, Louis Napoleon Bonaparte was able to become Napoleon III only because he had become the leader of the speculators . . ." Pareto cites many other instances, and then he goes on to discuss the relationship of the élites and changes in their composition. Here is a passage from the *Treatise*:

> Periods of rapid increase in economic prosperity are favourable to speculators, who grow rich and win places in the governing class if they do not already belong to it, but unfavourable to people who live on incomes more or less fixed. These latter drop behind, either because of the natural rise in prices or because they are unable to compete with the speculators in securing the favours of politicians or public. Effects are just the reverse in periods of economic depression.[1]

Pareto continues with some general observations. Thus he argued that when periods of rapid increase in economic prosperity are more the rule than periods of depression, the political élite gets richer in speculators, who thus contribute to class I residues. Correspondingly, it grows poorer in those people (Pareto calls them "gentlemen") who live on fixed incomes and who are strong in class II residues. Such a change in composition inclines the political élite to economic enterprise until such time as forces appear to counteract the trend. Such forces arise from the strengthening of class II residues in the non-governing élite who are outraged by the chicanery, graft and concupiscence revealed in economic and political intrigues, and who when strong enough

[1] *The Mind and Society*, Para 2310, p. 1644.

sweep the governing élite away. Here we see the equilibrium state of society being restored, for Pareto's social system is mainly a political system and his political system is largely concerned with élite members; hence his theory of the circulation of élites is integral to his general ideas about society being a mechanistic type of system.

Among the criticisms that have been made of Pareto's sociology is that which points out that economic, scientific and cultural developments over the past two centuries seem to have reduced the power of class II residues generally. In other words, the equilibrium state has not been achieved at the same level, but there has, rather, been a linear trend. Pareto refused to allow there had been a linear trend and in this he ran counter to prevailing contemporary notions. His reply was that this so-called trend is itself part of a higher level cycle; there are cycles of cycles it would appear. Talcott Parsons declares that his evidence, voluminous though it be, shows weakness, for Pareto has failed to define the conditions governing changes in the proportions of residues; nor has he anything to say about biological and genetic factors bearing upon these changes.[1] Certainly, we have to admit that his scheme is flexible enough to fit almost any set of historical events; a metaphysical strength but an empirical weakness. His work is impressive, uneven, sometimes unreliable historically, but highly suggestive and (like Weber, although in a very different manner) he has proved to be a means of providing contrasts to Marxist thought. His influence on political theorists and political sociologists is still strong.[2] However, his abiding influence on sociology is likely to be the way his work succeeded in stimulating discussion in the famous Harvard University seminar to which L. J. Henderson made such an influential contribution in the 1930s, a contribution which issued in his *Pareto's General Sociology* (1935); a book not so much about Pareto as about a physiologist's reflections on general system theory. Among those who attended that seminar were Talcott Parsons, who has discussed Pareto's work, together with that of Marx, Durkheim and Weber, in that

[1] T. Parsons, *The Structure of Social Action* (1937).

[2] See, for example, Raymond Aron's article, "Social Structure and the Ruling Class", *British Journal of Sociology*, Vol. I, Nos. 1 and 2, 1950.

"large cavernous" but important book *The Structure of Social Action* (1937), and G. C. Homans, whose influential book, *The Human Group* (1950), bears many of the signs of Paretean influence at a remove.

CHAPTER X

THE SOCIAL SURVEY TRADITION

In more than one country sociology began to take shape before the academic world took an interest in it; indeed, at times it developed despite the antipathy of the academics. This is especially true of the early social survey in Britain and the statistical enquiry in Germany. In the U.S.A. the proliferation of institutions of higher learning prevented those rigidities from arising that restricted the university to traditional subjects and that resulted in a display of disdain such as that of historians, jurists and others. Yet the social survey and the statistical enquiry have an exceedingly important place in the history of sociology, for it was from these developments that modern empirical sociology has very largely sprung; as we asserted at the beginning of this book this is one of the two main traditions that have informed the subject.

In many ways Britain was the pioneer in the field, for here there was a strong belief in the usefulness of the public investigation, the assembling of evidence and the detailed fact-finding enquiry. In Scotland William Creech published *The Statistical Account of Scotland* in twenty-one volumes between 1791 and 1799. The Editor, Sir John Sinclair, had invited ministers to contribute data about their parishes. A *New Statistical Account* was brought out on similar lines between 1834 and 1845. Reformers like John Howard at the end of the eighteenth century moved the House of Commons to prison reform by facts and figures skilfully presented in support of arguments. Edwin Chadwick had stimulated sanitary reform largely as a result of his investigation in Whitechapel into the causes of epidemic diseases, and his arguments backed by impressive evidence about the close relationship between disease and poverty. And although he was retired at an early age from active participation in government, he exerted great influence, down to his death in 1890, on reformist movements and legislation and on the compilation of data and evidence preparatory to it.

In the period to which this history of sociology is restricted we note the powerful influence of Florence Nightingale, who survived Chadwick by twenty years, and whose experiences in the Crimean War led to her indefatigable work collecting data in support of the reform of medical and hospital services, both civil and military. These and many others, who were members of the National Association for the Promotion of Social Science, helped to develop the tradition of fact-finding research, the compilation of data and the writing of reports directed to administrative and legislative purposes.

In the U.S.A. a somewhat similar movement had taken place. The thirty years preceding 1860 had shown a general enthusiasm for collecting data with a view to influencing policy-making. The years following 1860 were more critical in spirit, but even so Dr Grace Peckham could assert in 1885 that "the present age is a statistical age. There is a mania for gathering statistics on every conceivable subject. 'What are the statistics in regard to it?' is almost invariably asked, when any question comes up for discussion."[1] Statistics was, in fact, gaining popularity as a method, as is evidenced by the writings of General Francis H. Walker[2] and R. Mayo-Smith[3] on demographic matters, and more especially C. D. Wright,[4] who endeavoured to apply statistics to sociological data; and all the time there was an increasing desire to use statistical data for administrative purposes.

In Germany too, following in the Prussian tradition of administration, there were many investigations of a practical nature. The *Verein für Sozialpolitik*, which was founded in 1872, led the way to sponsoring social enquiries, and in the period from 1873 to 1880, when Bismarkian legislation was being prepared as part of the social insurance programme, many government fact-finding studies were carried out. Agricultural surveys had begun early in the century, and there was a postal questionnaire sent to landowners in 1874, which received, however, only a twenty per cent response. A survey on usury took place from 1886–7, and there

[1] "Influence of City Life on Health and Development" *Journal of Social Issues*, No. 21, 1886, p. 79.
[2] *Economics and Statistics* (1899).
[3] *Statistics and Sociology* (1895); *Emigration and Immigration* (1890).
[4] *Principles of Practical Sociology* (1899).

were many others.[1] This encouraged a somewhat pedantic scholar, G. Schnapper-Arndt, to publish a text in 1888 on the methodology of social investigations;[2] it was designed to promote more precision in such studies.

At this time there were also notable investigations of an empirical nature, resting on the careful collection of data, augmented by the analysis of statistics. Among these was Max Weber's famous dissertation on the condition of the farmworkers east of the Elbe,[3] published by the *Verein* in 1892. The Evangelical-Social Congress, a religious organisation interested in social questions, was founded in 1891. Modelled on the *Verein* it tried to work in the same tradition. Max Weber was a member of the Congress and obtained its support for another agricultural-worker survey he wanted to carry out, again by means of a postal questionnaire. Other organisations followed in this train and sponsored surveys and investigations of a fact-finding character. One development of interest was the investigation into religious beliefs by the Evangelical-Social Congress, under the direction of Pastor Max Rade. Not only were industrial workers directly questioned, but a rudimentary attempt was made to match a socialist group with a control.[4]

At the turn of the century, Georg von Mayr published a large three-volume work on social statistics.[5] Contemporary with von Mayr's deliberations was the empirical work of Ferdinand Tönnies who carried out many studies on crime and delinquency in North Germany, and did so with considerable statistical sophistication.

However, it was in Britain that the social survey was most effective in determining policy. Partly this was because of the established tradition of appointing Royal Commissions to investigate specific subjects which, of course, depended chiefly upon the cross-examination of witnesses, but partly also, it must be admitted, because academic prejudices in Britain were not so

[1] An excellent study of empirical sociological research in Germany is Richard Oberschall's doctoral thesis "Empirical Social Research in Germany 1848–1914, Columbia University, 1962, from which this information is obtained.

[2] *Methodologie Sozialer Enqueten* (1888).

[3] "Die Verhältnisse der Landarbeiter im Ostelbischen Deutschland" *Verein* 55, 1892.

[4] Oberschall, *op. cit.*, pp. 47 ff.

[5] *Statistik und Gesellschaftslehre*, 3 vols. 1895–1917.

effective as in Germany; the number of graduates in the country being small, amateur politics was therefore more down to earth and empirically oriented. Moreover, in Britain the social survey movement was initiated by wealthy philanthropists, and philanthropy cannot, with good conscience, be easily spurned; reports based on surveys were treated with respect by upper and middle class people because they were carried out by their own kind. Chief of these is the work of Charles Booth, the Liverpool shipowner.

CHARLES JAMES BOOTH (1840–1916)

Booth, a successful businessman, was jolted out of his middle class complacency to develop a concern for the widespread misery in which so many lived in Industrial England. The agent of this change was his wife, Mary Macaulay, a cousin of Beatrice Potter (later Mrs Webb) and niece of Lord Macaulay. According to Lord and Lady Simey,[1] Booth's biographers, this intelligent and well-read woman gradually led Booth to take up the cause of the poor, their sickness, wretchedness and boredom, despite his own business struggles and his ill-health. After failing to make any headway politically he decided that the entire question of poverty must be radically examined, and to this end he planned an investigation into its causes. It is interesting to note that his strong conservative disposition, and his correspondingly equally strong opposition to socialist ideas, led him at first to question the reports of the extent and severity of poverty in East London. Indeed he took to task both the Registrar-General, for his conclusions in the Census Report of 1881, and the authors of the Report of the Social Democratic Federation on poverty in the East End. The former, he showed, was inaccurate and often meaningless, and the latter, he felt, was exaggerated sensationalism. The current reports on poverty, he argued, were not only wrong but dangerous, for he was disturbed by the riots in London in the 1880s and he connected the two things.[2]

In preparing for his survey of poverty in London, Booth secured the advice and help of various friends. Yet whilst he attributed

[1] T. S. and M. B. Simey, *Charles Booth: Social Scientist* (1960).
[2] *Ibid.*, pp. 67 ff.

much to their help it must be said that he himself was the main planner. His idea was to trace a connection between poverty and well-being, on the one hand, and the conditions of employment on the other; also to describe the industrial peculiarities of London, and to focus attention on both the nature of work and the character of workers, and of the influence acting upon them.[1]

One well-known person to play a major part in this enterprise was Beatrix Potter, but after her marriage to Sidney Webb she ceased to be an active supporter. There was also a small staff of investigators. On a suggestion which originated from Joseph Chamberlain, Booth's plan included the use of reports from School Board visitors. These visitors of schools, of whom there were 250 in London, being in frequent contact with families, possessed a vast amount of information and experience. Booth and his helpers interviewed them and collected data about every family, with children, in 3400 streets. The work began in 1886 and the results appeared in the first edition three years later. As well as the data obtained from the School Board visitors there were reports on particular local crafts and industries like tailoring and particular aspects of the community like that on the Jewish population. Crucial to his argument is his conception of poverty. The poor he defined as those whose income is one pound or less per week for a moderate family. His classification of people according to their type of livelihood is interesting.[2] He lists various categories and denotes each by a letter; categories A, B, C and D constitute the *poor*.

H Upper middle class
G Lower middle class
F Higher class labour
E Regular standard earnings

D Small regular earnings
C Intermittent earnings
B Casual earnings
A Lowest class of occasional labourers

[1] *Ibid.*, p. 79.
[2] *Labour and Life of the People*, Vol. I (1889), p. 34.

Booth was not sentimental about the poor. He described them with a percipient eye; he was sympathetic but detached. His interest was directed especially to category B, those whose whole livelihood depended on their casual earnings; and he noted that people in this group were shiftless, pleasure-loving and unstable, that they demanded variety and excitement, and that they were essentially ill-disciplined. He argued that their competition depressed the standard of the group immediately above them, and concluded that if reform could take place to reduce casual earnings, i.e. to increase regular earnings, then this important cause of poverty would be remedied. Although category B represented only 7·5 per cent of the population of the East End it was having an effect, he argued, on the categories above, which accounted for over 22 per cent. Other factors to which he pointed included absence of work, death of a husband, sickness, accident and old age, as all contributing to poverty in categories C and D.

His first volume, *Labour and Life of the People, East London*, published in 1889, was followed by a second, two years later, *Labour and Life of the People, London Continued*, and by a third the following year on *Pauperism, a Picture, and the Endowment of Old Age, an Argument*. The second edition of his *Labour and Life of the People in London* in nine volumes appeared from 1892 to 1897. The final edition ran to seventeen volumes and was published from 1902 to 1903.

The upshot of all this immense labour on Booth's part was to demonstrate that the size of the problem had not been exaggerated, that private charity was irrelevant to its remedy and that only large planned state-originated action could meet the need. These conclusions, it should be added, were not drawn unequivocally by Booth, whose conservatism made him abhor anything that smacked of socialism. However, his work directly bore on later legislation which provided old-age pensions, unemployment and health insurance, free school meals, labour exchanges, and minimum wage levels. Yet Booth's work is not above criticism. Indeed, it would be surprising if a novel endeavour such as this did not have weaknesses. Booth's methods were not very reliable. His School Board visitors did not visit their families with a view to obtaining the required data, they merely reproduced it from their recollection, and of course some information they did not have because they had no need of it in their work. Again, there was room for variation in views about the degree of poverty a family suffered. It is by no means clear that all sources of income were accounted for, especially if there was a child earning. Moreover, it was argued by some that an income of twenty to twenty-one shillings was adequate for a family that was provident; it was improvidence which put some families on the wrong side of the "poverty line", but this depended too on the subjective attitude of the visitor. But the major criticism is that Booth did not accomplish what he set out to do, namely to show the link between conditions of living and type of employment; much data was collected which is relevant, but the connection is not made, except in the most general way. And this criticism may be related to an even more general one, namely that he had no sociological framework in mind in the first place. The fact is that seventeen volumes of data is far too many, and it would have been much less cumbersome and much more useful if data had been collected with a greater sense of theoretical relevance. Booth's was a great achievement, but it has ceased to be a model for sociological enquiry.

B. SEEBOHM ROWNTREE (1871–1954)

In 1899 Rowntree, manufacturer and philanthropist, began to collect material for his study of poverty in York. His book *Poverty: A study of Town Life* was published in 1901, the revised edition in 1902. This study, like Booth's, was directed toward obtaining an understanding of the nature and extent of poverty, but it displayed the advantages of further reflection on the problem. Indeed, it had become clear that the term had to be defined much more carefully than Booth had done. To facilitate his study, Rowntree made a distinction between what he called *primary* and *secondary* poverty. Primary poverty describes the condition of those people whose total earnings were not sufficient to obtain the minimum necessities for physical efficiency. To establish this base-line he consulted a number of British and American food experts. Secondary poverty describes the condition of those whose earnings would have been sufficient for the maintenance of physical efficiency, had not some part of them been absorbed by other expenditure, either useful or wasteful. This set of definitions was a distinct advance on Booth's work, for it provided a much more objective test. Indeed, he was particularly careful about itemising the necessities; food, clothes, lighting and heating, etc., allowing different weighting for families of different composition. His notion of the "poverty line", whilst open to discussion as to where it was to be drawn, did provide a measure and it did allow for comparisons to be made as between different populations, or the same population over a period of time. It was this latter that Rowntree was interested in doing.

In 1936 his York study was repeated and the results of the second survey were published in a book entitled *Poverty and Progress: A Second Social Survey of York* (1941). In this study he obtained information about earnings from employers rather than from his respondents, and he also estimated the earnings of children in the family. Moreover, he adopted a revised standard of defining poverty. Earlier in 1937 he had published a book called *The Human Needs of Labour* in which he re-estimated the expenditure required by a family to maintain itself in good health. He carried out a very careful study of the vitamins and calories required by a normal family and came to the conclusion that twenty shillings and six pence per week was sufficient to provide a family of two parents and three children with essential food. Added to this was a sum to cover rent, rates and fuel, garments and both household and personal sundries, and this brought the sum of money up to fifty-three shillings a week. His survey covered about 60 per cent of the population of York. He discovered that in terms of his definitions 17·8 per cent of the population of the city, i.e. 31·1 per cent of the working class, fell below this poverty line, as newly defined. This appeared to be an increase in poverty, for in the previous survey only 9·9 per cent of the population (i.e. 15·5 per cent of the working population) had come into this category. Yet his work was not strictly comparable, for he had altered his definition of poverty, raising the poverty line somewhat, and he had also defined the working class rather differently; moreover, the earnings of a family were not strictly comparable, some items being omitted and others included, whereas previously they were omitted. His ambition to produce material for comparison was seriously vitiated. This does not mean that no comparison may be made between the two periods in York, or for that matter between York and London, but we cannot speak with accuracy. On the whole, it does appear that there was less poverty in York than in East London at the turn of the century, and that poverty in York had declined by 1941.

Two other works of Rowntree may be briefly mentioned. One is a third study of York carried out after the war, entitled *Poverty and the Welfare State* (1951), and the other a general survey of life of people in England called *English Life and Leisure, a Social Study* (in conjunction with G. R. Lavers) (1951). The first of these two was a very short work, an essay in fact on the effect of the welfare state legislation enacted after 1936, on the incidence of poverty in York. The second of these works aroused considerable interest at the time, but it is not a systematic study; it is very vague and in its selection of data very biased; moreover, its arguments are somewhat tendentious. In attempting to paint a true picture whilst retaining some moral and conventional susceptibilities the authors laid themselves open to some sarcastic comments, like those in the review of the book in the *Listener* by Geoffrey Gorer about "interviewing prostitutes by proxy".

What we learn today from Rowntree and Booth is the use of techniques of investigation, and we also learn not to make the mistakes they made. In his biography of Rowntree, Asa Briggs[1] concludes by describing him as one of the small "group of 'amateur' sociologists to make thinking and feeling people aware of the bare facts of the 'social problem'". And he adds that it is difficult for us today to realise that large numbers of people at that time had to be given the evidence for its existence. In his later life he became concerned about old-age, and leisure, and at all times about unemployment. But he was handicapped both by increasing specialisation in the social sciences and by the growing complexity of these problems; problems that required, says Briggs, more than measurement.

[1] *A Study of the Work of Seebohm Rowntree 1871–1954*, p. 338.

Statistical Advances in Social Surveys

In 1915 A. L. Bowley and A. R. Burnett-Hurst published a report on their study, begun in 1912, of four towns: Northampton, Warrington, Stanley and Reading. Later on they added a study of Bolton, and their work thereafter came to be known as the Five Towns Survey. *Livelihood and Poverty* is not a large work; indeed, compared with other survey reports it is a book of modest size. This reflects notable advances in method. One of the most important of these is the introduction of sampling for the first time. Thus, in Reading, Bowley sampled 840 households out of a population of about 18,000 houses. Moreover, the aim of this survey was clearer than in previous ones. The investigators did not feel they had to collect a large amount of data, and therefore they were much more selective. The results were presented in tabular form and greater reliance was placed upon this kind of presentation than hitherto. The findings are more limited but they are also more cogent in argument and more telling in evidence. The authors had studied the work of Booth and Rowntree carefully and had learned much from their experience. They were anxious to present a more representative picture. Admittedly their survey contained no report on a very large city, but their towns ranged in size from 23,000 to 90,000 population and they argue that it is likely that their findings are representative of towns of up to 150,000 people. The industrial character of these towns varied, Stanley depending on coal mining, Northampton on the shoe industry, Warrington and Reading situated in different parts of the country having more varied economies. The topics selected included rents and housing, overcrowding, the composition of working class families, estimates of their earnings and poverty.

This survey was repeated in the year 1923–4 and a report was published under the title *Has Poverty Diminished?* This second study obviously aimed at comparing the situation ten years later with the original situation, but equally obviously there were bound to be some improvements in the methods employed. Sampling procedure was rather different, but nevertheless the results are comparable. Bowley estimated the degree of poverty by comparing the net income (i.e. after deducting rent and national insurance contributions) with the minimum standard of expenditure for the family in question; this included cost of food, clothing, household accessories, cleaning materials, light and coal. Bowley slightly modified the Rowntree standard of food, but he kept to the other items. He made the startling discovery, in his first survey, that one half of the households below the poverty line in Warrington and Reading, and nearly a half of those in York, and one third in Northampton, were living in poverty because the wages of the head of the household were insufficient to support a family of three children, and those in such a plight accounted for 13 per cent of the working class households studied. By the time he had completed his second survey he noted a remarkable improvement. Poverty had been halved. This was partly because real wages had increased but partly there was limitation in family size during this period.

Bowley's surveys are a landmark in the course of sociological research, if for no other reason than for his introduction of sampling technique; an advance in that aspect of sociological method that proved to be the precursor of many others. Previous surveys, excellent though they were in many ways, were carried out by busy men on a part-time and amateur basis; Bowley's surveys were the work of professionals. At the end of their book the authors discuss the methods they used and the degree of accuracy of their results. They indicate several sources of possible error. In the first place there is the collecting of information, which may be done in such a way as to incorporate the investigator's biases, but these, they say, should often cancel out as between interviewers or, again, in many cases there is an opportunity for cross-checking data from other sources. Secondly, errors may arise through inadequate categorisation. Thus it is important to define categories so that they are both exhaustive and clear. A study which begins with poor definitions of what is to be measured and compared very likely ends with distorted results. Thirdly, care has to be taken in sampling to ensure that the sample drawn is a random one, representative of the population being studied. In this connection also there is the problem of deciding how large a sample to draw. This, Bowley pointed out, depends upon the degree of error that is tolerable. If the sample is large there will be less error resulting from this aspect of the work than if the sample is small; thus did the notion of *standard error* develop, the limits within which the error that arises from the sampling process may obtain.

These advances were to prove of great value, not only to social scientists but to government departments, especially at first to the British Ministry of Labour. As far as social surveys are concerned, enthusiasm for them did not wane, but was rather increased by Bowley's success. Thus in 1928 a new survey of London Life and Labour was started, directly inspired by Booth's work but now directed by a committee and centred on the London School of Economics and Political Science. To be sure the sociological tradition at the school had been a philosophical one; this was reflected in the appointment of L. T. Hobhouse as first professor of sociology, then of Westermarck and later Morris Ginsberg, but the connection of the School with the Webbs was a strong one and it will be recalled that Beatrix Webb had assisted Booth. This new survey was financed by the Rockefeller Foundation, certain City of London Livery Companies and charitable organisations. This itself represents a new development, for money for research was becoming available; American foundations from time to time assisting in the advance of sociological research beyond the border of the U.S.A.

The nine volumes of the *New Survey of London Life and Labour* were published during the years 1930 and 1935 and they tell of the changes that had taken place since Charles Booth's time, in the social and economic conditions of the people. Indeed, the *New Survey* covered a greater area than Booth's had done and accordingly a greater population. This arose both from changes in the population of the capital and the movement of industry to the outer areas of the metropolis. The committee responsible for this work was aided by Bowley himself, and what is of particular interest is the comparison of methods; for whilst Booth's work was in some measure replicated, using the same methods, Bowley also carried out independently a study making use of his sampling technique.

Although ideas about what constitutes poverty may vary, and in fact have varied since Booth's day, the authors of this report wanted to make valid comparisons and consequently they accepted Booth's standard and applied it to their time. Bowley used the same criteria for his sample survey as he had used on the Five Towns Survey. The results show a fair degree of similarity. The main study found there was nearly half a million people suffering from poverty; it ranged from 10·6 per cent in East London to 7·2 per cent in the West. The sample survey covered only a limited area, but in it the main survey found 11·6 per cent in poverty, whilst the sample survey found 10·7 per cent; however, the figure Booth had given was 37·3 per cent. Poverty was also less concentrated than it had been. The causes of poverty come out much more clearly in this survey. Insufficient employment is a major cause, inadequate wages in relation to size of family another but lesser cause, but, the report concludes, it is still intermittent employment that gives rise to most difficulties.

This study endeavoured to say something about the less tangible factors, about the privation of space, fresh air, privacy and restful quiet, as the authors put it. These matters are related to overcrowding and in this connection the report has much to say about the density of the population in various districts and in types of housing.

The tradition of the social survey was now well established and so was the importance of its object, the study and measurement of poverty. In 1929 the Merseyside Survey was started. This was carried out by the University of Liverpool and covered the County Boroughs of Liverpool, Bootle, Wallasey and Birkenhead. Sampling technique was employed, every thirtieth working class household listed in the Voters' Register being selected for interview. This enterprise was also assisted by a grant from the Rockefeller Foundation and its aims were the same as the New Survey, i.e. the estimation of the extent of poverty and overcrowding, but some additional items were considered. Thus there is a discussion of the development of municipal housing, a survey of industries and investigations into selected industries and their attendant labour situation, the degree of labour mobility and the size of labour surpluses. The survey covers leisure-time pursuits, the incidence of church attendance, and so forth. Special studies were made of various groups and categories of persons, particularly those in need, like mentally deficient people, the deaf and the blind, epileptics and the physically handicapped. Altogether a total of nearly 7,000 families were investigated, and, like Booth's work the enquiries were made by school attendance officers. The report ran to three volumes and was published in 1934 under the title *The Social Survey of Merseyside*, D. Caradog Jones being chiefly responsible for this work.

Small Civic Surveys

This account has so far concentrated on the big social surveys concerned with poverty, for without doubt these were largely responsible for developing survey techniques and particularly for developing statistical methods. They also did much to orient sociology in Britain, where the social survey has remained a strong tradition in empirical social research. Yet there were numerous smaller studies which should be mentioned, although very briefly. In the early nineteen twenties a number of towns and cities made arrangements for descriptive surveys, some, more than others, making use of statistics. In mentioning a few at random we might begin with one of Ipswich in 1924, which was carried out under the auspices of the Local Committee of the Conference on Christian Politics, Economics and Citizenship.[1] This Committee first met two years earlier under the chairmanship of the Bishop of St Edmundsbury and Ipswich and consisted of clergy, schoolmasters, local councillors and others. The report dealt historically and descriptively with the city and went on to say something on health, housing, relief, education, defectives, art and science, commerce and industry, leisure, morality and religion. It was an honest attempt to describe the social life of the city, "warts and all"—we are told that there were 52 houses of ill-fame in Ipswich! About the same time, encouraged by Professor Abercrombie of the Department of Civic Design in Liverpool University, a survey was carried out at Cork in Ireland.[2] This was overtly related to town planning and the executive committee included engineers and architects. The report is accordingly slanted

[1] E. J. Gilchrist, *Ipswich: A Survey of the Town* (1924).
[2] A. F. S. Crawford, *Cork: A Civic Survey* (1926).

to include a discussion of the physical features, regional considerations, industries and docks, population and health, housing, natural zoning, communications, the cattle traffic, public buildings, open spaces, administration and municipal services. These two may be regarded as representative of small local surveys, which perhaps were of considerable local use. There were others of Norwich,[1] of Industrial Tyneside[2] and of Dublin[3] and Edinburgh.[4] Doubtless they enabled the citizens to have a better knowledge of their community. They directed attention to aspects of welfare and urban development in a constructive manner, but they had hardly any bearing upon the development of sociology except to reinforce in many laymen's minds that sociology is to be identified with fact-finding surveys of this kind.

We shall consider later in Chapter XVII some of the descriptive analytical work that followed the Second World War, and which also partly sprang out of this tradition. For the present let us briefly examine developments in the U.S.A. similar to those described above.

American Fact-finding Studies

Social problems like poverty and overcrowding were just as great in the U.S.A. at the turn of the century as they ever were in Britain, yet on the whole there was no body of amateur reformers of the stature of Booth and Rowntree either to engage in research or to stimulate public legislation. Some authors wrote pungently about the wretchedness of the poor, like Jacob A. Riis[5] who described slum conditions in New York in the 1880s, and Lincoln Steffens[6] who, fourteen years later, followed suit with another denunciatory book covering seven large metropolitan centres. The social survey was not, in America, an amateur pursuit, but a professional one. To be sure, it was a charitable foundation that

[1] C. B. Hawkins, *Norwich:* A Social Survey (1910).
[2] H. A. Mess, *Industrial Tyneside: A Social Survey made for the Bureau of Social Research for Tyneside* (1928).
[3] H. T. O'Rourke, *The Dublin Civic Survey* (1925).
[4] Marjorie Rackstraw (Editor), *A Social Survey of the City of Edinburgh* (1926).
[5] *How the other half lives* (1890).
[6] *The Shame of the Cities* (1904).

sponsored the first great survey, the Pittsburgh Survey of 1909–1914, but it was directed by Paul N. Kellog and carried out by trained economists and workers from social agencies. As Mark Abrams says, "In America an impersonal, businesslike professionalism filled the place long occupied in British society by the socially-minded middle class individualist."[1]

The first Pittsburgh Survey was concerned with wages, hours of work, work accidents and the whole gamut of topics relating to industrial relations. It studied family budgets, health matters, housing and sanitation, but also extended its scope to cover the examination of the local taxation system, the schools, hospitals, special institutions, and the administration of justice and crime. It was a massive undertaking, similar to Booth's in size but of greater scope. The six volumes were published in 1914 with the following titles, which indicate their contents: the Pittsburgh District—Civic Frontage; Wage-Earning Pittsburgh; Women and the Trades; Homestead, the Household of a Mill Town; Work Accidents and the Law; Steelworkers. Unlike Booth's study the American one did not result in beneficial legislation. Abram's judgement is just: "The measure of poverty, insecurity and wretchedness revealed was no less shocking but the findings made little impact on the prevailing doctrine that society's rewards were unfailingly proportionate to individual virtue".[2]

If the Pittsburgh Survey made little impact on legislators it nevertheless stimulated others to carry out similar studies of other towns. The Russell Sage Foundation helped by setting up a Department of Surveys and Exhibits and appointed Shelby Harrison as director. This department undertook surveys in Scranton, Pennsylvania, and in Newburgh, New York State; also in Topeka, Kansas, and in Springfield, Illinois. The Springfield Survey followed nine main lines of enquiry. It dealt with public schools, the care of the mentally defective, insane and alcoholic people, housing legislation and trends, public health, public and private charities, industrial conditions and labour relations, delinquency and the correctional system and, finally, the administration of the city and county offices. The authors stressed four steps: the investigation of the facts of local problems, the analysis

[1] *Social Surveys and Social Action* (1951), p. 115. [2] *Ibid.*

and interpretation of data, the formulation of suggestions and recommendations for action arising from their analysis, and the educational use of the facts collected and the recommendations made. Over nine hundred citizens helped in the Springfield Survey which was supported by leading professional and business people in the city. Public relations were well to the forefront. An exhibition was held, and we are told that "the city took over the survey". This work consisted of an examination of the records, both published and unpublished, of various organisations, visits of observation, written enquiries and interviews, and an examination of legislation.

In America the number of social surveys, all local in character, was enormous. By 1928 it was estimated that there had been 2,800 of them, the great majority being principally concerned with schools and education, health and sanitation, industrial work and labour relations, city planning, delinquency and correction, and housing. These surveys tended to be concentrated in the large cities of the east, such as New York, Cleveland, Chicago and Philadelphia, but there were some in California and even in Georgia. A wide variety of organisations, both official and private, interested themselves in this work. In their bibliography of surveys, Eaton and Harrison[1] say that "practically every type of private organisation interested in improving the conditions under which people live and work, and a large number of municipal, state and federal bodies have made the study of social conditions an important feature of their regular work". Essentially, they point out, the social survey in America was an enterprise drawing on the experience and skills of civic and social workers whilst engaged in their normal working activities, and of the engineer, the surveyor, the physician, the city planner, and the journalist and publicity worker—the last two being engaged "in interpreting facts and new knowledge in terms of human experience and presenting them in ways which will engage attention and stimulate democratic action".[2]

The history of the social survey is the story of a movement

[1] *A Bibliography of Social Surveys: Reports of fact-finding studies made as a basis for social action, arranged by subjects and localities* (1930), p. xxxvi.
[2] *Ibid.*, p. xxiv.

originating in a strong desire for a better understanding of the evil consequences of industrialisation, the emphasis being on poverty and housing. From the first it took on a positivistic outlook, stressing the importance of restricting attention to positive facts, and increasingly it was concerned with the collection of quantifiable data. From this came advances in statistical method which proved to be a permanent contribution to sociological research. The data that was collected then, today moulders on library shelves. It is seldom referred to, although on occasion, particularly in England, it assisted reformers and legislators. The truth is, it tends to be dull stuff. It is too factual. The data collected was for the most part assembled with insufficient theoretical interest and although laudable attempts were made in Britain to make comparisons, too often the writers allowed "facts to speak for themselves" not realising that facts never speak for themselves but for a point of view or in support of some hypothesis. The points of view are not clearly evident apart from a general humanitarian sympathy with those who suffer, and hypotheses are few in some studies and absent from others.

As the post-war period receded new influences came to be felt. These were attempts to write more interestingly about people and their lives, some being highly successful. There was also an awakening of interest in sociological theory and this was important for the development of community studies. For the present we shall leave the social survey tradition, a fact-finding enterprise with statistical orientation, to examine other trends and developments which later exerted an influence on it. Chief of these is the development of social anthropology.

CHAPTER XI

ADVANCES IN SOCIAL AND CULTURAL ANTHROPOLOGY AND THEIR BEARING ON GENERAL SOCIOLOGY

The difference between social and cultural anthropology is very largely the difference between European and American ways of looking at the subject, although it should be added that some works of European anthropologists are not dissimilar to those written on the far side of the Atlantic. Both traditions emerged from the older evolutionary type of anthropology. We have already mentioned the Englishman, Herbert Spencer, who helped to bring about the functionalist outlook, and we have also mentioned the American, Lewis Morgan, who attempted to describe the evolutionary law of cultural development. In Europe, and more particularly in England, social anthropology became on the whole the study of social relations in primitive societies, and later in more complex ones, and in this respect is hardly distinguishable from general sociology. In America the study of cultures persisted, that is to say anthropologists studied the entire body of custom in a society, much attention being paid to the history of cultures. Although over the years these two kinds of anthropology have enjoyed an academic autonomy, they have both had a bearing upon the development of general sociology. Indeed, they have inspired sociologists to take over their methods, albeit with modifications, and they have suggested new ways of looking at contemporary complex societies. In this chapter we shall review, very briefly to be sure, the salient features of the development of both social and cultural anthropology with the intention of showing the ways in which they have been able to exert this influence. What follows is not intended to be a history of social anthropology; for this the reader may with advantage turn to the work of R. H. Lowie[1] or look at a modern textbook on the subject, such as that of T. K. Penniman.[2]

[1] *The History of Ethnological Theory* (1937).
[2] *A Hundred Years of Anthropology* (rev. ed. 1965).

The Post-Evolutionary Period

Although evolutionary anthropology was not completely abandoned, and indeed today may be said to be enjoying a recrudescence,[1] the unresolved controversies over just how evolution has proceeded, together with a recognition of the defects of unilinear theories, led some scholars to be more interested in the raw data of ethnological studies than in abstract theories, or at least to ask new kinds of questions. Yet we must note some adventitious factors too. As the colonisation of Africa, parts of the East, Australia and New Zealand and the Pacific Islands took place, and as economic and social development followed, so missionary and educational services took shape. As a result of these, much better and more accurate accounts of local customs and practices were made available than travellers and traders had in earlier times provided. These were descriptions made by educated men used to observing people and their behaviour. Thus, some of the wilder speculations of armchair anthropologists were seen to be such, and consequently prejudices slowly began to die and a new interest in non-literate peoples was aroused. As new kinds of questions were asked about customs and institutions, investigators began to look for different kinds of information. There was, in short, a development in anthropological fieldwork as well as in theoretical orientation; both proceeded together. The chief names to note in this connection are those of Bronislaw Malinowski (1884–1942) and A. R. Radcliffe-Brown (1881–1955).

Already in 1898 an expedition led by a distinguished ethnologist, A. C. Haddon, had gone to the Torres Straits in the Pacific Ocean. Radcliffe-Brown, a student of Haddon himself, set off in 1906 to study the Andaman Islanders in the Indian Ocean.[2] Following Westermarck's visit to Morocco in 1900 and his later visits to look at the life and society of the people there, Malinowski who was his pupil also went overseas and spent nearly four years mostly studying the Trobriand Islanders and other Melanesian peoples.[3] To be sure this was during the First World War and he

[1] *Vide* W. Goldschmidt, *Understanding Human Society* (1959).

[2] *The Andaman Islanders—A Study in Social Anthropology* (1922).

[3] *Argonauts of the Western Pacific* (1922): *The Sexual Life of Savages* (1929). *Coral Gardens and their Magic* (1935).

did it to avoid internment, but he too had realised the importance of first-hand observation and the necessity to improve fieldwork techniques. As, for some years, these two men were between them responsible for training graduate students in Britain, it can be said that every social anthropologist in this country since then has received a rigorous training in methods of investigation.[1]

In America a similar shift in outlook took place. The great figure of the time was Franz Boas (1858–1942),[2] who took part in an expedition to Baffin Island in 1883, where he made a study of Eskimo customs.[3] In 1886 he began to study the Kwakiutl Indians of British Columbia.[4] He was responsible in succeeding years for training a large number of investigators, many becoming well-known anthropologists. Boas learned early that his original ideas about environmental determinism were unsound and that it was necessary to examine people's customs as a whole, but he learned also to note the variations existing within a culture, and he endeavoured to relate these variations to historical factors. His work, therefore, emphasised the study of cultures and also their history. Indeed, since his early influence on the subject, America has developed culture history to a high level. Still, this development is not without its critics. As Godfrey Lienhardt argues, it is a development having limitations as well as virtues, for it tends to encourage conjecture in the absence of written records.[5] Be that as it may, the point to note is that social and cultural anthropology represent different kinds of abstraction and hence somewhat different kinds of observation and analysis.

Functionalism in Social Anthropology

Functionalism is a dominant movement in social anthropology and one which has had a great effect on sociology generally. Yet it has come to represent a variety of views. Nevertheless, essentially

[1] E. E. Evans-Pritchard, *Social Anthropology* (1951), pp. 75 ff.

[2] *The Mind of Primitive Man* (1911, Revised 1939); *Primitive Art* (1927, Revised 1955); *Anthropology and Modern Life* (1932); *Race, Language and Culture* (1940).

[3] *The Central Eskimo* (1888); *The Eskimo of Baffin Land and Hudson Bay* (1901).

[4] *The Religion of the Kwakiutl Indians* (1930).

[5] *Social Anthropology* (1964), p. 26.

functionalism stresses the importance of seeing a human society as a differentiated whole of interdependent parts. It is believed that in examining a custom or usage the investigator should see how it contributes to a whole of which it is but a part, i.e. that its function should be described. The origins of this notion are various and need not be pursued here. Suffice it to mention that Fustel de Coulanges held it to be important to see interrelations in describing the ancient world, and he was not alone among the precursors of modern social anthropology, for Durkheim did so and his influence has been very marked; Franz Boas also held this view. It is noteworthy that both de Coulanges and Boas were historically minded; noteworthy because one of the attacks on functionalism is that it is anti-historical. To be sure, some of its exponents have disdained history, but this negative outlook is not part of functionalism. Malinowski, it is true, had no place for history, but the same cannot be said of Radcliffe-Brown, contrary to some statements he made that might suggest it, for he recognised perfectly well the importance of asking historical questions; indeed the writer can recall him describing himself as a social evolutionist. What Radcliffe-Brown objected to was guesswork; and his strictures on conjectural history, if perhaps somewhat too sweeping in their scope, were in principle justified.[1] Today, it is recognised the historical data available about many simple societies is more reliable than it was in his time.

The expositions of functional theory by Malinowski and Radcliffe-Brown differ, and we must examine each briefly in turn. Malinowski aimed to establish what he called a "science of culture". He assumed every culture to be an integrated whole, a unity in which every element has a contribution to make to its integration. The functioning of any institution, which is what he considered the elements to be, fulfils one or more human needs. His scheme of thought hangs on his classification of *needs*. By and large, he saw three different classes of needs: firstly, the biological needs for food, sex, protection, etc.; secondly, derived needs like law, economic organisation and so forth; and thirdly, integrative needs like knowledge, religion and magic. These ideas about needs reflect two aspects of the problem, for Malinowski

[1] *Structure and Function in Primitive Society* (1952), p. 3.

included both individual human needs and the needs of society and argued, for example, that religion and magic fulfil both needs. His scheme is not in common use today, although it should be added that one well-known textbook on social anthropology makes use of it.[1]

Probably more influential than Malinowski's thought has been that of Radcliffe-Brown, whose ideas about functionalism matured out of his early reflections on the writings of Montesquieu, Comte and Durkheim. Indeed, he was apt to speak of social anthropology at times as comparative sociology, for he perceived his subject as having theoretical implications far beyond the limits of the study of simple societies. Although he himself restricted his ethnological work to such societies, some of his students wrote about communities in advanced societies, for example, Horace Miner's study of the French Canadian community, St Denis,[2] and John Embree's book about a Japanese village,[3] both literate communities.

In a celebrated essay published in America in 1935 "On the Concept of Function in Social Science",[4] Radcliffe-Brown admitted that the term was derived from the analogy of organic and social life. Recalling Durkheim's view, that the function of a social institution is the correspondence between it and the needs of the social organism, he says he would prefer to substitute for the term *need* the expression *necessary conditions of existence*. This presupposes that there are necessary conditions for the existence and persistence of human societies, and it sets the sociologist the task of discovering what they are. We shall turn to this problem later in the book when we speak of functional prerequisites; for the present it is sufficient to note that Radcliffe-Brown was anxious to avoid basing functional analysis on biological needs, as Malinowski had done, and also to avoid a teleological interpretation, although it is difficult to see how he avoids the latter. The analogy between organic and social life, if made with care, was satisfactory

[1] R. Piddington, *An Introduction to Social Anthropology*, 2 Vols. (1952–7).
[2] *St Denis, A French-Canadian Parish* (1939).
[3] *Suye Mura* (1939)
[4] *American Anthropologist*, Vol XXXVII, 1935, reprinted with minor amendments by the author as Chapter IX of *Structure and Function in Primitive Society* (1952).

in his view. It immediately led him to speak about the *structure* of society, just as a biologist speaks about the structure of an organism. The task is to identify the elements of the structure; for the biologist these are cells, for the sociologist, according to Radcliffe-Brown, they are individual persons, In fact, of course, the units may vary, depending on the level of abstraction desired and what aspect of a social entity the sociologist is interested in. It is perfectly possible to speak of social systems of roles, or of social institutions, or of social groups. Radcliffe-Brown was unnecessarily restrictive in his formulation of the structure of a social system. However, for him the structure of a human community consisted of a number of people who enter into social relationships with one another, so that the set of relationships constitutes an integrated whole, having continuity beyond the bounds of human finiteness. "The social life of the community is here defined as the functioning of the social structure", and he continued, "The functioning of any recurrent activity, such as the punishment of a crime, or a funeral ceremony, is the part it plays in the social life as a whole and therefore the contribution it makes to the maintenance of the structural continuity."[1]

In this essay, to which we have referred, Radcliffe-Brown defined a number of concepts which, whilst they were used by others before him, notably by Spencer, were rendered more precise in sociological literature as a result. Functional analysis involves the concept of *structure*, which is defined as a set of relations amongst unit entities; the continuity of the structure is maintained by a *life-process* consisting of the *activities* of the units. It was with this equipment that he set the tasks for the sociologists. He pointed to three problems: firstly, that of deciding what kinds of structures there are, how they resemble or differ from one another, and how they are to be classified; secondly, that of discovering how they function; and thirdly, that of finding out how they develop over time and produce new forms.

Radcliffe-Brown was well aware of the dangers in his organic analogy, and he pointed to its limitations. In social life, unlike organic life, it is not possible to separate structure and functioning; one cannot dissect a society on a slab, as one can a body. Again,

[1] *Ibid.*, p. 180.

a social system, unlike an organic system, does on occasion change its structural type; any analogy with organisms undergoing metamorphosis is too far-fetched. Raymond Firth, in his excellent discussion of *function*,[1] argues that the association of the terms *structure* and *function* in Radcliffe-Brown's thought is an important contribution to the subject, and this is so not merely for social anthropology but for general sociology: indeed, it is now dominant in sociological thought. Firth also points to Radcliffe-Brown's use of the term *disnomia*, which led to the use of the concept of *dysfunction*, i.e. the manner in which functional relationships may have antagonistic effects and threaten the maintenance of the social system; this we shall discuss later in the book when considering the work of modern American theorists.

We have concentrated mainly on the thought of Radcliffe-Brown because, among other things, he influenced an entire generation of scholars in Britain. Thus most of the monographs written by men who carried out fieldwork in Africa are cast in the functionalist mould; a feature which facilitated the task of comparison. It was Radcliffe-Brown's aim to have material lending itself to this purpose, for above all he was keen to see comparative sociology flourishing. He wrote notable essays of this kind on kinship,[2] religion,[3] and totemism.[4] The works of British anthropologists like Evans-Pritchard,[5] Meyer Fortes[6] and Max Gluckman[7] show his influence, although the first of these three has expressed some radical criticisms of Radcliffe-Brown's view about societies being natural systems.[8] In the early nineteen thirties Radcliffe-Brown held a visiting professorship in the University of Chicago, and following this several American anthropologists were strongly influenced by his views on the subject; among them

[1] "Function" *Current Anthropology* edited by W. I. Thomas (1956), p. 239.
[2] *Op. cit.* See also *African Systems of Kinship and Marriage*, edited by A. R. Radcliffe-Brown and C. D. Forde (1950).
[3] *Op. cit.* (1952), Chapter VIII.
[4] *Ibid.*, Chapter VI.
[5] *The Nuer* (1940).
[6] *The Dynamics of Clanship among the Tallensi* (1945); *The Web of Kinship among the Tallensi* (1949).
[7] *The Judicial Process among the Barotse* (1955); *Custom and Conflict in Africa* (1955).
[8] *Op. cit.* (1951), Chapter III.

were Fred Eggan[1] and Sol Tax.[2] Yet on the whole American anthropology remained faithful to the tradition of culture history associated chiefly with the names of Franz Boas and A. L. Kroeber. Only in the past few decades has there been a movement toward looking at societies as systems, but then the interpretation has been in terms of cultural systems, and what is more it has been powerfully influenced by developments in psychology.

Cultural Anthropology in America

Under the guidance of Boas, cultural anthropology was idiographic; it emphasised the unique, but it was comprehensive in its outlook. Every item of the culture of a people was noted carefully; the term *culture* being used in a very broad manner to include all custom, i.e. the totality of learned behaviour, including material objects that were used as well as skills in the use of them. The elements of a cultural system are *culture traits*. The particular distribution and manner of diffusion of these elements constitutes the main goal of the investigator, and thus cultures are defined and so also are *culture areas*. Clark Wissler, who was an exponent of this concept, also described *culture patterns*.[3] Thus he was able to give an account of the patterns of Eskimo culture, but at the same time to see them all as representing a mode of adjustment to an arctic way of life, and this to be found in a culture area. Despite the historical outlook of cultural anthropology, with its emphasis on the unique and its tendency to enumerate rather than to discriminate among the elements of cultures, there were some notable insights into relationships which gave rise to generalisation. This is particularly true of the work of Boas and Kroeber.

At the same time as Radcliffe-Brown was teaching in the U.S.A. a new development in cultural anthropology took place. Incipiently, it was begun by Edward Sapir[4] who in his analysis of language and cultural behaviour spoke of *unconscious patterning*. It seemed to Sapir that it was possible to speak of a cultural style springing

[1] *Social Organisation of the Western Pueblos* (1950).
[2] "Social Organisation of the Fox Indians" in *Social Anthropology of North American Tribes*. Edited by F. Eggan (1937).
[3] *Man and Culture* (1923).
[4] *Language* (1921 and 1949).

from the scope and limits of language and thus producing a different style of culture from that depending on a different language. Here was a slight shift of interest in the subject. But the shift became a distinct movement with the production by Ruth Benedict of an article published in 1932 entitled "Configurations of Culture in North America".[1] The theme of this essay was incorporated in a book that became famous, *Patterns of Culture*, published two years later. Benedict's idea was based on an appreciation not only of language but of the psychological make-up of people. The source of her idea was European and derived especially from *Gestalt* psychology, the body of ideas about perception which emphasises the significance of the whole consisting of elements in a patterned relationship to each other. Mixed with her ideas also are some derived from the German philosopher Friedrich Nietzsche. What she did was to contrast two American Indian peoples, the Pueblo Indians who were sedentary and agricultural, and the Navahos who were migrant hunters and gatherers. She points up the contrast by declaring that they each had a quite distinct ethos; one was extrovert, ritualistic and restrained in behaviour, oriented to communal life, whilst the other displayed introvert characteristics, manifesting violent attitudes and having a marked individualistic outlook on life. She argued that they were representative of two general cultural types, what she called the Apollonian and the Dionysian. When Ruth Benedict first put these notions forward they received considerable criticism, for it was held to be invalid to attribute to societies or cultures the psychological characteristics of individuals, and the somewhat bizarre ideas of German romantic philosophy were not very palatable to empirically minded Americans. However, Boas supported her work in a preface to the book and there is no doubt that her work lies in the tradition of cultural anthropology. In fact, the notion of culture patterns is well established even though today there is rather more scepticism about the consistency of cultures than was displayed in her writings and in those of her intellectual successor, Margaret Mead.[2]

[1] *American Anthropologist*, Vol. XXXIV 1932.
[2] *Sex and Temperament in Three Primitive Societies* (1935).

Social and Cultural Anthropology

The influence of psychological thought, especially personality theory, has dominated cultural anthropology in the past two decades, but this is a subject we shall have more to say about later when examining the work of social psychologists. The bearing that social and cultural anthropology has upon sociological studies can be summarised as follows. Firstly, there is a growing conception of systematic theory, the notion that societies are to be regarded as systems, either social or cultural. This idea advanced a number of valuable concepts like *structure* and *function*, *social position*, *status* and *role*, and it focused attention on the task of defining more carefully the elements of the system. In social anthropology this came to be seen as a study of social institutions, and in cultural anthropology as a study of culture traits; but later attention was directed to the patterning of traits. There was also the growth in fieldwork techniques, an inheritance from Malinowski and Boas. These developments in both theory and practice combined to stimulate the examination of modern societies, or parts or aspects of them, using these ideas and concepts, and to do so by means of improved methods of observation and recording. In fact, the chief advance lay in the growing awareness of the importance of knowing what to look for, and of limiting data collection to matters of relevance. Let us now turn to some of these studies, which were stimulated by an interest in the developments which have been described in this chapter.

CHAPTER XII

DESCRIPTIVE SOCIOLOGY IN AMERICA

Although descriptive studies were affected by the developments in social and cultural anthropology, not only in America but later also in Britain, their origins lay elsewhere. We have already pointed out that the social survey tradition was the forerunner, but there was also another development, one that owed its insights to biology. This was the ecological approach to community development. It began with the work of a rural sociologist, Charles J. Galpin, who after studying at the University of Wisconsin, and for a time being active in the Christian ministry, became an official in the Department of Agriculture. Galpin made a notable contribution to rural sociology by his publication of *The Social Anatomy of a Rural Community* (1915),[1] where he reported the results of a social survey in which he had asked questions about the social habits of people in a rural area. What Galpin did was to ask questions about where the inhabitants shopped, where they went for entertainment, where their children went to school, and so forth, plotting the catchment areas on maps and comparing the areas within which one kind of activity took place with those in which others occurred. Although Galpin did not explicitly refer to ecological distributions, the measurement of them was, in fact, what his method amounted to. Here we may see the beginning of the determination of *natural areas*, a concept derived from ecological studies in biology. Much more explicitly ecological was the work of Robert Park and his collaborators. So before we examine the influence of anthropology on community studies we must look at the remarkable achievements of this group of sociologists, usually referred to as the Chicago School, led by Park, who was himself introduced into the University of Chicago by W. I. Thomas.

[1] Agricultural Extension Station Bulletin 34, Wisconsin, 1915.

Descriptive Sociology in America

ROBERT EZRA PARK (1864–1944)

Park was born in Pennsylvania but lived in the middle-west, graduating at the University of Michigan. For eleven years he was a newspaper reporter in Minneapolis, Detroit and Chicago, but he was also a serious academic, having studied at Harvard before going to Heidelberg where he submitted a doctoral thesis entitled *Publikum und Masse*. As a journalist he learned early that his editors would readily publish articles about communities, and especially about aspects of city life. Thus began his peregrinations around the strange and often foreign settlements of America's big industrial cities. In 1913 he was appointed to a lectureship in the University of Chicago, and later, in 1923, to the chair of sociology. Keenly observant, and with an eye for causes and coincidents, he set an example which later many of his students followed. In Germany he had been acquainted with the work of Simmel and consequently to some extent his interest was focused on interaction and types of relationships, and of course he was familiar with Simmel's great essay on the Metropolis. What Park did was to outline the task of studying the large metropolitan community, and to examine the nature of human behaviour in the urban environment. His original essay on this was published in 1916 in the *American Journal of Sociology*, but was later reprinted in the famous book, written in collaboration with E. W. Burgess and R. D. MacKenzie, entitled *The City* (1925). In this article he points out that whilst the city is an economic, geographical and ecological unit, it is something more; it is a culture area characterised by its own peculiar cultural type. As he put it: "The same patient methods of observation which anthropologists like Boas and Lowie have expended on the study of the life and manners of the North American Indian might be even more fruitfully employed in the investigation of the customs, beliefs, social practices, and general conceptions of life prevalent in Little Italy on the Lower North Side of Chicago, or in recording the more sophisticated folkways of the inhabitants of Greenwich Village and the neighbourhood of Washington Square, New York."[1]

[1] "The City: Suggestions for the Investigation of Human Behaviour in the Urban Environment", *Human Communities* (1952), p. 15.

Whilst Park's own personal predilection was for writing just this kind of anthropological description, he fell in with the developing ecological tradition and indeed did much to establish it. Greatly influenced by the biologist J. A. Thomson, who was, in turn, a Darwinian, Park argued that in the social system the individual members are involved in a process of competitive co-operation, which gives to their interrelations the character of a natural economy; this is the community, a term which denotes a habitat and its inhabitants. Thus any community consists of a population that is territorially organised, more or less completely rooted in the soil it occupies, and possesses mutually interdependent individual units in symbiotic relationships. He realised that the nature of this symbiosis was much more complex than the plant physiologist found and he was preapred to use the Spencerian term *superorganic* to recognise this. That a community is similar to an organism is seen when one considers its mechanism for regulating numbers and "preserving the balance between the competing species of which it is composed". Thus is the identity and integrity of the community preserved even as it changes and passes through the flux of history. The notion of ecological equilibrium is strongly brought out in Park's thought, for history may bring epidemics, invasions, new inventions and other factors which have their effects. The rapid changes which are the result intensify competition until a new equilibrium is achieved and competition is superseded by co-operation.

Two other ecological principles were perceived by Park to play their part in modern urban and industrial life, those of *dominance* and *succession.* Again, they are functions of competition. Thus, just as there are dominant botanical species in any habitat, so in the city the various natural or functional areas such as the slum, the rooming-house district, the central shopping area, the banking and commercial district and the industrial section all owe their existence to this factor of dominance and, he added, indirectly to competition.[1] For the struggle of industry and commerce for strategic positions in the city determines not only their own location but that of the other functional areas; the former are dominant. Park went on to discuss this subject in relation

[1] *Op. cit.,* p. 151.

to land values and natural features of the city. The principle of succession refers to the orderly sequence of changes which a city undergoes during its growth, for the growth of the city reflects the growth of the community it houses. There are determinate stages of development and each stage represents a new equilibrium state. It is all very similar to plant and animal ecology, although more complex.

In discussing the nature of this complexity, Park argued that society is organised on two levels: the biotic and the cultural. "There is a symbiotic society based on competition and a cultural society based on communication and consensus."[1] The latter rests on the former. Yet the situation of human life is even more complex than this elaboration allows for, as may be seen in the development of the many divergent systems of human interrelations that have become the subject matter of a variety of sciences. Human society is more than an ecological system, it is an economic, political and moral order.

Human ecology, as Park called his method of approach, was the basis for research into urban development. His chief lieutenant in this enterprise was R. D. MacKenzie, but he was also assisted by E. W. Burgess, with whom he wrote the famous textbook *An Introduction to the Science of Sociology* (1921), a book which reflected this approach to the subject and which for years was much used in university teaching in America. Burgess added greatly to the subject by elaborating his idea of city development in terms of concentric rings radiating from the core of a central commercial district. Thus, near the commercial core of the city is the industrial area with a ring of working class housing, then a ring of middle class housing of better quality, and in the suburbs the better type housing area with an outer commuter fringe. Of course not all cities display this pattern, nor do all go through the stages of development indicated, but there are many that do display this kind of structure, especially industrial cities at the turn of the century.

[1] *Ibid.*, p. 157.

The Chicago School of Sociology

Robert Park was a great teacher. The evidence for this is to be seen in the large number of books and studies produced by his students. It was said of him that he would much rather stimulate others to write many books than write one himself. What is perhaps most remarkable about his influence on others is not merely the manner in which he aroused interest in urban social life, but in the enthusiasm he created for writing about cities in an interesting way. He was a journalist as well as a sociologist, but a journalist who wrote well and insisted on others doing so too. Whilst anxious to develop some working concepts in sociology he avoided jargon, and at all times remembered he was writing about human life. Yet the principle of looking at social phenomena from the ecological standpoint was maintained in the work of his students as may be seen in the writings of E. R. Mowrer,[1] F. M. Thrasher,[2] Clifford Shaw[3] and H. W. Zorbaugh.[4] Let us briefly look at two of these studies.

Although Thrasher's book, *The Gang*, refers to as many as 1,313 Chicago gangs, his theme is that the gang must be studied in relation to its habitat, and this relationship is his principal theme. Thus there are definite areas within which gangs operate. They are found in a broad semi-circular zone about the central business district, and they form a sort of interstitial barrier between the business district and the residential areas of better quality. The gang is characteristic of those neighbourhoods which have a shifting population, which are encroached on by business and industry, and which are deteriorating residential districts; the gang, in short, is a phenomenon of human ecology. All this Thrasher documented for Chicago, plotting the gang areas on a map to show how gangs occurred in certain densities in certain interstitial areas.

Thrasher's definition of such adolescent gangs is as follows:

1 *Family Disorganisation* (1927).
2 *The Gang: A Study of 1,313 Gangs in Chicago* (1927, rev. edn. 1936).
3 *Delinquency Areas: A Study of the Geographic Distribution of School Truants, Juvenile Delinquents and Adult Offenders in Chicago* (1929).
4 *The Gold Coast and the Slum: A Sociological Study of Chicago's Near North Side* (1929).

"The Gang is an interstitial group originally formed spontaneously, and then integrated through conflict. It is characterised by the following types of behaviour: meeting face to face, milling, movement through space as a unit, conflict, and planning. The result of this collective behaviour is the development of tradition, unreflective internal structure, *esprit de corps*, solidarity, morale, group awareness, and attachment to a local territory."[1] There are, of course, variations in type. There is the diffuse type of gang, possessing little solidarity, meeting haphazardly but without any formal organisation or regular leadership. On the other hand, there is the solidified type of gang possessing more intense and extended conflict, enduring longer and displaying a high degree of morale and loyalty; these gangs are sometimes very tough and dangerous. There is a conventionalised type of gang, usually forming a club for dancing, athletics, or some form of pleasure-seeking. These are not necessarily delinquent, in fact usually they are not. But if a gang does not become conventionalised, says Thrasher, it will tend to become criminal, very often developing the features of a secret society with initiation ceremony, passwords, ritual, special codes, and so forth.

To some extent Thrasher was obliged to discuss the psychological make-up of gang members. Thus he considered the role of the romantic in the gang showing how there is sometimes utter confusion of the fanciful and the real. "A boy wants to save his family from foreclosure; so he steals the mortgage on his father's house and burns it. His motive is not understood, and he is sent to a reform school. By crawling a mile and a half in a sewer, he escapes, 'stows away' on a Danish ship, spends six months starving in France and Germany, finally lands in London, is deported to New Orleans, and bums his way home on the blinds. Two boys 'playing Indian' burn their companions at the stake. A boy of thirteen, carrying on a feud for over a year, deliberately shoots and kills his enemy, a boy of twelve."[2]

Perhaps the most interesting part of Thrasher's analysis is the relationship he sees between gangs and their locale, for their environment is a part of the city where there are unusual opportunities for amusement. Certain streets afford such opportunities, so do

[1] *Op. cit.*, p. 57. [2] *Ibid.*, p. 131.

canals, the riverside, newspaper alleys, amusement parks, and railroad tracks. One activity engaged in is the collection of junk, and of course selling it to dealers, some of whom have been known to encourage theft as well; and not only do they act as receivers, but the boys' parents do too. Again, there is the phenomenon of wandering. This reflects the lust for new experiences and the romantic outlook of many adolescents with few controls to keep them at home; it is essentially the compensation for the dull and sordid environment in which they spend their days. Much attention is given by Thrasher to gang warfare and its relationship to race and nationality, and he declares that the gang is "one manifestation of the disorganisation incident to cultural conflict among diverse nations and races gathered in one place and themselves in contact with a civilization foreign and largely inimical to them".[1]

Although this study by Thrasher begins with an ecological approach, in the latter half of the book the author is concerned mainly with descriptions of gang behaviour, and methods of maintaining control in the gang, type of leadership and the general structure of relationships within gangs, including the sex factor. In these descriptions there is much that is reminiscent of the work of the cultural anthropologist, for the author discusses the norms which govern behaviour and their source, the institutionalised practices, and the aims and purposes of gangs. Of course, as might be expected, a great deal of attention is given to the relationship of gangs to organised crime and the methods available to cope with this problem. Mainly, Thrasher examined the ways in which energies previously channelled into crime may be diverted into more harmless and even constructive directions. His work is thus very largely descriptive, based on his fund of experience and a lot of time spent in observing groups of young people of all ages. To be sure he attempted to give explanations, but these are cast in psychological and environmental terms; they are hypotheses which have been illustrated rather than tested.

Our other example from the Chicago School is Zorbaugh's book contrasting the two areas he calls the Gold Coast and the Slum which adjoin each other on the Near North Side of Chicago.

[1] *Ibid.*, p. 220.

As in the case of Thrasher's book, so in this there is an Introduction by Robert Park in which he declares hopefully that it is on studies such as these that programmes for reorganisation will be based, but he also refers to the similarity between such studies and that which anthropologists have made of the cultures of primitive peoples.

The Near North Side is an area of vivid contrasts, says Zorbaugh, and these are not contrasts merely between an old and a new part of the city, but between what is native and what is foreign, between wealth and poverty, and between vice and respectability, the conventional and the bohemian, luxury and toil. These contrasts are also extremes. What Zorbaugh has done is to examine the neighbourhoods in an area of Chicago adjoining Lake Michigan. Along the lake shore is an area of grand hotels and large houses where the wealthy families of Chicago life and interact among themselves. It is to be sure an area displaying a sense of community, but only in the sense that the wealthy families are clearly class-conscious and their society is exclusive. Various well-known devices are used to maintain this exclusiveness. The mores and folkways are much the same as those found in other parts of America and Europe among the rich and powerful; and these are documented carefully by the author. Perhaps it is wrong to say there was a sense of community amongst these people, for as a result of a questionnaire the author used he found that many of the inhabitants only had professional and limited social interests in the area, and indeed many spent a considerable time of the year away from the city; it is a fashionable place to have a town house and to live in during the social season, but that for some is all. The solidarity of the people, says Zorbaugh, is a solidarity of caste rather than of contiguity.

At the back of this fashionable area is the rooming house area, drab houses in drab surroundings, a nondescript world of shabby respectability. To the south it merges with the slum district. The whole of it is criss-crossed by business streets. At the better end the rooming houses are large, old-fashioned detached houses, their inhabitants are white collar workers, secretaries, clerks and the like; some are students. It is a population that turns over fairly often; not only those who rent rooms but the keepers of rooming houses also frequently change. These are not lodgings but rooms let to people. There are no common dining- or sitting-rooms to bring people together, nor are the rooming house keepers interested in those who rent rooms except in so far as they pay their rent. Consequently, there is a great anonymity and little social control. The author illustrates his theme by giving the account of the life of one lonely friendless girl. He shows in such a social setting how behaviour, when it is not routine, is impulsive rather than social; for relationships are few and ephemeral, quick and intimate, but casual and destructive.

To the west and south of the Gold Coast of Chicago is yet another area of dilapidated buildings, cafes and shops; it is the Latin quarter, a bohemian district frequented by artists and writers, mostly *avant garde*, poor and sometimes shiftless; it is also a student area. Whilst some sought its shelter because they wished to practice their art without the shackles of conventions, others are there because they sought the unconventional environment whilst having no art to practise. Thus does Zorbaugh pick out various areas in this Near North Side of the City; among the others is the "Rialto of the Half-World" bordering on the slum district; it is shabby by day but alive at night with its neon-lighted restaurants, cigar stores, pawnshops, cabarets and small dance halls. Here one meets the hobo, of whom Zorbaugh reckoned there were between three and five hundred thousand migrating through the city annually. Here also is the resort of the prostitute, the pedlar, the beggar and the small time criminal. Finally, he describes the slum proper. That district which has successively housed each wave of immigrants, the Irish, the Germans, the Swedes, the Sicilians, and which, when he was writing, was being invaded by Negroes from the South.

Zorbaugh's knowledge of this area of Chicago is very considerable and he describes the subtle differences between various districts with a wealth of colour, giving many case histories; it is very high class journalism and as a result Chicago of the nineteen twenties quickly comes to life in the mind's eye. To be sure there is discussion of how far there is a sense of community in these areas, the problem of social order looms large, and of course there is the final chapter on "Reform, Realism and City

Life". In this chapter he returns to the Gold Coast to examine the attempts made by some of its inhabitants to do something constructive for the life of the city as a whole; in these beginnings Zorbaugh sees some hope for the future of that great metropolis.

The Chicago School was thorough in describing urban life and dedicated in aiming to provide the basis for the reform and improvement of its local society. Starting out from an ecological standpoint, it appears to have developed a participant observer technique. The reports that were published read like the more popular type of cultural anthropological writing, but they have another quality as well; they have a sense of social purpose. The journalist-reformer, Robert Park, had imbued his students and colleagues with his own spirit. It is largely because of this quality, as well as because of the clear and colourful descriptions, that these books are still read today. To the ones already mentioned must be added others. Among the first was Nels Anderson's *The Hobo* and R. D. MacKenzie's *The Neighbourhood*, both published in 1923. Louis Wirth, who devoted himself to examining "urbanism", wrote a small work on *The Ghetto* in 1928, in which there is a general discussion of this social phenomenon as well as specific reference to Chicago. Somewhat lesser studies had been carried out by Paul Cressey, who wrote *The Taxi Dance Hall* and by Albert Blumenthal who wrote *Small Town Stuff*, both of which appeared in 1932, and also by W. C. Reckless who a year later brought out his work on *Vice in Chicago*. Of course it is necessary to mention the work of Park's collaborator, E. W. Burgess, who did so much to encourage the ecological outlook and who edited a series of papers in *The Urban Community* (1926), and with Park edited the even more famous collection entitled *The City*, published in the previous year.

Human ecology has suffered much criticism since Park and Burgess presented the notion. As in other cases the close analogies with biological science soon display the flaws in this kind of attempt. Chiefly, we should note the difficulty of relating organism to environment. As M. I. Alihan has pointed out, "Ecologists extend at will the concept of environment, so that more often than not it includes the geographical, physical, economic and social environments; and the result is that organism and environment merge into one another, so that the ecological organism is sometimes treated as though it were its own environment."[1] But whatever may be said by way of criticism of the enthusiasm of Park and Burgess for human ecology, the fact remains that they initiated a series of urban studies that proved to be an inspiration to American sociology.

Having given an outline of the Chicago School, which dominated American sociology for some years, it is necessary to retrace our steps for a while to look at a famous study, which although largely psychological in nature is also partly anthropological. It was accomplished immediately after the First World War and published between 1918 and 1921 in five volumes; it is *The Polish Peasant in Europe and America* by W. I. Thomas and F. Znaniecki.

The Polish Peasant

This massive study, which tends to be neglected today, is one of the most impressive pieces of sociological investigation ever carried out. The authors were obviously interested in a practical problem, namely the settlement of Polish immigrants in the United States. And it must be remembered that there were very large numbers emigrating from Poland to the U.S.A.; indeed, at one time the Polish community in Chicago was the third largest in the world, the others being Warsaw and Lodz. Yet practical problems were not in the forefront of their minds, for they explicitly say that sociology oriented primarily to social problems will fail to achieve anything worth-while.[2] They are exponents of a theoretical discipline, their aim is to describe and explain, although they were well aware that adequate explanation provides the basis for remedial action.

Thomas and Znaniecki start out with some views about the nature of sociological enquiry. They argue that it is possible either to consider the individual's dependence on the culture of his society and the social organisation it manifests, or to consider the manner in which the culture and social organisation depend on the individual, or to consider both. They prefer this last approach for they say they are able to look at the objective

[1] *Social Ecology: A Critical Analysis* (1938), pp. 243 ff.
[2] *The Polish Peasant in Europe and America* (2nd edn. 1958), p. 7.

cultural elements of social life, what they call for short *social values*, and also examine the subjective characteristics of members of the society, which they denote as the *attitudes*, both of these being correlated. Here then was one of the earliest attempts to carry out what amounts to a cultural anthropological study and relate it to the psychology of the people whose culture it is. They argue persuasively that whilst interested in certain social problems which occur both in Poland and in America, but which are exacerbated in the latter among the Polish immigrants, it is first necessary to make a study of the whole social system giving rise to these problems. Their analysis, therefore, was of Polish *peasant society* in Poland, in which they noted the changes that were taking place early in the present century, where necessary tracing them back and relating them to Polish history; and then they proceeded to examine the situation among Polish families and communities in the United States. The method they adopted was for the most part to examine documentary evidence in the form of letters written by Poles to their relatives in the United States and letters sent back to families and sometimes to others, such as the village priest. They made much use of one life-history, given in great detail, and also of court records in Poland. The wealth of data is most impressive, and so is the way it has been used.

It is not possible to do justice to the substantive findings in so short a span as this. It must suffice to say that they give a detailed analysis of the social values of the Polish peasant, his family structure and the normative order bearing upon his life. The function of various beliefs and institutions is traced, certain dysfunctions are noted in the context of discussion of incipient changes in the life of the Polish peasantry, and there is a penetrating analysis of the vicissitudes of the Polish peasant after emigrating, especially when the elderly members of an immigrant's family follow him to America, for then there is often severe disruption in the family, and members may be bitterly divided. The authors analyse the unfortunate effects of well intentioned social work practice on the family and discuss the sources of crime and delinquency among immigrants in terms of the breakdown of a system of relationships which is no longer viable.

The authors of this work began with the hypothesis that greater individualisation was occurring in Poland, but that this was vastly increased among the Polish immigrants. They ask how such a process is compatible with social cohesion. Their study suggests new questions. What forms of individualisation can be considered socially useful or harmful? What forms of social organisation allow for the greatest amount of individualism? They appear to perceive such individualisation as an intermediate stage between one form of organisation and another. In addition to these more general questions they ask others about abnormal behaviour: crime, vagabondage, prostitution and alcoholism, but they question if these are not the results of social conditions, and further ask: what precisely are these conditions? They answer in terms of a social and cultural system under stress.[1]

There are many aspects of this great work by Thomas and Znaniecki. There is the analysis of social systems, the definition of Polish peasant culture, the examination of the change from a peasant milieu to an urban one, the relationship between the sexes in two cultures, the relationship between parents and children and between immigrants of different generations. Yet the most outstanding feature is the methodological sophistication of the authors, their clearness of mind in planning the study, and the way in which the evidence is assembled to test hypotheses derived from the theoretical framework. Like members of the Chicago School, these authors too were interested in the fate of communities, in the problem of settlement in America's cities, and in the great American task of welding various nationalities into one nation, but they were much more conscious than Robert Park and his followers were of the importance of sociological theory, and they were much more adept at theoretical formulation. Most of the notions of functionalism, which social anthropology was largely responsible for producing, are implicit and incipient in their work, and the relationship between an academic discipline and social reform has seldom been better discussed. The holistic element in their argument had already been discussed by Thomas in the earlier work *Source Book on Social Origins* (1909).

One of the lasting contributions made by W. I. Thomas to

[1] *Ibid.*, pp. 78 ff.

sociological thought is enshrined in the concept *social situation.* His was the famous saying: "If men define situations as real, they are real in their consequences." The behaviour of men can only be understood when it is examined in its entire context. There is not only the social situation but the social situation as perceived by the actor. Thomas and Znaniecki tell of Polish peasants who travelled from western Poland to Germany to obtain seasonal employment, desiring to do as much piecework as possible although, on the Polish estates, they "accept only daywork and refuse piecework under the most ridiculous pretexts". The authors say that one might be inclined to think that the conditions for piecework were less favourable in Poland than in Germany, which is what the peasants themselves said, although the estate owners averred that peasants in Germany were more laborious because they were intimidated by owners and managers. But these explanations miss the point. "To be sure, the conditions are different; the whole social environment differs . . . The point is that the peasant who goes to Germany is led there by the desire for economic advance, and this attitude predominates during the whole period of season-work, not on account of the conditions themselves, but through the feeling of being in definite new conditions, and produces the desire to earn more by piecework." And they continue: "the peasant who stays at home preserves for the time being his old attitude toward work as a 'necessary evil', and this attitude, under the influence of traditional ideas about the conditions of work on an estate, produces the unwillingness to accept piecework".[1]

There is much to criticise in the formulations of Thomas and Znaniecki, and one of the best appraisals of their work may be found in the brief discussion of it by N. S. Timasheff:[2] a more extensive critique has been carried out by H. Blumer.[3] The central aim of *The Polish Peasant* was to establish causal relationships between phenomena, more precisely to determine the laws which demonstrate necessary relations between the units of social reality. This was to pitch the claim of sociology too high, and in

[1] *Ibid.*, p. 47.
[2] *Sociological Theory: Its Nature and Growth* (1955).
[3] *An Appraisal of Thomas and Znaniecki's: The Polish Peasant in Europe and America* (1939).

later years, as Timasheff notes, Thomas changed his mind and argued for the establishment of generalisation of lower certainty such as statistical probabilities. Both authors were social behaviourists, that is to say they held that the basic unit of sociological investigation is social action; in this they followed Weber. But it is action in a social situation that has to be explained, a social situation which can be analysed into the three elements: values, attitudes and the definition of the situation by the actor. Their emphasis, of course, was on the relationships between values and attitudes and their main hypothesis was stated as follows: "The cause of a value or an attitude is never an attitude or a value alone, but always a combination of an attitude and a value."[1] This accounts for the empirical fact that people may behave differently in the same situation in response to the same stimulus. Yet it is not for this part of their work that they are of particular interest today, so much as for their emphasis on studying the total situation in which a person lives. It is rather unfortunate that they allowed themselves to be side-tracked into discussions of personality types; itself a result of relying overmuch on the study of life-histories. It should be added, lest the wrong impression is gained, that neither author accepted the views of psychological behaviourism in their extreme form, but firmly believed that human beings act in terms of their knowledge of, and ability to respond to, symbolic actions directed toward them, with the consequence that it is invalid to explain human behaviour without reference to human minds.

Middletown Surveyed and Resurveyed

In 1929 Robert and Helen Lynd published their study *Middletown*, the name they gave to Muncie, Indiana. Its sub-title is *A Study in American Culture* and the foreword by Clark Wissler describes its origin; it was inspired by cultural anthropology. He declared it to be "a pioneer attempt to deal with a sample American community after the manner of social anthropology". The authors came to this city with the kind of outlook and approach that an

[1] *Op. cit.*, p. 44.

anthropologist would assume when visiting a primitive tribe. It was, of course, the first attempt to describe the life of a sizeable community in the round.

The authors' main concern was to ensure that they avoided viewing in a biased manner a culture they shared, and to devise a plan for studying such a highly complex entity as a city. It was from cultural anthropology that they received help in these difficulties, for they argued that there is a limited range of human activities, and to select these as the main descriptive categories, in common with the student of the primitive tribe, would be to provide an objective guide for their task. The six main activities they selected were: Getting a living; Making a home; Training the young; Using leisure in various forms of play, art, and so on; Engaging in religious practices; Engaging in community activities. This classification is the same as that of the anthropologist W. H. R. Rivers in his *Social Organisation* (1924). There was, however, a problem which assumed considerable proportions in this enterprise, for unlike the student of simple societies, the Lynds could not ignore the fact that the community they were studying was a changing one; or indeed, that it had developed greatly over the previous decades. They decided, therefore, to take the year 1890 as a base-line, partly because the records after that date were better and partly because the discovery of natural gas in 1886 set off a boom in the economy.

The investigating staff settled temporarily in the city in 1924 and their method was to compare the structure of the city in 1890 and 1924 rather than devote much time to the intervening period. This comparison enabled them to plot the main contrasts. They used the method of participant observation, visiting meetings of trade unions and political parties, and attending courts, school assemblies, churches and so forth. They examined files of old newspapers, court records, minutes of organisations and diaries. They compiled statistics of wages, employment, industrial accidents, church membership, library book circulation, etc. They interviewed citizens of all kinds, including ministers of religion, the Y.W.C.A. and Y.M.C.A. secretaries, and they visited and interviewed 124 working class families and 40 business class families. They also used questionnaires which were sent to over

400 clubs in the city and others to various schools. They collected a great amount of information.

It is interesting to note that the investigators soon found themselves thinking about the social divisions of the community and after much thought they came to the conclusion that it was reasonable to view this community as consisting of two main social groups, the working class families and the business class families. It seems almost by accident that they stumbled upon the social class structure of Middletown. Perhaps the prevailing egalitarian ideology of America had blinded them to the obvious, or perhaps their social anthropological approach had prevented them from perceiving this to be one of the outstanding features of modern industrial society. However, the fact of stratification did emerge.

In the Lynds' follow-up, *Middletown in Transition*, which was carried out ten years later in 1935 (the book being published in 1937), the authors were quite clear in their minds that the city had to be described and explained in social class terms. In fact the sub-title to the second volume is *A Study in Cultural Conflicts*; i.e. class conflicts. In the ten intervening years the population had grown from 36,500 to nearly 50,000 as a result of the economic prosperity that the area enjoyed; the emergence from the Depression was a major theme in the story. To be sure the authors use the same categories as before but with a difference. The chapter on "Getting a Living" is followed by one on "The X Family", for the authors had been criticised for failing to deal adequately in their first volume with the power and influence of this wealthy family; moreover, in the intervening period the influence of the X family had grown vastly, and had become obvious, as the wealth of this family was channelled into both public benefactions and industrial and commercial enterprises. The tracing of the ramifications of influence exerted by this family is one of the most fascinating aspects of the Lynds' second volume. One other feature to note is the new confidence the authors acquired in writing about the city, for they deal frankly with the ideological elements in the culture of Middletown, and of course, by implication of America itself.

The values of Middletown had not altered during the ten years but they had become firmer. The chief additions, they say, "are defensive, negative elaborations of already existing values, such as, among the business class, intense suspicion of centralising tendencies in government, of the interference of social legislation with business, of labor troubles, and of radicalism. Among the working class, tenuous and confused new positive values are appearing in such a thing as the aroused conception of the possible rise of government in bolstering the exposed position of labor by social legislation, including direct relief for the unemployed."[1] There is a frank appraisal of the political situation in Middletown and its dominant attitudes not only with respect to local politics but to the national affairs of the U.S.A. The Lynds' description is of a city "caught in its institutional conflicts, caught between past and future, and not knowing which way to move".[2] They close with R. H. Tawney's words about the ruling class of post-revolutionary Europe, ". . . they walked reluctantly backwards into the future, lest a worse thing should befall them".[3] This is a far cry from the anthropological approach, its detachment, its descriptive categories and its stable cultures, but that was the path taken to get to this present position. Sociology in this second volume of the Lynds has acquired some confidence both in its analysis and in choosing the subject for analysis.

The Yankee City Studies

It is perhaps curious that in the first of the six volumes which constitute the Yankee City Series there is no mention of the Lynds' *Middletown*, yet these volumes stand squarely in the tradition they inaugurated. After studying aboriginal people in Australia, Lloyd Warner turned his attention to a modern American community; indeed, he records telling his friends, A. R. Radcliffe-Brown and R. W. Lowie, that he was studying primitive peoples in order to understand modern man better. His plan was to select a suitable community; not one with marked disorganiation like Chicago, but one which had developed over a long period of time, possessing a coherent tradition. This was found in

[1] *Middletown in Transition*, p. 489.
[2] *Ibid.*, p. 510.
[3] *Equality* (1931), p. 127.

Newburyport, Rhode Island (pop. 17,000), henceforth known as Yankee City. The series deals with what is held to be a significant aspect of the life of a modern community "as it has been recorded and analysed by the combined and co-operative labors of a group of social anthropologists". The social anthropological approach comes out in the initial discussion in the first volume by Warner and Lunt, *The Social Life of a Modern Community* (1941), where the authors show how they began by considering the variety of structures, e.g. family, extended kin, age grading, because they loom large in anthropological studies. Yet the fact remains that the bulk of the book is about social classes, not about family, kinship and the other institutional structures usually found in a monograph on a primitive people. The methods and techniques employed have, on the other hand, greater claim to being those used by the anthropologist. The investigation was begun by four people, gradually increased in number, but the labour was divided. One person examined the high school system, another studied the rest of the school system, one investigator studied the French Canadians, Greeks, Poles and Russians in the city, another turned his attention to the Italian community, whilst one investigated the Jewish population and yet another the Negroes. The basic techniques used were the interview and first-hand observation but records, histories, biographies, diaries and other documents were also examined.

A superficial investigation of the values of Yankee citizens soon elicited the fact that they evaluated each other, and did so mostly in economic terms. There were "big people with the money" and "little people who are poor". Wealth alone was no sufficient criterion, there were other factors in the value system such as proper conduct. People were not only classed but they were often associated with an area of the city. Warner and Lunt arrived eventually at their famous sixfold class structure of Upper and Lower Upper classes, Upper and Lower Middle classes, and Upper and Lower Lower classes; a classification which was made on the basis of a variety of criteria economic, associational and residential.

The analysis of this community of social classes is thoroughgoing. After illustrating class norms in a series of profiles, some of which must surely be composite vignettes if they are not fictitious types, there is an analysis of the six classes according to sex and age, followed by a discussion of the ethnic composition of the community, and the ethnic ranking and social mobility. The residential areas and house types of the city are also studied in relation to the composition of the population, and the economic life of the city is outlined, followed by an examination of the ownership and control of property. Consumption patterns by classes constitute another chapter and there is a long section on the associations in the city and their membership, again by social classes. Reading habits and religious behaviour are discussed and then the social characteristics of the two upper and the two lower classes are described. It will be observed that as the book develops there is a movement from the general description that is associated with the anthropological monograph to the specialised topic of social class which is emphasised. E. A. Shils, in his survey of American sociology, maintains that this work by Warner and Lunt helped to re-define subject matters for investigation.[1] Certainly, it was a book which broke the new ground of social stratification analysis in America.

An important methodological contribution by Warner and Lunt is the use of informants to establish the character of the class structure in the community by asking them to rank a number of representative citizens. Having done this, Warner identified various social characteristics of these people, such as membership of cliques or associations; this enabled him to establish various criteria for assigning people to social classes, and also to obtain some idea of the distribution of the population according to classes. His methods were progressively refined and are described in his later work *Social Class in America* (1949).

The remaining volumes of the Yankee City Series are of variable quality. The second volume by Warner and Lunt, *The Status System of a Modern Community* (1942), is mainly concerned with the class complexion of the 357 associations that were investigated in Newburyport. The authors also try to identify relevant structures and conclude that there are seven: family, clique, association, school, church, economic, and political structures. They then

[1] "The Present Situation in American Sociology", *Pilot Papers*, ed. Chas. Madge, Vol. II, No. 2, 1947.

endeavoured to discover the positional system of the total community taking account of membership of structures. Approximately three quarters of the book consists of tables which are complex and abtruse. One is rather left wondering if the results justify the labour. There are no hypotheses formulated, and unless similar analyses were carried out in other cities and the results used for comparative purposes, it is difficult to see how this description could be of value to sociology. The third volume, *The Social Systems of American Ethnic Groups* (1945), is of more interest for it describes in some detail the social life of the various ethnic groups in Newburyport, showing in what ways they retain their cultural characteristics and in what ways they have changed and adapted to the American value system. Here the anthropological approach is noticeable and the descriptive categories are familiar, religious and associational. The fourth volume, *The Social System of the Modern Factory* (1947), is a monograph on a strike which profoundly affected the life of the city. The authors of this volume are Warner and J. O. Low, and they have documented in a most interesting way the development of this fairly general strike which bore on several productive enterprises. They looked at the historical setting as well as the current situation. Their analysis of the change in value of skills in the industry, the vicissitudes of the trade unions in organising workers, and the changes that had taken place in the status of the managers, go far in offering explanations of the strike and others of its type. What is of particular interest, however, is that in this work the authors go beyond Yankee City itself in their discussion and survey the entire national field, the clash of interests, the attacks on the dominant ideology, the growing complexity not only of commerce and industry but of government too. What began as a description of a single community has grown into an appraisal of an entire society. In a fourth volume by Warner entitled *The Living and the Dead* (1959), the largest of the six volumes, there is a study of the symbolic life of Americans. It is wide ranging in its scope and appeals to social anthropological concepts and explanations. The author discusses with a wealth of illustration political symbols, ideology, the myths about the foundation of the city, social class and status symbols, the part played by religion in the social life of the city and in particular the influence of Protestantism on the culture. Again, although the primary reference is to Newburyport, Yankee City is a representative city and the author slips easily into a discussion of the national culture of the United States.

The Tradition of Descriptive Sociology

It will be seen that this aspect of American sociology, which may be said to have begun in the last century with the description of Lawrence, Kansas, in *Introduction to the Study of Sociology* (1894) by Albion Small and G. Vincent, and which inspired other small community studies such as J. M. Williams' *An American Town* (1906) and N. L. Sims' *A Hoosier Village* (1912), has had a long innings. It led to the work of Galpin and thence to that of Park and his followers. The early influence of W. I. Thomas and Florian Znaniecki was strong on American sociology and has certainly stimulated others to use their methods. But it was *Middletown* and its follow-up, and latterly the Yankee City Series, that stand out in their influence on the development of the subject. The "contemplation of wholes", as E. A. Shils[1] describes it, is not congenial to the American academic temperament and the tradition has developed either by breaking the task of description down to what may be called inventory-making, a particularly sterile pursuit, or else using the community study to tackle a major, and often controversial, topic in American national life. Clearly, the nature of social stratification is an important topic in a society espousing egalitarian ideals, and it is controversial when the ideal is thought by some, but not by others, to have been realised. The nature of the ideology is a similar type of topic in a society where laissez-faire ideas are less and less obviously suitable for an advanced stage in the industrialisation process. One other major topic has been selected and this too may be seen to have emerged from community studies of a descriptive kind. This is the racial issue. It is incipient in Warner's discussion of ethnic groups in Newburyport but it began with two of Park's students: Franklin Frazier who wrote *The Negro Family in Chicago*

[1] *Ibid.*

(1936) and C. S. Johnson who wrote *The Negro in Chicago* (1922), but there were others, such as John Dollard's famous book *Caste and Class in a Southern Town* (1937), which is less about the small southern town in which the author lived whilst engaged in his researches than about the attitudes generally of southern people to Negroes and Negro reactions to them. In fact, the literature on race relations soon became independent of community studies and more aligned with developments in social psychology than with those in cultural anthropology. Community studies of a descriptive kind have not been abandoned, but they are fewer and more practically oriented. The inspiration they received from cultural anthropology did not in fact render them a growing point for sociology, for they have not produced any theoretical advance, only some progress in research techniques. One of the latest, *Plainville, U.S.A.* by James West, published in 1945, avowedly anthropological in orientation and perhaps the best known of the later works, is no exception to this judgement. Sociology has developed in other directions, in stratification studies, in an examination of race relations, in problem-oriented studies, in attitude measurement, and in theory development, to mention a few. Urban sociology is still a major factor in sociological teaching and research but it is much more oriented to town planning and in this respect the ecological tradition initiated by Park and Burgess is still alive, although much modified, as may be seen in the writings of J. A. Quinn[1] and A. H. Hawley;[2] this will be taken up again in Chapter XVI.

[1] *Human Ecology* (1950). [2] *Human Ecology* (1950).

CHAPTER XIII

THE ORIGINS OF SOCIAL PSYCHOLOGY

In order to give an account of sociology since 1940, it is first necessary to say something about the development of social psychology prior to the Second World War, for that war not only stimulated research into both social psychology and sociology, but it helped to break down the barrier between them.

The position of social psychology among the sciences of man has never been very clear. Moreover, what is taught under this heading is multifarious, at least as much so as in the case of sociology. Perhaps we are on fairly safe ground in saying that it is the study of individuals in so far as they are interacting with one another in a given environment. This means that the object of study is the effects of the human environment, both past and present, on behaviour.

Historically, the questions have been posed: what makes people behave in the way they do? How can we account for this or that action? Early psychological answers were usually monistic, that is to say the explanation was sought in the determination of a single principle governing behaviour. For William James it was habit,[1] for Gabriel Tarde it was imitation,[2] for Gustave Le Bon it was suggestion,[3] and for others, notably William McDougall, it was instinct.[4] These were the kinds of explanation given in the two decades which spanned the turn of the century, and whilst they aroused great interest at the time, and indeed in some quarters for some time afterwards, they are no longer today very seriously considered. This is partly because monistic explanations are unconvincing, partly because none of these theories could be tested, and partly because of the development of Freud's thought which, whilst based on a theory of instincts, went beyond this in its insights, and in recent years came not only to dominate

[1] *Principles of Psychology* (1890).
[2] *The Laws of Imitation* (Trans. 1903).
[3] *Psychologie des foules* (1895, Trans. *The Crowd,* 1896).
[4] *Introduction to Social Psychology* (1908).

psychological medicine, but also to exert an influence on educational psychology; of course, it has yet to be shown that psycho-analytic theory can be tested. But the climate of thought about human nature had been altering and early social psychological theories reflect these changes. Let us first look quickly at one of these early views, mainly so that we may note the extent of the change that has taken place in man's outlook; for the change is far-reaching.

Instinct Theories of Human Behaviour

We shall briefly consider the use of the concept *instinct*, as this has been the main monistic explanation in the past. Like much in sociology the source of this explanation also lay in biology. *Instinct* thus referred to whatever was inborn and unmodifiable in the organism and which was thus held to be responsible for behaviour. Biologists have done much work on the environmental factors which "trigger-off" behaviour sequences, and this suggests that various forms of non-human life have a range of alternative ways of responding to a stimulus, be it a threat of attack, a sexual advance, or a territorial invasion. But as biology advanced to an understanding of *imprinting* it became quite clear to some people that human beings do not behave in the same manner as animals do, and so explanation in terms of one or more instincts finally came to an end. Before this occurred, however, there was some competition in discerning the number and identity of instincts. McDougall was perhaps the best known of these writers, for he built a theory of social psychology on this basis. Thus, he linked a theory of emotions with that of instincts, as may be seen from his definition: "an instinct is an inherited or innate psychophysical disposition which determines its possessor to perceive, and to pay attention to, objects of a certain class, to experience an emotional excitement of a particular quality upon perceiving such an object, and to act in regard to it in a particular manner, or at least, to experience an impulse to such action".[1] McDougall listed twelve instincts and then added to them; other psychologists added more. In fact the procedure was to consider some

[1] *Ibid.*, p. 30.

discrete item of behaviour and then identify an instinct to account for it together with an appropriate emotion. Thus there was an instinct for flight with the emotion of fear; there was also a parental instinct, a reproductive instinct, a self-abasing instinct, and so forth, some of course being composite, as in the case of the religious instinct: "For it is clear that religious emotion is not a simple and specific variety, such as could be conditioned by any one instinct; it is rather a very complex and diversified product of the co-operation of several instincts, which bring forth heterogeneous manifestations, differing from one another as widely as light from darkness, according to the degree and kind of guidance afforded by imagination and reason."[1] It is an amalgam of curiosity, self-abasement, the parental instinct with its emotion of tenderness, and of flight with its emotion of fear.

"Lightly to postulate an indefinite number and variety of human instincts is a cheap and easy way to solve psychological problems," says McDougall, but it does not appear that he escaped from his own stricture. At any rate the criticism that fell on this kind of explanation and which was initiated by Knight Dunlap,[2] after the First World War, was severe and successful, in the sense that it helped to bring to an end the obsession with instinct-type explanations. They were not abandoned altogether—this could hardly be the case—but instincts came to be looked on as barely differentiated and they are now vaguely called drives, or needs, or vectors.

The abandonment of instinct theories represented also an awareness that interpretations in terms of heredity alone were unsound. Indeed, we may argue that to a very considerable extent social psychology developed in reaction to this type of thought. It is equally true to say, however, that today neither an extreme hereditary nor an extreme environmental position is tenable. Moreover, some psychologists, such as S. E. Asch, have seen a similarity in type of explanation between the two contenders, for both are atomistic explanations.[3] They leave too much unexplained and do so largely because the question they aim to

[1] *Ibid.*

[2] "Are there any instincts?", *Journal of Abnormal Psychology*, Vol. IV, 1919, pp. 307–311.

[3] S. E. Asch, *Social Psychology* (1952).

provide an answer to is too simply and crudely expressed. However, it is regrettable that public attention was concentrated on the instinct theory in McDougall's writings, for the other aspect of his work, that relating to the analysis of sentiments, had unjustly been relatively neglected. In fact, his study of sentiments, following that of A. F. Shand,[1] contained the seeds of later thought about human personality. Thus his self-regarding sentiment, which is one of a number he determined, describes attitudes taken by a person towards himself; a concept which raises the more interesting questions of self-perception and attitude formation, both of which were later to play a large part in social psychology.

CHARLES HORTON COOLEY (1864–1929)

Cooley, one of the early American social scientists, succeeded in presenting a view of human behaviour which avoided these errors. He based his thought on the recognition that men are born into communities and that the community is man-made. For Cooley, human society and the human being were complements, not to be thought of as in any way antithetical. His ideas were first incorporated in his *Human Nature and the Social Order*, published in 1902, where he says: "A separate individual is an abstraction unknown to experience, and so likewise is society when regarded as something apart from individuals." And he went on: "Society and individuals do not denote separable phenomena, but are simply the collective and distributive aspects of the same thing."[2] Similarly, heredity and environment are seen by him to be abstractions; society is an organic process.

The development of the individual person is part of the social process. Cooley spoke of a "looking-glass self" which consists of the propensity to imagine how others see us, the ability to estimate others' judgements of the self and the individual's own feeling about himself. This early view of the human personality as a social product antedated that of McDougall. It was much less popular, but we may say that whilst not very profound it presaged the

[1] "Character and the Emotions", *Mind*, 1896, see also his *Foundations of Character* (1914).
[2] *Op. cit.*, pp. 36 f.

later preoccupation of social psychology with the relationship of culture and personality.

Cooley was one of the first writers to discuss types of social groups, a subject that was later to loom large in the literature on social psychology. His book entitled *Social Organisation*, published a year after McDougall's textbook, discussed the differences between *primary* and *secondary* groups, a distinction which we shall refer to later when dealing with the development of group dynamics. In this work he endeavoured to relate social and psychological phenomena within a single framework and it is noteworthy that sociologists are apt to return to Cooley from time to time in order to discern in his works the origins of more recent developments in the subject. Nevertheless, it cannot be denied that at the time he wrote his views were uninfluential by comparison with those of McDougall. The change in ideas about human nature came about largely as a result of the work of Freud. It is interesting to note that Freud held firmly to the notion of instincts, although in justice it should be pointed out that the concept he uses (*Triebe*) was different in some respects from that of McDougall and others. But in fact he never abandoned this basis for his thought. Yet Freud's view of instinctive behaviour was a simple one, so simple indeed does it appear in retrospect that it was bound to give way to an appreciation of the modifying factors.

SIGMUND FREUD (1856–1939)

The part of Freud's great work which concerns us here is restricted to his contribution towards a theory of personality. This was itself a by-product of his interest in psychoneuroses, and mainly for this reason it is by no means either entirely coherent or complete. Yet its influence on both social psychology and cultural anthropology has been immense. We shall, perforce, have to give a brief exposition of his ideas about personality, or what he preferred to call *character*, acknowledging its very partial treatment.[1]

Freud, like his contemporaries Breuer and Charcot, was interested in accounting for some important observations relating to

[1] See S. Freud, *The Standard Edition of the Complete Psychological Works*, edited by J. Strachey (1953–1956).

the practice of hypnosis and the phenomenon of hysteria. All these clinicians, but Freud especially, had their attention directed to unconscious motivation. Thus concepts like repression, resistance, transference and anxiety were forged to assist in the task of description and explanation. In these early days Freud formulated his first instinct theory to account for hysteria. He held that sexual energy or *libido* sought an outlet and was manifested in two great drives, one for self-preservation and the other for procreation. These drives dominated the development of the personality from infancy to maturity. Inadequate outlets for the sexual drive were responsible for the psychopathological cases of hysteria and neurosis with which as a clinician he was primarily concerned. Prominent in his discussion of the obstructions of sexual drives is his Oedipal theory, a theory which aroused much controversy. He assumed infant sexuality and argued that the male child learns in infancy that the mother as a sexual object is forbidden him; moreover, he perceives the father as a rival and a threat, and with repressed hostility to the source of such threats the infant boy abandons sexual interests, and a period of latency ensues. This Oedipal phase, Freud thought, was a universal phenomenon. Today we are inclined to associate it with paternalistic cultures that have developed to a certain stage of civilisation. It is important to note, however, that in this theory instinctual drives are perceived to be modified by the human environment.

As time passed Freud tended to use the term sexual in a less specific manner, considering sexual energy to be present whenever any part of the body is the source of pleasurable feelings; for this purpose he used the term *libido*, perceiving it to have sexual origins. The parts of the body so endowed with the ability to provide libidinous sensations are the mouth, anus and genitals, and chronologically this is the order in which they become of interest to the infant. These three sources of pleasure, together with variable quantities of libido at different periods in the child's life, are the focus for his explanations about the development of character types. Fixation at any stage, even if it is a partial fixation, is responsible for the development of a type of character: oral, anal, or genital. The manner in which the child is raised and the emphasis on one or another erogenous zone sets the mould for the development of personality. Of course, Freud was apt to think that at a given age a child would of necessity be concerned with a particular erogenous zone, say the anal region, with, in this instance, attendant concern about cleanliness; maternal approval being secured by defecation at the required time. Development arrested at such a stage would produce an anal type of character, obsessed with tidiness and cleanliness, neat and methodical and probably cautious in manner, not very outgoing, perhaps rather close with money and far from exuberant or generous in his relationships.

All this and much more rested on Freud's assumption of instinctual development following the search for outlets for libidinous energy. It can be seen how Freud was led to emphasise the *pleasure principle.* Criticism of Freud's thought cannot be our chief concern here for it must of necessity entail a discussion of his ideas about neuroses. Our attention is therefore limited to his contribution to personality theory and especially in so far as it was brought into relationship with studies in cultural anthropology. However, for completeness we must mention Freud's second instinct theory, developed largely because the *libido* theory failed adequately to account for the aggression, mostly suppressed aggression, that he detected in his patients' lives. As a result of his experience treating soldiers during and after the First World War, suffering from what was then known as "shell-shock", Freud was inclined to place less emphasis on the sexual or procreative drives and more on the self-preservative ones. Indeed, he felt that the latter could also produce aggressive tendencies. It was from his reflections on these and other clinical phenomena that he came to posit a death instinct, which he saw as a universal tendency of organic life to return to an earlier inorganic state. Thus he still had two instincts to enable him to account for human development, Eros, or the life instinct made up of both sexual and self-preservative drives, and Thanatos, or the death or destructive instinct made up of aggressive drives partly directed towards the self. In many ways this second instinct theory was an improvement on the first, but there is much that it failed to account for even so, and the very emphasis on instinctual development prevented attention being properly directed to the human environment, for whilst the child is brought up by adults the treatment may well differ from one case to another. Freud did not explore the ways in which instinctual development might be modified by parental treatment.

In view of his emphasis on instincts one might wonder how it came about that psycho-analytic thought played such an important part in later cultural anthropological thought, for it seems to deny or at least prevent attention being given to cultural influences. Yet in fact the development of Freud's thought led others to pay more attention to the formation of character structures. The distinctions Freud made between oral, anal, genital and other composite character types stimulated others to speculate on the variations not only between individuals in any one society but between societies, where the contrasts made were between broadly defined types characteristic of different cultures. Moreover, the emphasis on the early years of infancy and childhood encouraged the notion that external as well as internal factors were at work in character formation.

The development of psycho-analytic thought went on within the limits set for it by Freud's assumptions, but there were others who departed fairly radically. Among them C. G. Jung developed a typology which did not depend wholly on instinct theory. He posited a basic dichotomy of introvert and extrovert types of personality with variations of each which could be respectively described as thinking, feeling, intuitive and sensational in subtype. One distinctive feature of Jung's thought is the view that personality enshrines the racial memory of mankind, albeit at an unconscious level, and that there are racial and collective factors in man's unconscious mind which determine or selectively guide his responses to his environment.[1] Another variation from Freud's work is that of Alfred Adler, whose discussion of personality development rests neither on a theory of instincts nor on a theory of primitive archetypes, but rather on the existence of social impulses or urges.[2] Whilst still holding the view that man has some inborn tendencies that determine his

[1] See C. G. Jung, *Collected Works*, edited by H. Read, M. Fordham & G. Adler (1953–etc.).

[2] *The Practice and Theory of Individual Psychology* (1927).

development, this at least was a move toward a recognition that the individual is a social being. The main modifications, however, came with the work of a number of American psychologists, sometimes known as the "neo-Freudians".

The Neo-Freudian Outlook

Trenchant criticisms of Freud's theory of psychoanalysis were made by Karen Horney (1885–1952) who attacked the instinctual basis of the theory.[1] She emphasised much more than traditional psycho-analysts the relationship between the child and his, or her, parents or parental surrogates. Beginning with an analysis of anxiety she argued that the condition of infancy is one of insecurity, and that the experiences of a child may be of intensified, or relieved, anxiety according to the experiences the child has of the human and non-human environment, but chiefly the former. This enabled her to develop a theory of neuroses in terms of certain needs like the need for affection and approval, the need for some restriction in the scope of life activities, the need to exploit others, the need for prestige, etc. These needs she describes as neurotic because they are irrational attempts to find solutions to the problems of disturbed social relationships. Horney did not see any difference in kind between the normal and the neurotic personality, merely a difference in degree; and this led her to point to the nature of the society that is found in Western Europe and North America, for she saw it as productive of certain neurotic traits.[2]

Similarly, Erich Fromm (b. 1900), who like Horney was also born in Germany but later emigrated to the U.S.A., stressed the propensity for man to be lonely and isolated.[3] This tends to be a condition of modern urban and industrial civilisation. It provides a problem for mankind as it represents in a sense the growth of freedom from which man is trying to escape. Fromm's writings are coloured greatly by his preoccupation with the rise of the Hitler regime in Germany and the development there, and elsewhere, of totalitarian governments. Why, he asked, does this

[1] *New Ways in Psychoanalysis* (1939).
[2] *Neurotic Personality of Our Time* (1937).
[3] *Escape from Freedom* (1941).

kind of government come about? Surely, it is both desired and detested? Like Horney he differentiates the needs of the human being. In Horney's analysis there were ten neurotic needs, in Fromm's analysis of man there were five needs which arise from his condition as both animal and human. They are the needs for relatedness, transcendence, rootedness, identity, and for a frame of orientation. These needs are the product of evolution rather than something culturally defined, yet their satisfaction depends on the nature of man's social arrangements, on the institutions of society. For the adjustment that the human personality makes to his social and natural environment is a compromise between his inner needs and the outer demands. This kind of analysis led Fromm to examine types of social environments, and more particularly the periods in history when major changes in social structures take place, as when the feudal structure of Europe gave way to the Capitalist Era, for it is at such times that the social character of a people suffers dislocation, and feelings of alienation are prevalent until new roots are discovered and a social character is formed more in keeping with the new way of life. In his later work, Fromm takes a definitely normative position, for he believes that his psychological analyses enable him to specify the social conditions which are most conducive to the development of the best personality structure, that which is, in other words, truly human.[1]

H. S. Sullivan (1892–1949) has exerted considerable influence on the practice of psychological medicine in the U.S.A., but has also, despite the unsystematic nature of his writings, influenced personality theorists. His major contribution has been to emphasise what he calls the interpersonal theory of psychiatry.[2] His view is that personality cannot be conceived apart from situations in which the person acts and interacts with other persons. The distinctively human quality of man lies in his interpersonal life, and such human interaction may even alter the physiological characteristics of a person. Biological features are thus subordinated to social ones in Sullivan's thought. Like the other neo-Freudians, and of course like Freud and Jung too, Sullivan

[1] *Man for Himself* (1947); *The Sane Society* (1955).
[2] *The Interpersonal Theory of Psychiatry* (1953).

conceives of the human personality as an economy of energy in which there is always a striving to reduce tensions. This is the common basis of all these theorists of personality development for they are concerned with the phenomenon of anxiety. Where they differ is in their determination of needs and their perception of the factors affecting these needs. They represent historically a movement from an emphasis on instincts to a consideration of the social milieu; progressively psychologists came to see that an understanding of the structure of social activities and the formation of normative structures is the key to an understanding of man's personality, or character formation. This then was the development in psychology which took place alongside a new awareness in cultural anthropology of the process of socialisation. It was a development which from time to time directly influcnced anthropological studies and was influenced by them, and as a result the nature of much sociological investigation was given a new orientation too. Let us turn to the developments in cultural anthropology that were taking place at this time.

Culture and the Development of Personality

It was not so much Freud's clinical writings, containing the elements of his theory of personality, which initially interested anthropologists after the First World War, so much as the first of Freud's so-called "sociological works". These are a trio of small books which endeavour to offer explanations of cultural phenomena. They are *Totem and Taboo* (trans. 1918); *Civilization and Its Discontents* (1930); and *Moses and Monotheism* (trans. 1939). The first of these sparked off some interest for it tried to provide, in psycho-analytic terms, an explanation of totemic religions and a large part of the body of custom connected with regulating the relationships between the sexes and between kinsfolk. It was around this book that discussion and controversy in America and Germany about the Oedipal theory centred. In Britain in the early 1920s C. G. Seligman[1] endeavoured to arouse some interest

[1] "Anthropology: A Study of Some Points of Contact", *Journal of the Royal Anthropological Institute,* Vol. 54, 1924. "Anthropological Perspective and Psychological Theory", *Journal of the Royal Anthropological Institute,* Vol. 62, 1932.

among social anthropologists in psychological theories, especially those of Jung, and in 1924 Malinowski contributed an article entitled "Mutterrechtliche Familie und Oedipus Komplex" to *Imago*, a journal to which Freud also contributed, following this up with a series of books heavily oriented to psycho-analytical thought, among them being the little-known book entitled *The Father in Primitive Psychology* (1926), the better known work *Sex and Repression in Savage Society* (1926), and the still more famous one, *The Sexual Life of Savages* (1929). In the second of these studies Malinowski developed Freud's theory of totemism to cover the case of a matrilineal society in Melanesia, showing in this case that the ambivalence, which Freud made so much of in the son's relationship to his father, is split up into love for the father and hatred for the mother's brother, who in such a society stands juridically in *loco parentis*. One other link is to be found in the work of the psycho-analyst G. Roheim who carried out field studies in Australia and Somaliland and published a report entitled "The Psychoanalysis of Primitive Culture Types",[1] but his work was not at the time very influential.

The main advance came with the work of Margaret Mead, who, following her contemporary Ruth Benedict and building on the studies of Sapir, did most to arouse interest in the socialisation process in simple societies. Her first work, *Coming of Age in Samoa* (1928), became a best-seller; it was followed two years later by *Growing up in New Guinea*. Even more popular, although rather less scholarly, was her book *Sex and Temperament in Three Primitive Societies* (1935), based on data she and R. Fortune collected on their expedition of 1931–3 to New Guinea. In this book she shows that temperament is not an innate set of dispositions, but a variable that depends upon the conditioning factors in child-rearing and which in turn depends upon the normative structure of the society in question. In illustration of her theme she contrasts the gentle, domesticated Arapesh who emphasise the virtues of co-operation and gradual growth, and where both men and women appear to pursue an identity of maternal kinds of roles, with the recently cannibalistic Mundugamor, whose general outlook is described as one of hostility, harshness and fear.

[1] *International Journal of Psychoanalysis*, Vol. 13, 1932.

The manner of child-rearing in each society is contrasted. The institutions of the two are seen to differ in significant respects, and these features are shown to be correlated with predominant differences in temperament. For good measure Mead goes on to give a brief description of the Tchambuli, in which again there are marked differences from these other two peoples, and among whom, she would have us understand, there are sex roles remarkably different from those we are familiar with, where the men sit around seeking admiration and the women engage in hard work and tend to manage affairs both domestic and communal.

Dr Mead's main interest is in sex roles; on this subject she has written extensively,[1] but the main interest of her work from the point of view of the history of sociology lies in the manner in which she incorporates the assumptions of analytically oriented psychology, the stress she lays on methods of child-rearing, especially the manner of suckling infants, and the ways in which the social institutions and customs of different peoples are shown to reflect their characteristic personality structures. Throughout her works there is a refrain about modern western civilisation, for she is anxious to show that the things we take for granted are variables in the life of humanity. Dr Mead is not only an ethnologist but both a critic of the West and an exponent of the place of women in society. "Historically our own culture has relied for the creation of rich and contrasting values upon many artificial distinctions, the most striking of which is sex." And she continues, "It will not be by mere abolition of these distinctions that society will develop patterns in which individual gifts are given a place instead of being forced into an ill-fitting mould. If we are to achieve a richer culture, rich in contrasting values, we must recognise the whole gamut of human potentialities, and so weave a less arbitrary social fabric, one in which each diverse gift will find a fitting place."[2] The influence on both sociologists and psychologists of Mead's studies in socialisation has been immense and with it of course there came a fillip to cultural relativism. The change from McDougall's emphasis on inborn characteristics to

[1] See *Male and Female: A Study of the Sexes in a Changing World* (1949).
[2] *Loc. cit.* (1935), p. 322.

cultural relativism is one of the major revolutions in the social sciences.[1]

The relationship being established between cultural anthropologists and psychologists, or, perhaps more precisely, psychiatrists, was made firmer by some of the former submitting to psycho-analysis. The developments which followed took the form of psycho-analytically oriented studies of simple peoples, such as that of Cora DuBois among the Alorese;[2] other studies of North American Indians were made specifically to consider personality development. But the most notable contribution to this tradition came with the publication in 1939 of Abram Kardiner's book *The Individual and His Society: The Psychodynamics of Primitive Social Organisation.* This was the outcome of a series of seminars held in New York by the author at which psychiatrists and anthropologists collaborated; among this number were Cora DuBois, Ralph Linton[3] and Ruth Benedict. It was in this crucible that the concept of *basic personality* was forged; a concept that in the ensuing years was almost to initiate a new branch of the social sciences. Although referring to various studies of simple peoples, like those of the Trobrianders and the Zuni Pueblo Indians, the main analysis was of the Marquesan people of Polynesia and the Tanala of Madagascar, both described at some length by Linton but analysed in psycho-analytical terms by Kardiner. His procedure is to distinguish *primary* from *secondary institutions*, for he argues that it is important to discern the characteristic unconscious constellations produced in individual members of a society by the socialising process, i.e. by primary institutions. The constellations are themselves expressed in secondary institutions like art forms, religion, folklore and so forth. The description of these psychological constellations constitutes a description of basic personality. The primary institutions produce it and the secondary ones reflect it. This work was followed by another, published in 1945, entitled *The Psychological Frontiers of Society*, in which the author makes use of material supplied by Linton on the Comanche Indians, and by Cora DuBois on the Alorese; and there is a report by James West on the village

[1] See Gardner Murphy, *Historical Introduction to Modern Psychology* (rev. edn. 1949), pp. 410 f.
[2] *The People of Alor* (1944).
[3] See his *Cultural Background of Personality* (1945).

in the middle-west he called *Plainville* and about which he wrote a book of that title.[1] The analysis is by Kardiner who developed the theme of the earlier work but emphasised psychopathology. Indeed, he noted maladjustments in cultural development from the study of personality characteristics. This development is of interest because the main preoccupation of psycho-analysis with neuroses is manifested in the discussion of basic personality. It also relies heavily on clinical experiences for it is assumed that those institutional facts which moulded the personality of psychoneurotics in Western countries are of similar significance generally.

We shall leave this particular development in social psychology for the present, but return to it later when discussing the influence of war-time research in sociology. For the present let us look at other pre-war developments in social psychology.

Attitude Studies

Although the most notable advance in social psychology prior to the Second World War was to be found, as we have indicated, in seeking an understanding of the relationship of personality to culture, there were other important developments taking place, although as yet they were incipient ones. Thus we must note the study of attitudes. This concept of *attitude* was attractive to many people for it was a higher order concept than had been used before; it represented a break with instinct theories of human behaviour and it lent itself to the development of techniques of measurement.

It is not difficult to see how in America practical problems gave orientation to social research, for the problem of attitudes towards ethnic groups loomed large as a result of the entry of waves of immigrants from Europe after the First World War. Prejudice displayed by one group to another was frequently seen and early attitude studies were often directed to this topic. E. Bogardus[2] was one of the first to carry out a study of this kind. He put a number of questions, concerning forty different nationalities, to 1725 American subjects, arranging the questions so that they

[1] *Plainville U.S.A.* (1945).

[2] *Immigration and Race Attitudes* (1928). See a précis in T. M. Newcomb, E. L. Hartley *et al. Readings in Social Psychology* (1947).

represented progressively intimate enquiries about associating with persons of different nationalities. Bogardus was able to show that Swedes, Englishmen and Germans were preferred to Arabs, Chinese and Turks, both in respect of the less intimate as well as the more initimate types of relationships. The simple technique he used proved very popular, and his work was repeated.

Interest in attitude research received a fillip as a result of the invention by L. L. Thurstone and E. J. Chave of a way to measure attitudes.[1] Thurstone set himself the task of providing, within a wide range of extremes, a series of intervening positions representing equal units of measurement. His method is known as that of "equal-appearing intervals". It entailed using a number of people as judges, whose task it is to assign scale values to each item in the attitude test. This is done by collecting a large number of statements representing a wide variety of opinions on the subject in question. These are then given to the people selected to judge and they are asked to distribute them in, say, eleven piles according to the degree of appreciation or depreciation expressed in the statements. To obtain a single value to represent the position of a statement on the eleven-point scale, the median of the positions assigned to the statement by all the judges is determined. This median is the scale value of the statement. The results may then be checked by testing on a larger sample than the judges represent, in order to see if there is internal consistency. The statements surviving this test may now be used as a measure of other people's attitudes to the object in question. Of course, a lot may depend on the attitudes of judges in the first place, and their selection may be a highly important factor. On the other hand, it must be mentioned that E. D. Hinckley, and later on other investigators, found that the attitudes of judges did not influence the scale values. What Hinckley did was to use Southern White Americans who were prejudiced against Negroes to assign scale values to statements about Negroes. He then compared these to the findings of North Americans who were not noticeably prejudiced; he discovered little difference.[2]

[1] *The Measurement of Attitudes* (1929).

[2] "The influence of individual opinion on construction of an attitude scale", *Journal of Social Psychology*, Vol. 3, 1932.

Further work on this by C. I. Hovland and M. Sherif[1] indicated Hinckley had, in the process of his testing, eliminated extreme judges. Methods such as Thurstone's have been used to measure attitudes to Jews, to Negroes, to the Church, to war and of course to political programmes and parties.

Attitude testing always depends upon respondents being truthful, but their major disadvantage lies in the fact that they rely on verbal responses to questions, and it is by no means safe to assume that a verbal response betrays a deep-set and persistent attitude. In fact, the particular social situation in which a respondent is asked questions may well determine the kind of response evoked. Nevertheless, the growth of attitude studies represents an attempt to render social investigation more precise, and certainly the gain to investigations into prejudice was considerable. Thus we find investigations like that of Eugene L. Horowitz helping to answer the question of how prejudice develops.[2] Horowitz believed that prejudice is learned and accordingly he studied its development in children, taking prejudiced attitudes towards Negroes as his subject. He devised three simple tests, two of them made use of a page of photographs of children, four being of white and eight being of Negro faces. The first test consisted of asking children to rank the faces in order of preference, the second test involved asking children to pick the faces of the boys with whom they would like to do things, and these were specified and involved varying degrees of intimacy. Rather similar was the third test which consisted of a number of photographs of boys engaged in activities as a group; each was duplicated with the difference that one copy contained the photograph of a Negro boy. The test was to discover if an activity would be rejected solely because of the inclusion of a Negro. These tests were then given to children in different schools, at different ages and in different parts of the U.S.A. Thus Horowitz applied the tests in a New York all-white school, with a retest six months later, in one

[1] "Judgemental phenomena and scales of attitude measurement: item displacement in Thurston scales", *Journal of Abnormal and Social Psychology*, Vol. 47, 1952.

[2] "Development of attitudes toward Negroes", *Archives of Psychology*, No. 194, 1936. See précis in T. M. Newcomb, E. L. Hartley *et al.*, *Readings in Social Psychology* (1947).

grade of a mixed white and Negro school, and among a small number of children of communist parentage, also in a town school in Tennessee and in schools in both urban and rural Georgia. The tests lent themselves to quantification of results. It became quite clear by comparison that each test had a characteristic growth curve for the period investigated, that intercorrelations among the tests increased with advance in age, that geographical location made no difference, that the small group of white boys in the mixed school in New York showed about as much prejudice as the boys in the all-white school, that Negro boys in the mixed school appeared to have accepted to some extent the standards of the white majority group, and that the small group of communist children showed no apparent prejudice against Negroes. Horowitz concluded "In the course of this presentation, it has been found necessary to contradict many of the oft-repeated cliches current in the discussions of the race problem. Young children were found to be not devoid of prejudice; contact with a 'nice' Negro is not a universal panacea; living as neighbours, going to a common school, were found to be insufficient; Northern children were found to differ very very slightly from Southern children. It seems that attitudes toward Negroes are now chiefly determined not by contact with Negroes, but by contact with the prevalent attitude toward Negroes."[1]

Attitude studies developed greatly in the ensuing years and the interest in racial attitudes, especially anti-semitism, grew as a result of the persecution of the Jews in Germany. We shall return to this later in the next chapter. For the present let us examine briefly some other developments in the inter-war period in social psychology. Among these was the interest in small groups, especially of children who of course provide an easy source of subjects for study, and we may note also how the use of experimental and quasi-experimental procedures was introduced in this way into sociological investigation. The study of the behaviour of people as members of small groups has burgeoned into a great efflorescence in recent years; here we shall merely look at the early sproutings.

[1] *Ibid.*, p. 517.

Small Group Studies

To a slight extent small group studies arose out of interest in psychoanalysis. Thus we may note the observations made by Susan Isaacs of children in her Maltinghouse School at Cambridge.[1] But experimental psychologists had already undertaken numerous studies of children's behaviour in group settings, many of these being listed by G. Murphy, L. B. Murphy and T. M. Newcomb in their influential book *Experimental Social Psychology: An Interpretation of Research upon the Socialization of the Individual*, the revised edition being published in 1937 and the original by the first two authors in 1931. Prominent in their treatment is the investigation of the learning process in social situations on which they cite thirteen contributions, studies of aggression in children of which they cite forty-seven contributions, and of competition among children on which they cite fifteen contributions.

To take an example from early studies of behaviour in groups we shall refer to J. F. Dashiell,[2] whose work followed that of other investigators[3] and built upon them, so that it reflects the beginnings of cumulative work in the field. What Dashiell did was to examine other people's effects on the task performance of students engaged in solving mathematical problems and other tasks. Some of his students worked alone, thus providing controls, some worked alone but in the knowledge that other students elsewhere were at that time also working on the same tasks, yet other students were striving to excel in a collective situation, and still others were working under close supervision by spectators. Dashiell's hypothesis was that in company his subjects worked faster than when alone; but accuracy of work proved also to be a factor in the situation.

The study of what Cooley called *primary groups* was carried out in a somewhat unsystematic manner by the Chicago sociologists. Thrasher's study of gangs in that city,[4] J. Landesco's detailed and penetrating study of the inner working of a single criminal

[1] *Social Development of Young Children* (1933).
[2] "An Experimental Analysis of some Group Effects", *Journal of Abnormal and Social Psychology*, Vol. 25, 1932.
[3] See J. Klein, *The Study of Groups* (1956). Ch. 6.
[4] See Chap. XI. *Op. cit.*

gang,[1] and Clifford Shaw's study of delinquent boys[2] were in fact all first-hand investigations into groups; but whilst interesting there was no systematic theory behind these studies, nor any consciousness that there was a body of coherent knowledge of groups to draw on—only a passionate interest in describing the way people lived. To be sure many insights were derived from them and these were incorporated into remedial measures; their works are still read because they illustrate sociological truths, but the tradition did not advance and subsequent work by sociologists using their methods has been largely repetitive. But at the same time as these studies were being made, Mary Parker Follett was writing in America about business administration, writings which pointed again and again to the use to be made of voluntary association and the manner in which informal relationships affect formal procedures.[3] However, the first study to be concerned with normal everyday working groups, as distinct from experimental groups of children or students, was the Hawthorne Works Study in the Western Electric Company's branch of that name, a five-year study carried out by the Department of Industrial Research of the Harvard Business School from 1926 onwards under the direction of Elton Mayo.[4] Here the investigators were from various disciplines and psychology was no more prominent than any other social science. The results of this lengthy research project have become famous. It is particularly interesting because at first emphasis was on the effects of physical factors, such as lighting, on work performance, and it only later became apparent that social and psychological factors were of primary importance in bearing upon productive output. Financial incentive schemes appeared to be rather less important than the worker's evaluation of his or her work and the social milieu in which that work took place, i.e. the people with whom a worker performed the required tasks. The character of the intimate group seemed to determine a set of attitudes which in turn bore directly on efficiency, obedience

[1] *Organised Crime in Chicago* (1929).

[2] *The Jack-Roller: A Delinquent Boy's Own Story* (1930); *The Natural History of a Delinquent Career* (1931).

[3] *Creative Experience* (1924). See also *Freedom and Co-ordination* (ed.) (1949).

[4] *The Social Problems of an Industrial Civilisation* (1945).

to rules and orders, as well as general satisfaction. In the Relay Assembly Experiment Group a small number of women workers were separated from the larger body of workers and put in a room by themselves with the member of the research team investigating their activities; it was discovered that their output displayed an almost continuous rise over a given period during which time varying changes in methods of payment and conditions of working were made. The one factor that remained constant was the smallness of the group and the stability of its membership; this was largely a function of the loyalty developed, itself a result of the interest displayed in the group by management and the research team, which consulted them before making any change.

In another study in the same factory, known as the Bank Wiring Observation Study, a group of men were observed as they wired banks of terminals. This study showed that where a group of workers do not enjoy very good relations with management they will tend to restrict output in accordance with often quite elaborate systems of rules and enforcing sanctions. These studies have made a great impact on management studies; as far as social psychology goes they stimulated interest in small group research, laying the emphasis on what G. C. Homans, one of the investigators, was later to call sentiments of liking.[1] In short, small group studies were reoriented toward an investigation of feelings by members of groups for each other and the satisfactions they received from their task performance.

Although we have said that in this early work on small groups use was made of experimental techniques mostly derived from general psychology, the fact remains that in many cases there were serious deficiencies in the designs. This is so of the Western Electric Company studies, for, as E. A. Shils points out, these enquiries were not set up in a way that allowed for rigorous testing of hypotheses about membership in a small group.[2] In fact, the membership of the group was a residual variable, and historically the investigators only became aware of it after other variables had been examined by industrial psychologists. Social

[1] *The Human Group* (1950).

[2] "The Study of the Primary Group", *The Policy Sciences: Recent Developments in Scope and Method*, eds. D. Lerner & H. D. Lasswell (1951).

psychology had yet to develop a framework of thought that was distinctive, or a conceptual scheme from which hypotheses could be derived. This was to come. But it did not emerge until a variety of studies had been carried out in many kinds of situations, for the most part under the pressures imposed by war-time needs. It is to these that we shall now turn, for the war gave sociological, as well as psychological studies a great fillip, and it was the more socially defined enquiries which benefited most.

CHAPTER XIV

SOCIOLOGY IN WAR-TIME

In the immediate pre-war years sociology, in some European countries, was in the process of being suppressed. In Germany, for instance, Tönnies was retired from active work at Kiel University by the National Socialist regime, others like Max Horkheimer were obliged to emigrate to escape the persecution of the Jews. Social research was generally restricted and sociology in particular was almost forbidden, or where it was allowed to exist it was rendered innocuous. In Italy an incipient development of the subject was extinguished. The advent of the war and the occupation by the Axis powers of the greater part of Europe brought sociological investigation to an end. In France the toll was devastating, for many sociologists were political opponents of the Vichy regime. One of the most outstanding of French scholars, Maurice Halbwachs, died in a concentration camp, others like Bettelheim were more fortunate and survived this experience. In his case we are especially grateful both for his survival and because of the valuable contribution to our understanding of the social and psychological processes connected with terror and hardship which Bettelheim subsequently made.[1] But if the subject suffered in some countries as a result of the war, in other places sociological and social psychological studies were stimulated as a result of its demands. Indeed, the war provided unique opportunities for investigations that would have been unthinkable in peace-time. To be sure it was in the U.S.A. that this was most noticeable, but to a definite, although lesser extent this was true also of Britain. There were two main aspects of this. Firstly, there was a set of urgent problems mainly connected with military operations, chiefly problems of morale among both soldiers and civilians, together with problems of communication especially between allies but also in connection

[1] B. Bettelheim, "Individual and mass behaviour in extreme situations", *J. Abn. & Soc. Psych.*, Vol. 38.

with internal propaganda aimed to bring about changes in civilian attitudes and habits. Secondly, there were problems which arose in the consideration of post-war plans. In this respect there was the question of American policy in Japan in the event of a Japanese surrender, and there were also problems regarding the resettlement of soldiers on demobilisation and especially of former prisoners of war. These problems broadened out into general ones concerning post-war reconstruction, which in some areas was a major undertaking. Thus in the Netherlands sociology gained great strength from the necessity to devote a large proportion of the national resources to rebuilding and planning new communities, and in this instance was helped by the establishment of a Ministry of Social Security which actively sponsored social research. Although in this chapter we shall say something of these post-war developments, we shall be chiefly concerned with the research that was stimulated directly by war-time conditions and needs.

American and British Servicemen

One of the most impressive works ever to be produced in the U.S.A. appeared in four volumes, three in 1949 and the last in the following year. They were collectively known as *Studies in Social Psychology in World War II*, but the first two volumes are better known as *The American Soldier*.[1] This great work was the report of four years' activity of the Research Branch of the Information and Education Division of the U.S. Army. It is a record of the attitudes of the American soldier during the Second World War together with a discussion of the techniques used to study these attitudes. It was essentially the result of team work, and it may be said to illustrate a stage in the movement from individual work to collective effort in sociological research, for many people took part in these studies. After the war the Army handed over the punched cards used in these attitude studies to the Social Science Research Council, set up in 1946, so that under its independent auspices the data could be analysed and these volumes published.

[1] S. A. Stouffer *et al.*, Vol. I, *The American Soldier: Adjustment During Army Life* (1949), Vol. II, *The American Soldier: Combat and Its Aftermath* (1949), C. I. Hovland *et al.*, Vol. III, *Experiments on Mass Communication* (1949), S. A. Stouffer *et al.*, Vol. IV, *Measurement and Prediction* (1950).

The advantages enjoyed by the staff of the Research Branch were many. They had at their disposal in Army personnel a large cross-section of people and, what is more, people who were organised in a manner enabling them to be accessible to the team. Moreover, the prevailing conservative attitudes towards social research were rapidly broken down under the pressures of necessity. If information was to be available to the military decision-makers then facilitics had to be made available to the team to secure the required data.

It is interesting to see how the team was recruited, for some, like S. A. Stouffer who directed the work, came from universities, but some came from government departments, whilst still others came from industrial and commercial undertakings, and from this last group came a tendency to make use of the techniques of polling organisations such as those of Gallup and Roper. Indeed, it may be noted in passing that the use of sample survey techniques had been advanced more by commercial corporations than by academics in the years preceding the war. Reliance on public opinion and market research techniques was considerable.

The theoretical influences on the work of the Research Branch were varied. The authors of this work admit to four main sources of ideas: (1) the literature on dynamic psychology with its Freudian and neo-Freudian overtones, (2) the general body of organised knowledge called Learning Theory, (3) social anthropology and sociology in so far as it contributed to discussion of cultural variations and dwelt on socialising processes in childhood, the development of role theory and studies of social stratification and social mobility, and (4) sociological contributions in the study of social institutions, with particular reference to social control and social change, and also sociology's distinctive quality of refusing to reduce social phenomena necessarily to individual behavioural acts.

The first two volumes are concerned with the attitudes of soldiers as they were determined by their responses, but the third volume considers the changes in responses and these are studied in the framework of controlled experiments. The fourth volume is devoted to the concept of social attitudes, their measurement and prediction. The range and content of these attitudes are so great that it would be impossible within the limits of this survey of sociological works to do justice to these volumes. All that can be accomplished is to give some idea of the kind of problems the Research Branch dealt with and some of their findings, and to this end we shall consider very briefly one or two selected examples.

The first volume is devoted to "Adjustment during Army Life". The task of establishing indices to measure adjustment took the form of examining four areas of attitudes; these are personal esprit, or the expressed sense of well-being which a soldier displays in his verbal responses to questions about himself; the manner in which he displays a personal commitment to the Army; the degree of satisfaction shown with his status and job in the Army; and the kinds of evaluative remarks he makes about the Army. Having arbitrarily settled on these attitudinal areas the investigators estimated the personal adjustment of soldiers and endeavoured to relate their results to the men's education, age, and marital status. They describe the variations in adjustment according to the type of military experience men had had, e.g. those with overseas service, those who had suffered poor health in the Army, and those with different kinds of treatment in terms of leave and recreation. They also investigated the nature of social mobility in the Army and the soldiers' reactions to promotion opportunities. The U.S. Army had rapidly expanded from about a quarter of a million in 1940 to over eight million in 1945; there had thus been many opportunities for promotion. It was in conjunction with this last study that the authors introduced the valuable concept of *relative deprivation*. Thus they were able, not only to show the existence of different attitudes towards promotion, but to explain why they did not apparently fit the facts. Among the non-commissioned officers of the Military Police, who had completed only part of their high school education, there were many more favourable views about their promotion chances than among their counterparts, of similar educational attainments, in the U.S. Air Corps where in fact the opportunities for promotion were very much better than in the Police. It was one of Stouffer's chief contributions that he was able to use the concept of *relative deprivation* to explain this phenomenon.

For he argued that the Military Police N.C.O. felt more highly rewarded when he compared his promotion with the 83 per cent of those with similar education in his part of the Army who had not been promoted to N.C.O. rank, than the Air Corps N.C.O. who compared his rank with only 53 per cent of those with similar education who had not been promoted.

The second volume of *The American Soldier* is sub-titled "Combat and its Aftermath". This volume discusses the morale of combat troops including flying personnel, and dwells in particular on the factors which enable men to resist stress. It includes analyses of attitudes of non-combatant troops to the war and to others engaged in fighting, and also the attitudes of combat troops toward non-combatants. Finally there is a series of discussions on the attitudes of soldiers to demobilization and the principles which were held officially to guide such procedures. The third and fourth volumes are concerned with methodology, in the sense that the third volume is an essay on mass communication, with special reference to the use of films by the Army; accordingly it is focused on learning theory and perception, whilst the fourth volume is a lengthy discussion of attitudes and their measurement.

The strength of *The American Soldier*, says E. A. Shils,[1] lies in the analysis of both the influence of membership in primary groups, such as the basic operational fighting units, on the behaviour of individual soldiers, and in the factors which promote or obstruct the formation of small primary groups and the acceptance of membership in them. What emerges from these studies, he argues, is that "in the main identification with specific secondary symbols is not enough nor are clearly defined commands enough to make military organisation an effective mechanism for moving men to action".[2] The fact is that we are led in this study from macro- to micro-sociology. Not that the authors of this great work were necessarily led themselves to see this, but the implications are clear—the emphasis is on the study of small groups. Moreover, R. K. Merton and Alice S. Kitt in a long essay of appraisal have pointed to the implications of this study for

[1] "Primary Groups in the American Army" in *Continuities in Social Research: Studies in the Scope and Method of "The American Soldier"*, edd. R. K. Merton and P. F. Lazarsfeld (1950).

[2] *Ibid.*, p. 25.

reference-group theory.[1] Most of the appraisals point to the cumulative element in the work: the initial hypotheses lead to more refined ones, the relationship between research and theory is constantly demonstrated and thus new ideas emerge. Not only has this work facilitated the study of social attitudes but it has enhanced research in both the field of social groups and in that of role theory. Attitude studies, as a result, are not conducted in a psychological limbo but are carried out within a social context which relates attitudes to social structures.

On a much more modest scale a number of studies of attitudes of soldiers, but especially relating to the selection of candidates for officer training, were carried out in Britain; mostly they were sponsored by the War Office. To a large extent this was the work of a group of psychiatrists who were sensitive to environmental and group influences on decision-making. Among these studies we may mention those by A. T. M. Wilson,[2] later to become Director of the Tavistock Institute of Human Relations, and his colleague E. Trist, the present Director.

Studies of Culture at a Distance

The necessity to understand the enemy, both for purposes of propaganda policy and for preparation for the administration of occupied territories on the cessation of hostilities, increasingly led both the American and British governments to sponsor cultural studies; these came to be known generically as studies in national character. Of course there were the popular stereotypes of other peoples, but much of the writing that helped to sustain, if not create, such stereotypes was too superficial and anecdotal. In the U.S.A. the Office of Naval Research set up a Human Resources Division which supported a series of studies by financial grants. In Britain the War Office Directorate of Military Intelligence sponsored research connected with psychological warfare and made use of Army psychiatrists for this purpose. It is interesting that in the U.S.A. the people working on national character

[1] "Contributions to the Theory of Reference Group Behaviour", *supra* p. 40 ff.

[2] A. T. M. Wilson, "Some aspects of social process", *Journal of Social Issues*, 1951.

studies were mainly social anthropologists and sociologists, whilst those in Britain were mainly psychiatrists. The consequences were not surprising, for in America the approach generally was to see a relationship between social systems on the one hand and personality systems on the other, to focus attention on the connections between personality and some aspects of social life, and so to describe, often with great insight, patterns of shared behaviour, the ethos of a people, and the system of cultural values detected in behaviour. In short the question asked was: how does culture shape the individual personality? In Britain the question tended to be differently phrased, for psychiatrists came with strong attachments to psycho-analytic ideas. They were much more interested in the structure of personality. The emphasis was not so much on culture as on personality, and how certain personality types have influenced national behaviour. This difference does not reflect a national bias in the social sciences, for in America some of the investigators were British anthropologists, and at least one American sociologist was advising the British War Office.

The result of this bias in America was to advance sociological studies of national units at the expense of personality theory, and one may agree with Alex Inkeles and D. J. Levinson[1] when they say that it was under the pressure of policy-making that an analysis of collective ideas took the place of a study of individuals, for national character is assumed, not demonstrated. The question "What modes of personality, if any, are present in a nation?" was not asked. Yet what was accomplished is of great interest. Perhaps the most famous work to come from this tradition was Ruth Benedict's *The Chrysanthemum and the Sword*, 1947; the sub-title of this work is "Patterns of Japanese Culture". This study was carried out when Dr Benedict was employed by the Office of War Information as were also Alexander Leighton, Clyde Kluckhohn and Nathan Leites, all of whom published contributions towards studies of national character. Clearly, the enigma of Japanese behaviour presented a problem to the American government and some systematic work which would

[1] "National Character: The Study of Modal Personality and Socio-cultural Systems", *Handbook of Social Psychology*, Vol. II, ed. G. Lindzey (1954).

interpret Japanese attitudes and behaviour was a necessity. What Benedict did was to delineate the apparent contradictions in Japanese national character and show that nevertheless they could be reviewed in such a way as to show they possess consistency. To be sure, to Western eyes, they appeared both loyal and treacherous, disciplined and yet sometimes insubordinate, avid to learn from the West yet deeply conservative, aesthetically inclined and yet militaristic; but her profound analysis of the value system of the Japanese people sheds light on all these contradictions. The value placed on hierarchy, the deeply ingrained attitudes of respect, reflected in the peculiarities of the Japanese language, the sense of obligation and the importance of repaying debts of all kinds, the whole set of beliefs and ideas surrounding the notions of *gimu* and *giri* were described with a clarity and insight that is truly remarkable. She and her colleagues were able to influence the policy-making of the military authorities to such an extent that this must remain one of the most notable occasions when sociological study has been of great political significance. For it was on the basis of this and cognate studies that the decision to retain the Emperor, as head of state, was made; a decision of far-reaching importance, in the first place, for effecting a general surrender of scattered Japanese forces in the East and, in the second place, for post-war reconstruction of Japanese society.

Yet Benedict's study was not done first hand. That is to say, whilst relying on a pre-war study by John Embree[1] of Japanese rural life and especially family life, she had to rely on interviews with Japanese Americans, Westerners who had lived for a long time in Japan, and on the literature of the country and the films it had produced. Similarly, other studies were also carried out "at a distance" and among them were studies of Rumanians, Russians, Syrians, Italians and Chinese.[2] These were all originally inspired by Ruth Benedict who inaugurated a series under the title of *The Columbia University Research in Contemporary Cultures*.

Geoffrey Gorer, an Englishman who studied cultural anthropology with Benedict and Mead, and who was associated with the Columbia University project, published a small book in 1948

[1] *Suye Mura: A Japanese Village* (1946).

[2] M. Mead and R. Metraux (eds.), *The Study of Culture at a Distance* (1953).

entitled *The Americans: A Study in National Character*, parts of which had appeared earlier in British and American popular journals. This was clearly an attempt to provide the British with a guide to an understanding of their American allies, for Gorer was attached during the War to a British Mission in Washington. It should be recalled that the British knew very much less of the Americans then than they do now. The obvious similarities of the two people obscured a number of profound differences, so that unintentionally difficulties arose as collaboration became increasingly a more important item in the war effort. Gorer's book followed another by Margaret Mead published in the U.S.A. in 1942 under the title *And keep your powder dry* (the English publication went under the more prosaic title of *The American Character*, 1944). Mead, like Benedict on Japan, had concentrated on an analysis of values, using the same kind of culture pattern approach, but incorporating some notions that sprang from analytically oriented psychology. Gorer's approach emphasised psychology more. Thus, for example, in discussing American attitudes to Europe he argued that Europe is their rejected "father", and that America is perceived as a motherland rather than a fatherland. His study of raising children in the U.S.A. appealed strongly to psychoanalytic notions. To be sure there are interpretations of American life in other terms: their liking for mechanical analogies, their egalitarian ideology and so forth, but the psychological component of the study is marked. This became even more pronounced in his later work on Russian national character. Indeed, the full title of that book runs *The People of Great Russia: A Psychological Study*; it was published in 1949 and written in conjunction with John Rickman, a psychoanalyst who had spent two years as a physician in Russia during the Revolution. Rickman contributed vignettes of Russian peasant life, Gorer the analysis of Russian attitudes and their genesis. The emphasis on child development is marked and herein we must mention the insights Gorer claims he obtained from postulating the "swaddling hypothesis", a belief that the widespread practice of swaddling babies influenced profoundly their basic responses. He argues, for instance, that this restriction on infant movement allowed for expression only through the eyes, that it set up a basic angry rage pattern as a result of frustration, but the periodic unswaddling of the infant for feeding and bathing allowed for intense relief, so accounting for an alternative pattern of exhilaration and freedom. It is in terms such as these that Gorer explains the moods of Russian people and interprets the behaviour of these people both individually and collectively.

The work of H. V. Dicks[1] on German prisoners of war, carried out between 1942 and 1946, was directed to discovering something of the connection between character structure and political ideology. This was part of a larger piece of work of which the aim was to survey German morale, but it was also oriented to devising a means whereby the future Allied Administration of Germany could distinguish between Nazis and non-Nazis, without recourse to the crude criterion of whether they were members of the National Sozialistische Deutschlands Arbeiter Partei, for formal membership of the Party was clearly enjoined on many by virtue of their profession.

Dicks started out to examine a number of hypotheses, and it will be seen that his psycho-analytic background played a large part in their formulation. Firstly, he supposed that "German prisoners who held Nazi or near Nazi beliefs and ideology with conviction and fanaticism, had a personality structure which differed from the norm of German national character in the sense that they embodied this structure in more exaggerated or concentrated form". Secondly, he supposed that "Nazis or near Nazis were likely to be men of markedly pregenital or immature personality structure in which libido organisation followed a sado-masochistic pattern, based on a repression of the tender tie with the mother and resulting typically in a homosexual paranoid (extra-punitive) relation to a harsh and ambivalently loved and hated father figure, with its attendant sadism towards symbols of the displaced bad portion of this figure . . ."[2] Dicks used a scheduled interview technique but also carried out lengthy non-directed interviews. The kinds of information he elicited provided data on parental predominance in childhood, religious attitudes,

[1] "Personality Traits and National Socialist Ideology: A War-time Study of German Prisoners of War", *Human Relations*, Vol. III, No. 2, 1950.

[2] *Op. cit.*, pp. 113 f.

and types of solutions of the oedipal phase of development. His analysis in psycho-analytic terms seemed to confirm his hypotheses. About ten per cent in the armed forces were of the fanatical core, but never less than thirty-five per cent were supporters of the Nazi ideology, and even those not sharing the high syndrome which he denotes as the *F syndrome personality* (i.e. the fanatical personality type), had a substantial number of traits in common. If they did not have the aggressive paranoid activism of the fanatical core, they nevertheless had a propensity to subordinate themselves to strong authorities.

It is interesting to note that at the time this report was published T. W. Adorno and his colleagues were publishing *The Authoritarian Personality*, that outstanding study of a personality type of the kind that Dicks was describing. This too was inspired by the war-time need to understand the phenomenon of the Fascist or Nazi fanatic and to discern the roots of this type in the cultural milieu of the Western world. To be sure the work of Adorno and his colleagues was more in the nature of a trait analysis, and Dicks' work much more psycho-analytically oriented, but both stemmed from the same imperatives, and both threw light on a series of problems, less on the general topic of national character which tended to be dropped in the post-war years, than on personality theory; for the complexities of the latter and the peace-time needs of therapeutic techniques replaced the needs of war-time. In any case the social and cultural anthropologists who had started this line of enquiry turned to other things. Dicks' own work continued in relation to a study of Russian deserters from the Red Army and prisoners of war held by the Germans and released by the Western allies,[1] and Margaret Mead's studies continued, although these came to be increasingly concerned with personality development in childhood[2] and in studies of technical change and its effects on personality development.[3] The reason for this trend is not difficult to see, for what was needed in national character studies was a method for arriving at the modal personality.

[1] "Observations on Contemporary Russian Behaviour", *Human Relations*, Vol. V, No. 2, 1952.

[2] M. Mead and M. Wolfenstein (eds.), *Childhood in Contemporary Cultures* (1955).

[3] M. Mead (ed.), *Cultural Patterns and Technical Change* (1953).

In war-time this was under-emphasised and under pressure of circumstances more attention was devoted to the study of cultural patterns. To establish a relationship between culture and personality it is necessary to have a better theory of personality than at present obtains. This was increasingly seen to be the case, and after the war the emphasis shifted therefore in the direction of personality studies.

Britain: Self-analysis through Mass-Observation

The war not only gave rise to pressing problems connected with military aims and administrative needs, but it focused people's attention on what was to happen after the war. The reconstruction of society after war-time dislocation and bombing, after the development of new techniques and more especially new patterns of behaviour, new institutions, greater employment of married women, social mobility in the armed forces, and general geographical movement; all of these, if not new, were on such a scale as to require a long hard look at the kind of society that was to emerge after the war. Nowhere was this more so than in Britain, for nowhere had the changes been so far reaching, and the measure of this was the Labour Party's landslide victory at the polls in 1944 which cast aside the great war-time leader Winston Churchill and invested with power a party committed to a big programme of radical reform. What was the effect of this political change on British Sociology? Clearly, it was a new social awareness. Partly, this was discernible among the *avant-garde* before the war broke out. An instance of this may be seen in the establishment of Mass-Observation by Tom Harrisson and Charles Madge in 1937. This was an attempt to marry social anthropology to journalism in the interests of revealing Britain to its inhabitants. Using information in all parts of the country Mass-Observation collected data for use in reports and articles, some published directly, others in magazines and newspapers.

The first report was of the Coronation of King George VI in 1937, but Harrisson had embarked on a study of the city of Bolton in Lancashire a year earlier, and it was there, as well as in London, that the organisation set up a centre. During the war

Mass-Observation carried out a number of studies for the Ministry of Information and for the Admiralty, but latterly it has become a market research organisation, whilst still retaining certain non-commercial interests. A selection of titles of reports includes: *Britain*, 1939, a Penguin Special written by the founders, *Clothes Rationing* (1941), *War Factory* (1943), *Britain and her Birth-rate* (1945), *Exmoor Village* (1947), *On Sunday* (1949). In 1961 Harrisson published a review of this organisation's work in *Britain Revisited*. In his review, Harrisson justifies the work of Mass-Observation by saying that in the early 'thirties there was little in the way of a bridge between the organs of supposed power (by which he means the press and radio) and the mass of non-vociferous people of the land. The situation in the 'sixties is obviously better in that market research and public opinion polls have helped to convey the attitudes and opinions of the masses to government and other bodies. Mass-Observation helped to pave the way for this development in Britain. It was essentially a data-collecting organisation, but it did have the inestimable value of emphasising observation. Indeed, Harrisson makes much of the ornithological interests of many of its supporters. Sheer observation is usually underestimated in modern sociology where questionnaires and interviews bulk large, but the practice of observing what people *do* has repaid the effort made again and again. It was unfortunate that the enthusiasm behind this venture was so diffuse and that there was so little sociological theory to direct attention and assist in the formulation of problems; indeed the effort may well seem disproportionate to the results. It is doubtful if the Mass-Observation movement did more than stimulate people's interests in social enquiry. It fed the left-wing political elements, and in some ways it fitted into the Fabian tradition, but as far as sociological investigation is concerned it was akin to market research and public opinion polling, which developed greatly after the war, rather than sociological investigation proper. In fact, under modern American influences raw empiricism has declined in Britain and this has adversely affected Mass-Observation.

The war, of course, also stimulated a variety of enquiries not all of which were sociological in character although they made use of social survey techniques. Mass-Observation used these but augmented them with a more anthropological type of enquiry. But the social survey came into its own, for governments required information and the sampling technique was found most useful. Thus besides the work set in motion by the American services, to which we have briefly referred, there was a large range of studies in both Britain and America covering many aspects of civilian government. In Britain the Government Social Survey was founded, originally called the War-time Social Survey. This was set up in 1941, and whilst it did not initiate studies, nor does so today, it was and is used by other government departments. During the war it began by investigating morale and endeavoured to assess the effects of government propaganda. This aroused some criticism at the time and investigators came to be popularly known as "Cooper's snoopers" (after the Minister of Information, Mr. Duff Cooper). Consequently, attention was redirected to more factual matters, to making enquiries about recruitment to the services, the employment of married women, the use of blood donors for transfusions, the use of agricultural land, recruitment to the mines and, at the end of the war, the demand for service medals, for in Britain these had to be applied for by those entitled to them. Today, the Government Social Survey meets some of the needs of departments like the Ministry of Health, the Home Office, the Board of Trade and also some other bodies like the Medical Research Council, which is government-financed. But it was the war that clarified the need for this government service and, if it is mainly factual and eschews theory, much of its data is of sociological significance, and the refinements in social survey technique which it has helped to bring about are of abiding value for the prosecution of sociological research by other bodies.

Resettlement of Prisoners of War

One of the neatest studies of resettlement concerned repatriated British prisoners of war, some of whom had been incarcerated since 1940, having been captured whilst effecting the evacuation of the main British Army units at Dunkirk. Clearly, this was a special problem, for these men had been away from their families and their local communities for many years, but it was the prototype of problems which were likely to arise during general demobilisation. Thus in 1946 A. C. T. W. Curle,[1] a social anthropologist interested in dynamic psychology, undertook a study of prisoners of war returned to Britain from Germany. The study was an attempt to measure the effectiveness of the Civil Resettlement Units which had been set up on the advice of social scientists attached to the British Army. A pilot unit had been set up early in 1945 and twenty were in existence by the end of that year. The exercise Curle undertook was to define de-socialisation, examining the various factors affecting the prisoner of war, not only from the time he was captured but taking account of the experience of enlistment, of being separated from family and community, of being increasingly integrated into a military unit, of the sudden deprivation of social ties and the task of maintaining prescribed identity in a prisoner of war camp despite attempts by captors to wean him away from his allegiances. The Civil Resettlement Unit (C.R.U.) was an attempt to provide a transitional community between that of the prisoner of war camp and the man's home and civilian surroundings, it was an attempt to help a man adjust to a family that had altered, children growing older, new ideas, forgotten or half-remembered work tasks, social ties, and so forth. Providing a set of criteria for measuring social adjustment with reference to control groups in the population, suitably matched for age, family structure etc., Curle, on the basis of extended interviews and psychiatric assessments, compared those ex-prisoners of war who had been through a C.R.U. with those who had not, and he found a significantly higher proportion of well-adjusted men in the sample who had attended a C.R.U. Moreover, the proportion of men who were "well-settled" in their community seemed to be higher in the C.R.U. group, which suggested greater integration as well as indicating that more men had been beneficially influenced.

This study is of interest because it introduced a method of

[1] Adam Curle, "Transitional Communities and Social Re-connection: A Follow-up Study of the Civil Resettlement of British Prisoners of War" Part I, *Human Relations*, Vol. I, No. 1, 1947. Adam Curle & E. L. Trist, "Transitional Communities and Social Re-connection, *Human Relations*, Vol. I, No. 2, 1947. See also A. T. M. Wilson, "The Serviceman comes home", *Pilot Papers*, Vol. I, 1946.

making a personal assessment of individuals on the basis of modern dynamic psychology, but it also analysed the structure of the social environment of the men, their families, their army units, their prisoner of war camp relationships and the structure of the C.R.U., for the C.R.U. was a deliberate attempt to provide a therapeutic community, designed to act as a bridge between the authoritarian regimes of both the Army and the prisoner of war camp on the one hand and the democratic civilian community on the other. Thus men volunteered for a C.R.U. It was essentially an information giving unit. Discussion groups were a notable feature in which free expression of views and opinions was encouraged, those taking a lead in the activities being both civilian and military personnel. The units organised visits of observation to factories, to places where there were social activities and other outside places of interest. Weekend leave was frequent, so that men could get to know their families again gradually. The hierarchical distinctions of the Army were minimised, with commensality and recreational facilities for all ranks, both staff and ex-prisoner of war members. The C.R.U. was designed to minimise anxiety, to help and inform, and to permit gradual resettlement. The findings of this study are very suggestive, for the principles upon which the C.R.U. was set up for ex-prisoners of war might well be applied to the resettlement of other kinds of people—civil prisoners, mental patients from hospital, those who have been institutionalised in homes from the sub-normal, and so forth. The particular categories used by the author of this report may also be used in a general appraisal of the problems of *normal* people who fall short of the highest category of social settlement. Indeed, the study is suggestive for many aspects of therapeutic community enterprises.

CHAPTER XV

THE ORGANISATION AND PROFESSIONALISATION OF SOCIOLOGY

The conditions which favour popularity are not necessarily those which advance scholarship. A popular theory may prevent a sounder one from being considered, a common prejudice may direct the course of development in research into blind alleys, or a politically controversial movement may deter the sober-minded academic world from accepting a line of thought and study that could with profit be disciplined by criticism and by methodological refinement. Sociology has suffered from bouts of popularity followed by periods of distrust. This is true of the effects of popular thought at the end of the eighteenth century. At first Montesquieu's work was taken seriously, then put aside. Comte's work was tentatively considered by J. S. Mill but by few others, so that it failed to have lasting influence on English thought; it had none at all on German scholars. Spencer's great popularity in the nineteenth century in Britain, a popularity that was even greater in the U.S.A., whilst encouraging the study of social institutions may nevertheless be said to have inhibited the development of quantitative empirical sociological research by excluding it from the universities. The first developments of sociology in both Britain and America in the universities were in the form of evolutionary anthropology and sociology, and the latter was strongly opposed in Britain to Geddes' urban empiricism, whilst in Columbia University, New York, Giddings was intolerant of developments not in accord with his own brand of psychological evolutionism. Only in social anthropology did evolutionary speculation lead to field studies and this only took place because of the arrival in England of Malinowski, after partial restriction by Australia during the First World War, with notebooks full of observations of primitive people in the Pacific.

The latest bout of popularity came after the Second World War, in the early 1950s in Germany, and in the 1960s in Britain. In the New World the popularity of sociology grew steadily from the ending of the war, and has been exceptional in Canada during the 1960s. It was this popularity which carried it into the universities and established it as part of undergraduate courses of study. Thus, to often exaggerated views as to the usefulness of sociology, has been added the opinion that it has educational value. In Britain one might almost say it is beginning to occupy the place once held by Greats at Oxford as a suitable training for administrators. But popularity has been the bane of the subject. Too many have expected too much and have consequently been too disappointed. Useful it may be, both with respect to research findings and as a means of informing youth of the nature of the society they are part of, but seldom does it have a very direct and cogent bearing on the important problems of our times, and even less often do research findings in sociology absolve politicians and administrators from making decisions that offend some section of the community. Yet despite the disadvantages of popularity sociology has grown in stature as a subject for study. How has this come about? The answer, as E. A. Shils has pointed out, lies in its incorporation into the university as a subject for research and teaching.

The coming of age of sociology partly depended upon it abandoning political interests. In the past it has been variously conservative and radical, sometimes even socialist in orientation. Sociology also has had to shed its propensity to be a substitute for religious belief, not always very successfully. It has come to be respectable largely because it is seen to be a useful aid in administration and to be in the main a descriptive and statistically oriented kind of enquiry. The expansion of university education meant also that it has been perceived to be useful as a subject for study by those without any special interest in the natural sciences nor possessed of any great introspective sensitivity to the arts. Of the increasing numbers of young people entering the universities since the Second World War many are interested in the general social problems of our times. They have a tendency to be active rather than contemplative. They are sociable and sensitive to human and social needs. Sociology has thus come to be an operational science, rather than a political one in itself, although the hope that it is ultimately useful politically is never extinguished. If it has ceased to be obviously a substitute for religion it has in fact joined other scientific enterprises in offering a way of life to a generation that accepts without question the basic philosophical postulates upon which modern science rests, but this is merely to say that large sections of the modern world accept "scientific" philosophy as a belief system. To be sure, sociology has become manipulative, to use Shils' term,[1] as it has become more restricted in its scope and as it has concentrated on more practical problems, themselves cast in a largely administrative frame of reference. Where sociology is concerned with larger themes, where it examines institutional behaviour in broad terms, where it considers civilisation as a whole, the approach of its practitioners is not political but academic, not committed but detached.

All this change in the status and nature of the subject is the direct result of the institutionalisation of social research in universities and institutes and the use of the findings of such research as content for teaching at the higher levels of the educational process. Sociology was for long kept out of the universities. In Britain and Germany it was perceived to be a radical movement and in Germany especially it suffered from the reaction to the *Kathedersozialismus*, i.e. to those who used their academic positions to advance the ideas of Lorenz von Stein and Karl Marx. But even in the U.S.A. its acceptance by the universities was slow and it was largely relegated to the liberal-arts college rather than developed in the large university.

The State of Sociology prior to the First World War

The development of the modern university in Germany, as Shils[2] has pointed out, has fostered the systematic progress of academic subjects generally. A number of factors may be detected. Thus there is the emphasis of the German university on the definitive work, the textbook, revised many times and growing larger and more impressive in its detailed contents and range of thought, providing a principal means of instruction on the one hand but

[1] E. A. Shils: 'Epilogue" in *Theories of Society* (1961), eds. T. Parsons, E. A. Shils, K. D. Naegele, and J. R. Pitts. [2] *Ibid.*

advancing the organising of a department of knowledge on the other. It cannot be said that this led directly to the development of sociology in Germany, for this is clearly not the case, but the general pattern of higher education in Germany profoundly influenced American university practice, where the textbook is an important vehicle for instruction in sociology today and has been since Giddings wrote his *Principles of Sociology* (1896), Ward his *Pure Sociology* (1904), and Ross his *Social Psychology* (1908). The organisation of a subject around the professor, of which the textbook is an outward manifestation, meant that some sort of centralised control was exerted. To be sure, a special slant or the advance of some particular aspect of the subject occurred in one university and distinguished it from a different emphasis in another, and to this extent there was introduced an element of rivalry, but it all helped to stimulate the progressive organisation of the subject in environmental circumstances of criticism. In this way a degree of unity was imposed on sociology, for in circumstances of criticism any special emphasis must take contrary views into account. There has to be agreement on the areas of disagreement, and a defence within the university of a basic unity of the subject in arguments with representatives of other disciplines over the share of resources. The introduction of sociology as part of the curriculum in liberal-arts colleges, in contrast to be sure with the total absence of the subject in the curricula of the German gymnasium, the French lycée and the English grammar school, meant that large numbers of American students were introduced to the subject and a proportion of these went on to university to carry out postgraduate work in sociology. In America sociology courses were introduced in Boston University in 1883, in William and Mary College in 1885, in Indiana University in 1886 and in the University of Wyoming a year later. It was introduced into Brown University in 1890, where Ward taught. A number of colleges, including Oberlin and Vassar, took it up in 1891, but it was not introduced into Chicago and Cornell until 1893. This may be regarded as the first stage of university development of sociology in America. The second stage dates from a decade later and included the widespread introduction of sociological teaching in liberal-arts colleges, where there was a rapid increase in student numbers, but development may also be seen in universities which give a liberal-arts type of education. Subventions for rural sociological research by the state encouraged its development in agricultural and land colleges. The energetic Albion Small probably did more than anyone to establish sociology in the U.S.A. His appointment to the first chair of sociology in Chicago, the founding of the *American Journal of Sociology* under his editorship in 1895, and his establishment of the American Sociological Society in the same year under the presidency of Lester Ward, represent an important point in the history of sociology in that country. In 1889 Franklin Giddings was elected to the chair of sociology in Columbia University, New York, and from then onwards Chicago and Columbia dominated the field, becoming the main centres for research and graduate work; indeed one may say that very largely these two centres have been responsible for the staffing of sociology departments, at the higher levels, throughout the U.S.A.

In Britain, France and Germany sociology might knock loudly on the door, but the doors of the universities, with but few exceptions, were firmly shut against it. In Germany, unlike America or even France, sociology did not have a clear place in the academic world. It was for long associated with other social sciences like economics (itself largely historical in character) and political science,[1] and indeed the social sciences generally were largely philosophical in content, especially was this true of the sociological component. Weber and Tönnies endeavoured to move in an empirical direction and Weber in particular dealt with the problem of values in an attempt to found a value-free discipline suitable for academic study. The high point of sociological development prior to the First World War was the establishment in 1909 of the Deutsche Gesellschaft für Soziologie. The members, like Max Weber, were interested in carrying out research of a sociological nature but came from other disciplines. Another outstanding step was the appearance of the *Archiv für Sozialwissenschaft und Sozialpolitik*, the organ of the Verein für Sozialpolitik, itself founded in the nineteenth century; this sponsored and co-ordinated social

[1] L. von Wiese, "The Place of Social Science in Germany", *American Journal of Sociology*, July 1951.

research on a broad front, including some sociological research. Max Weber had much to do with the editorial policy of the *Archiv*. But prior to the First World War there was no specifically sociological university chair; Weber himself occupied a chair of economics.

In France Le Play had been encouraged by Emperor Napoleon III, and his *La Réforme Sociale* founded in 1881 was influential; but it was Durkheim who succeeded in introducing sociology into the universities, firstly at Bordeaux where he held a chair of pedagogy, and later in Paris. His founding of *L'Année Sociologique* in 1898 was one of the most important steps in the development of academic sociology in France. In it he reviewed German works like those of Tönnies and commented on Spencer's work in England. The journal ran until 1912. It has been described as one of the most comprehensive and scholarly reviews ever published. Durkheim was succeeded at Paris by Célestin Bouglé, formerly professor of social philosophy in the University of Toulouse, who espoused the ideas of Simmel. He was anti-historical in his sociological views. Although the author of a famous work on caste entitled: *Essai sur la régime des castes* (1808), he did little to present sociology as an organised body of knowledge. The Durkheimian tradition dominated much of French sociological thinking, despite Bouglé, through the works of Mauss and Halbwachs. We should also recall the work of René Worms, that indefatigable organiser of sociological discussion, who founded the *Revue International de Sociologie*, of which he was the editor until 1926. This journal was somewhat anti-Durkheimian in sentiment. It served the Institut International de Sociologie, established in 1893, of which Worms was the general secretary. Both offices passed on Worms' death to Gaston Richard. But sociology did not thrive much outside Paris. In Belgium Émile Waxweiler was director of L'Institut de Sociologie Solvay from 1901 to 1916. This was, and is, one of the best organised and financed research institutes in Europe. In Italy the *Revista Italiana Sociologia* was founded in 1897.

The organisation of sociology in England may be said to date from the founding of the Sociological Society of London in 1904 under the presidency of Viscount Bryce. In April of that year a meeting was held in the London School of Economics and Political Science, part of the University of London. Bryce, in his opening address, pointed to various branches of social enquiry which could come within the purview of the subject; prominent among them was eugenics. He argued that the Society would "survey with the eye of science the whole field of human activity".[1] Bryce went on to say that there was no systematic treatise on sociology which would show the unity of these various kinds of enquiry, not even a book by a German scholar. He also noted how poor were British universities by comparison with Continental and American ones in their provision for social research. It is perhaps interesting to note the kinds of papers submitted to the first conference of that Society. Eugenics as a study was defined by Francis Galton, Civics was discussed by Patrick Geddes, the position of women in early civilisation was the subject of a paper by Westermarck, and the relationship of sociology to other social sciences was the content of a paper sent to the meeting by Durkheim; and this was further discussed by Victor Branford and M. E. Fauconnet. The committee of the Society was chaired by L. T. Hobhouse, the rival of Geddes for the newly established chair of sociology at London and the first in Britain. The dispute over the chair spilled over into the Society; this issue was both a matter of personalities and policy. To be sure, Geddes' exuberant manner and enthusiasm went against him and Hobhouse's sweet reasonableness probably won him the position, but Hobhouse represented the philosophical side of sociology, speculative and evolutionary, whereas Geddes was a social engineer, interested in urban planning. For over forty years the Hobhousian tradition dominated sociology in the London School, being supported by Westermarck and later by Morris Ginsberg who succeeded Hobhouse. Both Hobhouse and Westermarck were appointed to chairs in 1907. The administrative and reformist tradition did not enter the academic world in Britain until after the war but then it was through the inspiration of Charles Booth whose firm, A. Booth and Company, founded a chair of social science in his memory at the University of Liverpool, the first occupant being Sir Alexander Carr-Saunders who held it from 1923 to 1937.

[1] *Sociological Papers* (1905).

The Inter-War Period

The ending of the First World War did not bring in its train a marked growth in sociological research and teaching. Some new influences made themselves felt. Pitirim Sorokin and Nicholas Timasheff escaped from Russia to the U.S.A.; and Georges Gurvitch likewise escaped to settle in France. Florian Znaniecki migrated from Poland at this time, but returned later for a while before finally settling in America. In Germany there was a resurgence of interest in sociology. The Deutsche Gesellschaft für Soziologie held five congresses between 1922 and 1930: in Jena in 1922 where the discussion was about revolutions; in Heidelberg in 1924 to discuss sociology and social policy; in Vienna two years later when among the topics were democracy, natural law and the theory of social relations; in 1928 in Zurich where the Society discussed competition, social change, *verstehen*, and the origins of art; and lastly in Berlin in 1930. In Cologne the famous quarterly was founded in 1923. Originally it was entitled *Kölner Vierteljahrshefte für Soziologie*. It was edited by C. Eckert, H. Lindemann, Max Scheler and L. von Wiese. Publication ceased in 1933 at the instigation of the National Socialist German Workers Party, when that party came to power. The back numbers of the journal and those of the *Archiv* were destroyed by members of the party. But during the inter-war period K. Thurnwald edited nine volumes of the *Zeitschrift für Völkerpsychologie und Soziologie* and this provided a vehicle for sociological communication until it too was suppressed. K. Dunkmann's *Archiv für Angewandte Soziologie*, founded in 1925, survived until 1935.

In Britain the Institute of Sociology was established the same year that sociology was being suppressed in Germany, for in 1933 it took over the *Sociological Review*, formerly published by the Sociological Society of London. Victor Branford, a railway company director and a keen reformer, was closely associated with it. The president of the Institute was the anthropologist and psychologist R. R. Marett. Under the influence of Patrick Geddes the old Society had derived its inspiration from the work of the Frenchmen Le Play and Demolins, and this was carried over. The Society was domiciled in Le Play House in London which was mainly financed by Branford; it was after his death that the Society and Le Play House became transmuted into the Institute. Its success was limited. The Society, which preceded it, had deteriorated greatly in the 1920s, and at first the Institute proved more successful. It received support from the academics. Both Morris Ginsberg and T. H. Marshall took part, and Marshall edited the conference reports on *Class Conflict and Social Stratification* (1938), which ought to be more widely known than they are. But even so, the older interests which stemmed from Geddes' writing and lecturing, worthy in aim but undisciplined, idealistic but intellectually feeble, still persisted. If the academics were rather distant, philosophical and insufficiently empirically minded, then the members of the Institute, like those of the Society, were too varied in their interests, and the aims and purposes of the Institute were too inchoate. It has been said that Patrick Geddes was responsible for the rejection of empirical sociology by the British universities, that his strong views, immoderately expressed, led to the subject being perceived by other scholars as "a science, a philosophy, a religion, and a social programme primarily dependent upon Messianic leadership",[1] although it is interesting to note that the sober and cautious Booth publicly supported him. In the University of London the teaching of sociology continued on a small scale but with few practitioners, a situation which lasted till after the Second World War and which resulted in a chronic shortage of teachers of the subject when sociology at last gained admittance to other British universities.

If sociology had scarcely taken root in Britain, neither had it had much success in Italy, where slight beginnings were crushed under the heel of Mussolini's fascism. Moreover, it was unpopular in academic circles. The prevailing liberal idealistic philosophy of Benedetto Croce found it uncongenial. Croce himself spoke scathingly: "Sociology . . . a name which stands censured as an inelegant hybrid of latin and greek" and he dismissed it as "this diseased science". The fact is that he perceived it to be ahistorical if not anti-historical. In Japan the writings of some American and German sociologists were used in universities for teaching the

[1] H. Becker and H. E. Barnes: *Social Thought from Lore to Science* (1938, 3rd edn. 1961), Vol. II, p. 812.

subject; those of Ward, Giddings and Cooley especially, then later those of Simmel, Weber and von Wiese. Here we may detect a changing political allegiance from early pro-American sentiment to that change in outlook which led Japan to join the Axis powers. However, a Sociological Society was founded in 1927. In the following year a South-Eastern Sociological Society was founded in China to advance the subject and it published a quarterly journal. Its international outlook was soon abandoned and the following year it was replaced by the National Chinese Sociological Society, a Society which sponsored surveys in rural areas and carried out population investigations.

The main advance in the academic organisation of sociology came in the U.S.A., where the early gains were consolidated. Sociology was a subject taught in many colleges and universities both at undergraduate and graduate level. It had gained greatly as a result of the growth of the Chicago School under Park, then under Burgess and later under Everett C. Hughes. The Sociological Society grew slowly in numbers but, compared with the membership of other societies, they were impressive. In the University of Southern California the *Journal of Applied Sociology* was founded in 1921, based on the carlier *Sociological Monographs* begun in 1916. Later it was renamed *Sociology and Social Research*. After that "Nestor of American sociologists", as the *American Journal of Sociology* referred to its editor, Lester Ward, had died in 1913, the Journal's policy began to change from an emphasis on grand theory to one on methodological problems and the use of statistics. Formerly, there had been a degree of urbanity in the policy and contributions were sought from other countries as well as from American scholars. Foreign articles appeared in translation, including Simmel's, but these ceased and a more parochial outlook prevailed, and still prevails. When Faris, and later Burgess, took over the editorship the Journal manifested a greater interest in North American urban studies, and under Herbert Blumer race relations in the U.S.A.[1] were its chief concern.

[1] See Ethel Shanas, "The American Journal of Sociology through fifty years", *American Journal of Sociology*, Vol. 50, 1945.

Sociology after World War II

In the last chapter we saw the effect which war-time had upon sociology, how it stimulated research into matters affecting morale, social organisation, leadership and readjustment. We saw also the hope placed in it by those who turned their attention to post-war reconstruction. The war gave sociological development a fillip, but so also did the aftermath of war. In the Netherlands, for instance, where the sociological tradition had for a long time had close associations with geography, post-war reconstruction presented many problems which, it was thought, sociology could help to solve. The Dutch tradition, established by Steinmetz in Amsterdam, emphasised the manner in which environment conditions human life. *Sociography* was his creation. (At Utrecht it was called *social geography.*) A lot of work had been done in this field by H. N. ter Veen and others. This was a tradition that continued after the war on a large scale, for the Dutch people had a lot of reconstruction to effect. The economic crisis of the 1930s had predisposed governments to think in terms of planned development. The destruction of central Rotterdam by the Luftwaffe and the flooding of the polders during the German retreat made planning all the more an obvious necessity. Thus sociography led easily to the development of urban and rural studies oriented to planned development. Practical social problems of an unusual kind had presented themselves, for example: what does one do with a fishing population deprived of its sea? Such a question had arisen before the war when the land of the Zuiderzee had been reclaimed, but after the war there were large population movements and resettlement problems abounded. The use of sociologists was recognised. Chairs of sociology were established in the State Universities of Utrecht, Leiden and Groningen, in the Amsterdam Municipal University, in the Roman Catholic University of Nijmegen, in the School of Economics at Tilburg, and in the Rotterdam School of Economics. The Roman Catholic institutions tended to emphasise a Thomistic philosophical approach rather than the empirical one which so strongly marked the others. Most of the departments of sociology borrowed heavily from the American tradition as regards problem formation and methodological techniques. But both Roman and Reformed Churches also had sociological research institutes to carry out empirical studies related to pastoral work and to church organisation. The Netherlands also sponsored an International Social Science Institute in The Hague in which some lectures are in English, and this Institute draws students for advanced and specialised courses from many countries, including under-developed ones. There are in the Netherlands a number of publications assisting the development of sociology: a guide and reference book *Sociologische Gids*; *De Sociologisch Bulletin*; *Mens en Maatschappij* (Man and Society), and *Tijdschift voor Economische en Sociale Geografie*, which supports the sociographic tradition of Dutch studies.

Similarly, post-war reconstruction in Poland favoured the development of sociology despite the general antipathy to the subject which communism displays. Before the war Ludvik Krzywick (1858–1941) had occupied the first chair of sociology at Warsaw. A sociological research institute had flourished at Poznan and a review was published by the University. This was revived in 1947 under the title *Przeglad Sociologiczny*. Ecological studies of cities were undertaken and also rural sociological studies. Many of them were related to the task of enabling refugees to settle and adapt to their new surroundings. Analyses of social stratification have also been made. The Polish sociologists have made much use of case-histories and life histories and here we see a connection with the famous work of Thomas and Znaniecki referred to in an earlier chapter. To a large extent this was the work of Josef Chalasinski, the author of a four volume work on the Polish peasantry and its younger generation. Departments of sociology were established in the Universities of Lodz, Lublin, Warsaw and Wroclaw in addition to the re-establishment of the subject in Poznan. Clearly, much of the research relates to problems of town and country planning, but some attention is given to industrial relations research and to family studies. Today Polish sociology is prominently represented in the international congresses by Jan Szepeczpanski.

In Finland, like most Scandinavian countries, sociological research has tended to be oriented to criminological topics. Dr Veli

Verkko, who held the chair of sociology in Helsinki University from 1948 until his death in 1955, was prominent in analysing criminal statistics. In Sweden, where the first chair was founded at Uppsala and occupied by Torgny Segerstedt, the subject grew out of social philosophy. Criminology has been prominent; urban and rural studies have been carried out by Bengt Rundblad, and there is some interest in small group studies. *Acta Sociologica,* published in English, first appeared in 1956 and provides a vehicle for communicating research reports. In Denmark sociology received a powerful fillip when Theodor Geiger migrated in 1933 from Munich eventually to take the chair of sociology at the University of Aarhus in 1938. Geiger's social stratification studies are well-known contributions to the subject. He spent the war period in Sweden but also visited Canada, and his wide contacts gave a breadth to Danish sociology which has been of great benefit to it. The Westermarck Society provides a means whereby Scandinavian scholars can collaborate and publish their researches. The transactions of the Society appear in English, being published in Copenhagen.

Although in Germany, under Weber's influence, sociology might have followed the impressive lead he gave, the fact is that it was ruthlessly suppressed by the National Socialist German Workers' Party. German sociology had been mainly theoretical, historically oriented, comparative and analytical. Its affinities with philosophy gave rise to the *Wissenssoziologie* of Max Weber, Max Scheler and Karl Mannheim, probably the most notable contributors to this development. But this particular tradition was an oppositional one. Subsequent development in this field was mainly American. In Germany folklore replaced sociology during Hitler's regime. Three veteran sociologists survived the war: Alfred Weber (1868–1958) who laid the foundation stone of the sociocultural school of sociology at Heidelberg, Leopold von Wiese (b. 1876) at Köln and Alfred Vierkandt (1867–1953). Max Horkheimer and Theodor Adorno returned after the war from the U.S.A. to the J. W. Goethe University of Frankfurt, where the former became Rector of the University and the latter Director of the Institut für Sozialforschung. Despite their acquaintance with American empirical sociology the two scholars made their first post-war contributions to the philosophical tradition of German sociology by writing *Dialektik der Aufklärung*, published in Amsterdam in 1948. Another émigré to return was Helmuth Plessner who accepted the chair at Göttingen and whose *Zwischen Philosophie und Gesellschaft* (1953) reflects the same tradition. However, new developments were taking place. Professor Joseph Hoffman, of the Department of Economics in the University of Munster, with foreign support helped to establish the impressive Sozialforschungsstelle in Dortmund, part of which is a sociological section set up under the direction of Dr Otto Neuloh, a research centre mainly oriented to industrial and urban studies and which publishes *Soziale Welt*. Thus before any research institute was established in Britain for sociological research there were two post-war creations in Germany, both well housed in new buildings. German sociology was off to a good start. Moreover, in Hamburg the Trade Union Academy sponsored sociological research into family structure directed by Helmuth Schelsky, later to be called to the chair of sociology in the University there. In 1946 the German Sociological Society reassembled for its first congress; after this, empirical sociological research began to gain ground. A year later the *Kölner Zeitschrift für Soziologie* resumed publication under the editorship of von Wiese and in 1955 this famous journal added to its title "*und Sozialpsychologie*". In 1956 Otto Abel founded the *Zeitschrift für Agrargeschichte und Agrarsoziologie*. Other periodicals to be established include the series of books published by T. Adorno and W. Kirks called the *Frankfurter Beiträge zur Soziologie*, and the *Dortmunder Schriften für Sozialforschung* which contains reports of the Sozialforschungstelle, the *Göttinger Abhandlungen für Soziologie* edited by H. Plessner, the *Soziologische Gegenwartsfragen* edited by Boetticher, Neundorfer and Schelsky, and *Sociologus* edited by Hilde Thurnwald which caters for both anthropologists and sociologists. By this time there were, in addition to those mentioned, several other journals and also a number of research institutes.[1] By this time chairs of sociology existed in the Universities of Berlin, Köln, Frankfurt, Göttingen, Hamburg, Kiel and Tübingen. The Evangelical and

[1] Max Horkheimer: *Survey of the Social Sciences in Western Germany: A Report on Recent Developments* (1952).

Roman Catholic Church Colleges had incorporated sociological teaching into their curricula and so had the universities where there was no specific chair of sociology; it was by this time taking firm root and was looking outward. More and more foreign works appeared in translation during the 1960s, and frequent reference was made to American and British research reports. In West Germany sociology had arrived; the same could not be said for East Germany, where the German Democratic Government permitted only the communist ideology to prevail, a feature that was painfully apparent whenever their delegation attended an international congress.

In France sociological research was facilitated through the Centre National de la Recherche Scientifique which has thirteen sections for the human sciences. Here sociology and demography are set together. This parent body was responsible for the Centre d'Études Sociologiques set up in 1945 under the direction of Georges Gurvitch, directed now by J. Stoetzel. Other research organisations to be mentioned include the Centre d'Études et de Recherches Sociologiques of the University of Toulouse and the Laboratoire des Sciences Sociales of the University of Aix-en-Provence. In the academic world the Licence de Sociologie as a university degree dates from 1957.

In Britain the development of sociological research and teaching received a modest but significant fillip in the universities as a result of the acceptance by the University Grants Committee of the report of the Committee set up by the Government in 1945 under Sir John Clapham. £1,250,000 was allocated for the period 1947–1952 and the annual rate of expenditure rose thereafter. The development of departments of sociology in most universities (Oxford and Cambridge dragged their feet) is recorded by A. B. Cherns[1] and an account of the principal characteristics of this advance by Alan Little.[2]

A notable post-war development has been the establishment in London University of a Centre for Urban Studies under the directorship of Mrs Ruth Glass. The growth of the number of

[1] "Organized Social Science Research in Great Britain", *Information*, Vol. I, 1962.

[2] "Sociology in Britain since 1945", *Information*, Vol. II, 1963.

sociological journals in America and Britain was noticeable in the 1940s and the 1950s. *Human Relations* was jointly sponsored by the Tavistock Institute of Human Relations in London and the Research Centre for Group Dynamics, formerly of the Massachusetts Institute of Technology, Boston, and later domiciled in Ann Arbor, Michigan. The *British Journal of Sociology* appeared in 1950, ably guided in its early years by D. G. MacRae. The old *Sociological Review* was taken over by the University College of North Staffordshire (later Keele University) and a biannual new series appeared in 1953 in different format under the same name; this was a distinct improvement on the old series which, under war-time conditions and the rather indiscriminate editorship of Alexander Farquharson, had declined into a rag-bag for all kinds of articles only some of which could be said to be sociological. The Institute of Sociology disappeared, but the British Sociological Association was founded in 1951, although it did not have its own journal until 1967, when the first number of *Sociology* appeared, edited by Michael Banton. In the same year an applied social science journal was founded, the *Journal of Social and Economic Administration*, edited by M. H. Cooper and sponsored by the University of Exeter.

In the U.S.A. the war had brought sociology very much into the public view, and it had greatly advanced in the universities. The American Sociological Society was moved to break with the *American Journal of Sociology*, with its Chicago connection, and established its own organ, the *American Sociological Review*. Rural sociologists split off and a new journal *Rural Sociology* appeared. The American Sociological Society drew up a new constitution and in 1962 changed its name to the American Sociological Association; it had a membership of six thousand, but the *Review* enjoyed a much larger readership than this. Sociological studies were organised in leading universities in separate agencies. Thus the Bureau of Applied Social Research is part of Columbia University, New York, and the National Opinion Research Center is at the University of Chicago, but some agencies are independent of the departments of sociology; such is the case with the Institute for Social Research. Moreover, research was on an increasingly large scale. H. L. Zetterberg records that in 1954 the average cost of a research project was $3,900.[1] It is interesting to note that the largest sums for research were provided by the foundations and the government. Research was increasingly being sponsored by the great research organisations, by the Rand Corporation, itself sponsored by the American Air Force, by the U.S. Department of Defence, by the Central Intelligence Agency, but above all by the big Foundations, especially the Ford and Rockefeller Foundations.[2] The Ford Foundation financed the Center for Advanced Study in the Behavioral Sciences at Palo Alto, California, instituted in 1954, which brings a small number of distinguished scholars to the U.S.A. to meet a selection of American scholars and to enable them to take part in seminars of a multi-disciplinary kind. On a smaller scale the Foundation sponsored other similar ventures such as, to mention one example, the Inter-collegiate Program of Graduate Studies at Claremont Graduate School in California. The emphasis was increasingly on multi-disciplinary research. This had already been reflected in the establishment at Harvard University of the Department of Social Relations, under the chairmanship of Talcott Parsons, the Institute of Human Relations at Yale University and other institutes and research centres in the Universities of Minnesota, North Carolina, Cornell, Washington, and Vanderbilt University in Tennessee. Indeed, "social relations" and "behavioral sciences" were terms which emerged at this time. Indicative of the consolidation of the social sciences was the new revised edition in 1968 of the *Encyclopaedia of the Social Sciences*, originally published in 1933. Significant also as an index of the consolidation and organisation of sociological studies is the plethora of textbooks which appeared in the decade beginning 1955, and other works of reference such as the *Handbuch der Soziologie* (1956) edited by Werner Ziegenfüss, *The Dictionary of the Social Sciences* (1964) edited by J. Gould and W. L. Kolb, and *A Dictionary of Sociology* (1968) edited by G. Duncan Mitchell.

In other countries sociology advanced on a modest scale;

[1] "Organized Social Science Research in Great Britain", *Information*, Vol. I, 1962.

[2] For a description of the changes in the organisation of research and especially its collaborative nature, see H. L. Zetterberg, *Sociology in the U.S.A.: A Trend Report* (U.N.E.S.C.O. 1956).

in Latin-America several universities developed sociological teaching, some founding chairs. In Japan a journal called *Social Research* appeared in 1947, and partly under American occupation influences departments of sociology appeared in Japanese universities. In Canada, New Zealand and Australia journals were published, although only in Canada did the universities take the subject in the fold on any large scale. In Australia, especially, psychology predominated and sociology gained admittance in only a few places. Nevertheless, by the mid-twentieth century it was well represented in Europe, both North and South America, the Far East, and even in some communist countries, e.g. Poland and Roumania, and later in the Soviet Union itself where Professor Osipov guides its affairs under the central control of the Academy of Sciences.[1]

National developments have since led to the growth of international relationships between sociologists. In September 1949 a meeting was held in Oslo under the auspices of U.N.E.S.C.O. as a result of which the International Sociological Association was born. Since then the Association has held a number of conferences, well attended by sociologists from all over the world—in France, the Netherlands, Italy, U.S.A. and elsewhere. On a smaller scale nationalistic restrictions were overcome, for the growth of the subject may be observed in the publication in 1960 of the *Archives Européennes de Sociologie* and in 1964 of *Sociologia Ruralis*, the journal of the European Society for Rural Sociology.

The twenty-year period from 1947 represents the general acceptance of sociology into the universities, the awareness of the importance of substantial financing of research, mainly multi-disciplinary in nature, and the increasing awareness by other disciplines of the necessity of sociological research to complement their own work. The academic organisation of the subject led to the establishment of learned societies, which in turn helped to establish professional rules of conduct. This has still far to go, but a beginning has been made. Complexities in modern administrative problems have doubtless also aided the growth of the subject, for there is more and more need for operational research, and the

[1] For an account and appraisal of sociological studies in the U.S.S.R., see A. Simirenko, *Soviet Sociology* (1967).

study of organisation has thus come to be a significant part of sociological research. Sociology is more and more being applied, consultative work is being carried out, and thus organisation of the subject is being followed by the professionalisation of those who practise it.

CHAPTER XVI

MACROSOCIOLOGY

I: *Social Change*

We have endeavoured to narrate the history of sociology up to the end of World War II and have considered the effect which that war had on sociology; now it remains to bring the story up to date. However, major political and military events, whilst having some bearing on the course of the development of the subject, are not the only ones, and, indeed, the development of thought tends usually to follow its own rather conservative course despite world-shaking events, for a scholar does not usually take up a subject *de novo*, but rather his thought is shaped over a considerable period of time and even his early decisions as to what will constitute a life's work, perhaps especially his early decisions, are unlikely to be modified much in the process of being worked out. Thus when we review post-war sociology we still see that its origins lie in the past, in traditions that were moulded by the Enlightenment, by the writers who saw in the comparative study of social institutions a field ripe for harvest, by those imbued with the optimism of the idea of progress, an optimism that was tempered rather than destroyed by two world wars, and by those who see in the subject a means of demonstrating the need for, and the manner of effecting, reform in political and social structures; above all, amongst those who, liking to see things in the large, have pursued sociology in the grand manner, but perhaps with more erudition, with greater refinement of concepts and with altogether more subtlety of thought. In this chapter we shall trace, albeit very quickly and superficially, some of the main strands in this more complicated tapestry which is the history of sociological thought since the war.

Macrosociology is the term given to the endeavour to study and compare total societies and cultures, or major aspects of them. It is the tradition of Comte, Marx, and de Tocqueville, of the evolutionists from Spencer to Hobhouse and of comparative sociologists like Maine and Westermarck, and indeed of some of the historians—Gibbon, Niebuhr and Mommsen to mention a few. What these writers had in common was the belief that they were describing changes in human society of either an evolutionary or progressive kind, or at least, if they were writing just history, that theirs was a narrative of linear development, perhaps not progressively altogether good but at least progressive in some sense, political or economic or technological. But in the twentieth century there was a recrudescence of an older tradition, one familiar to the Greeks but notably shared only by Giabattista Vico in the late seventeenth century,[1] an oddity standing between the Greeks and the moderns. This was a tradition of seeing a cyclical pattern in the history of mankind. And yet, whilst we may see a continuity of tradition it also remains true to say that but for World War I this might not have been revived. What the war did was to check the optimism of the Victorians and sometimes almost to reverse it. If civilisation was not progressive, and if its death could be encompassed by the human mind in prospect at least, some thought there was evidence that it might not be the end of civilisations; a new one might arise on the ruins of the old. Civilisation, therefore, was perceived to be not some unitary thing but a category or class of social life of which there were different forms existing at different times, or even coterminously. The scholars who have turned their minds in this direction have not always spoken of *civilisations*; some speak of *high cultures* or *world cultures*, but they are agreed that it is reasonable to think about human social life on a large scale in such terms. Here we shall briefly mention a few of the more prominent: Oswald Spengler, A. J. Toynbee and Pitirim Sorokin. The tradition in which these writers stand is the speculative one, and in these writings we may see some of the best of this tradition.

OSWALD SPENGLER (1880–1936)

Spengler's great work *Der Untergang des Abendlandes* was published between 1918 and 1922; the translation *The Decline of the*

[1] *Principi di una scienza nuova* (1725, 2nd edn. 1730, 3rd edn. 1744).

West was published in 1926. It was very much a post-World War I contribution to the subject, but its roots lay in the past for it owed much to Hegel; moreover it is highly likely that Spengler obtained the broad outline of his view of world history from the Russian scholar Nicolai J. Danilevsky (1822–1885), whose article "Russia and Europe" was published in a Russian journal *Zaria* in 1869; this is the view taken by the two distinguished Russian born sociologists P. Sorokin[1] and N. S. Timasheff.[2] But if Spengler's ideas belong to the last century the tradition has extended into this one in the work of both Toynbee and Sorokin, and, indeed, much in the development of their thought can be said to be mid-twentieth-century sociology.

Danilevsky had advanced the notion that Europe and Russia each belong to different "historic-cultural types", that these types are alien to each other and that this accounts for the persistent hostility of Europe to Russia and to the suspicion of Europe held by Russians. In pursuing his argument he determined a number of such types, each possessing its own history, and each an entity in itself, with its own growth and decay and even death. There was an Egyptian civilisation, a Semitic one, the Chinese, the Hindu-Indian, the Iranian, the Hebrew, the Greek, the Roman, the Arabic and the European civilisations. Spengler has a very similar breakdown of world history into units which he calls "high cultures". These are organisms having a life cycle of birth, childhood, youth, manhood and senescence. In its last phase a high culture becomes a civilisation; this last stage may be prolonged and, by comparison, the earlier stages may occur in quick succession. Spengler refers frequently to the art forms of a high culture to illustrate prominent features of each stage of its development: "It is a young and trembling soul, heavy with misgivings, that reveals itself in the morning of Romanesque and Gothic", or again "Childhood speaks to us also, and in the same tones, out of early Homeric Doric, out of early Christian (which is really early Arabian) art and out of the works of the Old Kingdom in Egypt that began with the Fourth Dynasty."[3] He looked for

[1] *Sociological Theories of Today*, (1966) p. 187.
[2] *Sociological Theory: Its Nature and Growth*, 3rd edn. (1967), p. 271.
[3] *Op. cit.* (1926), p. 107.

homologies in cultures and found them: the development of the classical style in the ancient world and the development of mathematics in the modern world, Pythagoras as the contemporary of Descartes, Archytas of Laplace, Archimedes of Gauss. Similarly, he saw the Ionic and the Baroque as homologous, Polygnotus corresponding to Rembrandt, Polycletus to Bach.[1]

Spengler's work is difficult to classify without qualification as sociology. It is a philosophy of history deeply influenced by Nietzschean ideas, an interpretation of cultures and especially of Western Culture; it is also pessimistic. Its value, from the sociologist's standpoint, is to be discerned less in its breadth of vision than in its holism, its use of comparison and the suggestive, albeit vague, references to the social bases of religious movements. This last item especially was to focus the attention of Toynbee on the emergence of high religions at certain stages in the disintegration of cultures. Above all it is his cyclical view of spring, summer, autumn and winter in each great spiritual epoch that places it in the recent tradition of macrosociological thought; a tradition that is intellectually late in the history of modern thought because sociology has been generally a vehicle for optimistic linear theories of social development, theories which have had a tenacious hold on the imagination of modern man.

ARNOLD J. TOYNBEE (b. 1899)

A Study of History was published in twelve volumes from 1934 to 1961 and represents one of the most massive undertakings in the attempt to see an intelligible pattern in the history of the human race. Like Danilevsky and Spengler, Toynbee envisages an analysis of a number of intelligible units of history; they are called civilisations and are greater than nation-states but may be determined as a result of tracing the relationships between nation-states over space and time. Such units of history are, he says, the social atoms with which students of history have to deal.[2] It is a more sensible unit than the nation-state, which has to be seen in its context, the context of its civilisation. It follows that there is a slighter continuity between civilisations than there is between different

[1] *Ibid.*, p. 112. [2] *Op. cit.,* Vol. 1., p. 45.

periods of the history of any one nation-state. However, this facilitates rather than detracts from the ability to make comparisons, to discern the affiliations of civilisations, such as the Western and the Hellenic, and to see the parallels in the development of those extant and those that have passed away or are partially present in fossilised form like the societies of Monophysite Christians of Armenia, Mesopotamia, Egypt and Abyssinia, or the Jews or the Parsees, or the Jains of India, or fragments of them.

In Toynbee's scheme of things human societies began as primitive societies. In some cases these then developed into Primary Civilisations. Such was the case with the Egyptian, Andean, Mayan, Sumeric, Minoan, the Indus Culture and the Shang Culture—all primary civilisations. Then in each one of them there developed a rudimentary high religion, itself the product of an internal proletariat, possibly of more than one as when the internal proletariats of the Egyptiac and Sumeric civilisations produced the rudimentary high religions of Osiris and Isis; and of course a civilisation may produce more than one, for the worship of Tammuz and Ishtar was a Sumeric product too. From the *primary* is derived a *secondary* civilisation. Thus the Yucatec emerged from the Mayan, the Babylonic from the Sumeric, the Syriac from the Hellenic, the Sinic from the Shang culture. Then we see the development of high religions proper. Thus the internal proletariat of Babylon gave birth to Judaism and Zoroastrianism, the Indic internal proletariat produced Hinduism, the Syriac produced Islam, whilst the internal proletariat of the Hellenic civilisation produced the worship of Isis, Cybele, Mithraism, Manichæism and Christianity. On the other hand the dominant minority of Hellenism gave birth to Neo-Platonism, and the Sinic internal proletariat took over Neo-Taoism from the Sinic dominant minority. There then takes place the formation of Tertiary Civilisation: the Hindu, Iranic-Arabic, an abortive Far Eastern, Western, Orthodox Christian, an abortive Scandinavian and others. These in turn gave rise to secondary high religions such as Kabirism, Sikhism, Brahmō-Samaj, Baha'ism, the Almadīyah, Bedreddinism, Christian sects, the T'aip'ing, etc.

It will be seen that Toynbee uses concepts like *dominant minority* and *internal proletariat* in a general way. The discernment of these groupings is of the essence of his sociological treatment. Dominant minorities like the Samurai, the Confucian literati, the Incas, the Persian grandees, and many more are distinguished by their ability to found universal states. Out of twenty civilisations that have broken down, no less than fifteen have passed through this stage on their way to dissolution. There was thus an Hellenic universal state in the Roman Empire, an Andean one in the Empire of the Incas, a Minoan one in what Toynbee calls the "thalassocracy of Minos", a Sumeric universal state in the Empire of Sumer and Akkad, a Babylonic one in the Empire of Nebuchadnezzar, an Egyptiac one in the "Middle Empire" of the eleventh and twelfth dynasties, a Russian Orthodox one in the Muscovite Empire, the Tokugawa Shogunate in Japan and others. Internal proletariats may also be discerned, their contributions being a high religion. Within the fractions of a disintegrating civilisation Toynbee sees there are groupings of people who are in it but not of it. Their mark is a feeling of being disinherited and hence they are resentful. It begins on the spiritual plane but extends often to the economic and material plane. In the Hellenic civilisation, for example, the internal proletariat consisted of disinherited and uprooted members of Hellenic society, partially disinherited members of alien civilisations and primitive societies conquered and exploited without being torn up by the roots, and doubly disinherited elements who were conscripted as slave labour and deported to work on distant plantations. Of course, sometimes such an internal proletariat rebels and is ferocious in its savagery, but on other occasions its response is far from violent. Thus the Hellenic proletariat produced the early Christian Church, a development that led eventually to the conversion of the dominant minority. Toynbee's discussion of the interplay of dominant minority and internal proletariat, the attempts to found universal states and the rise of high religions, is set against a sociological study of historical social classes, their formation and change. In addition, he considers the effects of external proletariats in the drama of challenge and response which is the history of the great civilisations of the world.

The nature of cultural change is central to his whole theme. The drama of a civilisation lies in the way in which a challenge evokes a response. There are many sources of stimuli; they may be found in "hard" environments, the exploration of opportunities in new territory, blows such as sudden defeat in war, frontier conditions with people pressing and threatening, the fruits of adversity which include discipline and resourcefulness. The fact that there are variabilities in the rate of cultural change witnesses to the power of men to shape their destiny despite all the factors that are given; there is no iron law of social change, but there are some fundamentals that can be discerned and described, and it is with these that Toynbee is concerned. His story is one of the fate of disintegrating civilisations. Of the twenty-eight he considers, including the arrested ones, eighteen are dead and nine of the remaining ten, he declares, can be shown to have broken down. Such breakdowns are to be described in terms of failure in creative power on the part of a minority which afterwards becomes a *dominant* instead of a *creative* minority, an answering withdrawal of allegiance and mimesis on the part of the majority, and a consequent loss of social unity in the society as a whole. Toynbee traces typical responses to challenges, responses which fail in the end, whilst temporarily prolonging the process of disintegration. Such disintegration proceeds unevenly; there is a series of "routs and rallies" but these seem to follow a pattern of their own. Thus he argues that there are "three and a half beats", and this pattern may be traced in the history of a number of civilisations; our own not having yet completed the process and present challenge still, he hopes, about to evoke a response. Stimulating as Toynbee's work is, there is one feature which lends restraint to its influence on modern sociologists. His work manifests a belief in the guiding hand of Providence, as it is understood in the Christian tradition, and this and the material which he discusses is thus constrained into a particular line of argument, not necessarily acceptable to the sociologist *per se.* His work, like Spengler's, is a philosophy of history. It is in the same spectrum of thought as that of the philosopher R. G. Collingwood, as argued in his treatise *The Idea of History* (1936).

This view of history contrasts sharply with what Toynbee calls the antinomianism of historians, and to be sure many historians disdain to take part in this kind of intellectual analysis; but it is of the essence of sociology to compare and to generalise, even if today most sociologists are chary of predicting, seeing prediction as little different from prophecy. Foremost among the critics of such philosophies of history is Sir Karl R. Popper whose analysis of what he calls "pro-naturalistic" theories of historicism includes trenchant attacks on the linear progressivist and evolutionary writings of the last century, but also a more restrained but derogatory analysis of Toynbee's work.[1] Linear theories are easily dealt with in so far as they aim to put forward a theory of social change in terms of progress, for necessarily based on world history they generalise about one particular instance. Cyclical theories, formed from an analysis of several cultures or civilisations, are less easily disposed of; but essentially Popper argues that today social change depends upon the development of science, and as science is essentially unpredictable, then so is the course of future events. His view is a popular one among sociologists, most of whom appear to favour an atomistic approach to the subject and to match the antinomianism of the historians by being anti-historical in their sociological writings. But one of the main factors has been the concentration of the sociologist's attention on more manageable topics for study. The intellectual climate of the modern university is not congenial to broad and philosophical thought, and to engage in this for a lifetime can soon lead to isolation in the academic community. Such was largely the fate of Pitirim Sorokin. For whilst Spengler was a German schoolmaster writing in a congenial philosophical environment, and Toynbee a classicist and historian writing in an English environment where historical studies enjoy high prestige and where still he is regarded as a kind of historian by most academics, Sorokin was a professor of sociology in St. Petersburg and later, after the Russian revolution, in America for a short time at the University of Minnesota and later for most of his life at Harvard. In this empirical and unphilosophical academic environment he became gradually separated from the mainstream of sociological research. Indeed, he had to witness sociology developing in Harvard quite

[1] "The Poverty of Historicism", *Economica* (1944–45) republished as *The Poverty of Historicism* (1957).

separately and outside his own department and himself denied, until in advanced age, the presidential chair of the American Sociological Association. His work, massive and erudite, and one of the great achievements in the history of sociology, lies comparatively neglected. Occasional lip-service may be paid to its erudite qualities and the complexity of its analysis, but it is seldom referred to by other writers; indeed, one recent *Reader* on social change contains no mention of his work.[1]

PITIRIM S. SOROKIN (1889–1968)

Although his ideas about social and cultural change have been expressed in various writings throughout his life the definitive statement of them is to be found in his major work *Social and Cultural Dynamics* (1937–1941). Sorokin sees the task of the sociologist to be mainly that of discerning different kinds of *social systems* and analysing them, but he also is aware of *cultural systems* and indeed of *cultural super-systems*. Thus whilst one may describe and compare, for instance, organised groups like a trade union or a professional association or an institution like a university or a church, both these kinds of phenomena are social systems. A cultural system in his usage is the sum total of that which is created or modified by the activity, conscious or unconscious, of a plurality of individuals interacting with each other and conditioning one another's behaviour.[2] This is a very broad definition and is similar to the broad and general use of the word by American cultural anthropologists. It would seem that a cultural system is any consistent system of meanings, a philosophy, a religion, a science, an epic poem or a symphony. However, one of the important points in Sorokin's discussion is that social systems cannot be properly regarded as integrated; they may be, but frequently they contain elements which are not. Thus he makes use of the term *congery* to indicate that there are other elements. This is especially true of cultural systems and most particularly of cultural super-systems. Elements may therefore form a congery by virtue of spatial or mechanical adjacency, as often happens in

[1] A. & E. Etzioni, *Social Change; Sources, Patterns and Consequences* (1964).
[2] *Op. cit.* (1937), Vol. 1, p. 3.

architectural styles, or by indirect association through a common external factor, as when an arctic people make use of snow shoes, large heating stoves, felt boots and so forth, because of the intense cold; here the various items could be replaced by others without necessarily forming or reforming a system—they are a congery. Sorokin allows that cultural items may be causally or functionally related, although in varying degrees, and beyond this the items may, he argues, be integrated in a logico-meaningful manner; in other words the elements are so well integrated that we say they constitute a harmonious or consistent whole, e.g. a Bach cantata, a Rembrandt painting, or Chartres Cathedral. The recognition by Sorokin that human cultures are not tidy means that it is less easy for him to say something general about them than it is for a Spengler or a Toynbee, but he does provide some categories for this purpose.

Systems, says Sorokin, may be categorised broadly as *sensate, ideational* and *idealistic*. The ground for this classification is provided in his argument that there is a type of reality which is apprehended as true by the people who share a culture. In other words Sorokin anchors his classification in people's beliefs. The term *belief* is included in *knowledge*, for at the roots of all knowledge there are beliefs and it is the major premise that is the key to the identification of a culture. For him the keys are to be found in faith, reason, the senses, and in mixtures of these. His analysis of various types is complex and subtle, for he considers, for example, the ideational culture under the sub-categories of ascetic and active, and the sensate under the sub-categories of active, passive and cynical, but these do not exhaust the categories and accordingly Sorokin allows for mixed types of mentality and culture. This classification of cultures is justified by an analysis of a very large amount of data which is annotated in the first three volumes of this work. His analyses cover art history, philosophies, wars and revolutions and many other features of social history which may be used as indices of the perception of reality.

Sorokin's analysis aims to answer certain questions about cultural systems. How does a culture change? What spatial and temporal uniformities may be detected? What rhythms and periodicities do cultures manifest? Why do cultures change? Why are there rhythms and periodicities? Why are there fluctuations and trends and cycles? But his main point is to score the super-rhythms, the movements from ideational to idealistic to sensate, and to indicate the overall uniformity: crisis-catharsis-charisma-resurrection. Perhaps the main impression to be gleaned from a perusal of this work is Sorokin's sense of the complexity of cultures. He is less willing than Spengler and Toynbee to be assured about the existence of clear principles governing the formation and change of cultures, but he does claim to have picked out some significant features, to have shown how certain themes dominate and above all to confirm the view of these other writers that cyclical patterns may be discerned and traced in some detail. Sorokin himself has criticised the views of Spengler and Toynbee in his *Sociological Theories of Today* (1966), and in the same work defended his own views against his critics.

Other Writers on Social Change

Brief mention must be made of the work of the distinguished American anthropologist, A. L. Kroeber (1876–1960), who carried out an investigation of the manner in which high cultures change. He not only denied the validity of monocausal theories of change, but in fact was reluctant to generalise at all. His work, *Configurations of Cultural Growth* (1944), is therefore largely descriptive and analytical. Alfred Weber (1868–1958) in Germany in his great work *Kulturgeschichte als Kultursoziologie* (1935) argued that the sociologist must attempt to grasp the historical process in its wholeness so as to be able to say something about the nature and destiny of man. There are distinguishable processes—some are social, others civilisational and others cultural. Man's will brings about changes in the social structure, but these are themselves influenced by cultural factors as well as by the constraints imposed by the civilisation which is a product of his endeavours. Mainly these are technical but not entirely. Civilisation is a progressive matter and the achievements are cumulative. Culture is creative and hence contains the unique, not easily replicated without loss or transformation. Moreover, periods of creativity may alternate with periods of sterility; assuredly, he asserted, there is no inevitability and hence no set of general laws governing cultural change.

Among other writers on macrosociology of social change are F. Stuart Chapin (b. 1888) who wrote a book *Cultural Change* (1928). Similar in outlook is the work of W. F. Ogburn (1886–1959) entitled *Social Change* (1922), in which the material culture of a society is distinguished from the socio-cultural aspects, with a discussion of the discrepancies between the rates of development of the two. Material culture is advanced, non-material culture lags behind; hence the description of Ogburn's view as the *Cultural-Lag Theory*, a view partly reminiscent of Alfred Weber; but compared with the latter's and also Sorokin's, the analyses of these two writers are much less subtle and the range of data they consider is much narrower and altogether slighter. On the whole the contributions made at the macrosociological level of social change, or at least the most impressive ones, have been by writers of the past or by men now in advanced old age. The subject still excites interest, but not in the same way; nor does it appear that there are authors capable of comprehending the enormous mass of data that a Toynbee, a Sorokin or a Weber spent their lives in mastering. One recent attempt to provide a theory from the social behaviourist standpoint is that of D. Martindale, whose *Social Life and Cultural Change* (1962) involves five major case studies drawn from the period 900–200 B.C., in ancient China, India, Israel and Greece, and the Modern West. Social change theory today is rather the subject for the essay, sometimes elegant and thoughtful, examples being G. and M. Wilson's *The Analysis of Social Change* (1945), and W. E. Moore's *Social Change* (1963); also M. Ginsberg's (1958) Herbert Spencer lecture published in *Essays in Sociology and Social Philosophy*, Vol. III (1961). Other essays may be found in *Explorations in Social Change* (1964) edited by G. K. Zollschan and W. Hirsch.

II: SOCIOLOGICAL THEORY

The late C. Wright Mills maintained that for the working social scientist neither method nor theory is an autonomous domain. He went on to point out, quite rightly, that method is related to a range of problems. Theories, he said, are like "the language of the country you live in: having the ability to speak the language is nothing to brag about, but it is a disgrace, as well as an inconvenience, if you cannot speak it".[1] Yet whilst this is true it is also the case that during the past twenty years there have been developments in the way sociologists envisage their task which stem from the theoretical reflections of a few of their number. In this section, accordingly, we shall briefly consider some of the more influential writings on sociological theory.

The main impact of social anthropology on the development of sociological research in both Britain and America, which we referred to in Chapter XI, was reflected in the orientation provided by Malinowski and Radcliffe-Brown, and is loosely referred to as *functionalism.* Very largely through the writings of Talcott Parsons this has come to be a major feature in sociological discussion, but it is largely an Anglo-American product, for Parsons was introduced to this orientation by Malinowski at the London School of Economics, whilst Radcliffe-Brown,[2] the English social anthropologist, exerted some considerable influence in Chicago on some American scholars. With inspiration from Pareto and other sources, L. J. Henderson led a discussion of systems in equilibrium at Harvard in a seminar attended, among others, by G. C. Homans and Talcott Parsons. Through these channels and many others there developed a new interest in systematic sociology: an interest that has grown and has come to dominate the sociological scene but which has also given rise to opposition as it moved from being a challenge to orthodoxy to becoming an orthodoxy itself.

The origins of functionalism lie in the works of both Spencer and Durkheim, even if its latest and most powerful protagonists are Parsons and Kingsley Davis. Parsons is also to some extent the historian of this line of thought. This may be seen in his *Structure of Social Action*, which was first published in 1937. Although

[1] "On Intellectual Craftsmanship", *Symposium on Sociological Theory*, edit. Llewellyn Gross (1959), pp. 24–26.

[2] See his posthumous work reconstructed from lectures given in seminars at the University of Chicago: *A Natural Science of Society* (1957), and also an article published at the time "On the Concept of Function in Social Science", *American Anthropologist*, 1935, pp. 394–397.

neglected at the time, it was reprinted in 1949, by which date it was having a considerable impact on some leading sociologists such as R. K. Merton[1] and Marion Levy[2] in America, and on others, e.g. trans-Atlantic like E. A. Shils, or English like W. J. H. Sprott.[3] Principally, of course, this work was a means of focusing interest again on social theory, in the attempt to present "a single body of systematic theoretical reasoning the development of which can be traced through a critical analysis of the writings of this group";[4] "this group" consisted of the nineteenth-century English economist Alfred Marshall, together with Emile Durkheim, Max Weber, and Vilfredo Pareto. His was an attempt to show that in fact these writers in their several ways had all been advancing contributions resting on a common basis, contributions to a theory of social action. Parsons' argument is anti-positivist in outlook and unifying in aim. But what eventually emerged in Parsons' thought was an affirmation of the functional view of Radcliffe-Brown, variously represented in British and American anthropology, not the least, and perhaps not obviously, by such an influential writer as Ruth Benedict in her own country. His exposition, denoted by the term *structural-functional analysis*, was given widespread attention through the publication of his articles in *Essays in Sociological Theory: Pure and Applied* (1949), Revised Edition 1954 especially chapter XI; and more especially in his later work *The Social System* (1951). In his earlier work Parsons had identified the principal sociological problem as the same as Hobbes; it was the problem of social order. How is order maintained? Clearly the Spencerian answer left something to be desired (Durkheim had done much to demolish it), but Parsons thought that in studying the individual unit act the basis could be laid for the study of the integrative function of the system of common values. In his later work, *The Social System*, this was followed up by an analysis of institutionalised forms of behaviour, which necessitated a study of social systems and their

[1] See his *Social Theory and Social Structure* (1951 rev. edn. 1957).

[2] See his *The Structure of Society* (1952) for an attempt to analyse modern complex society in functional form.

[3] See his review of the reprint of Parsons' *Structure of Social Action* in the *British Journal of Sociology*, Vol. 1, 1950, also his Mason Lectures *Science and Social Action* (1954).

[4] *Op. cit.*, p. v.

interpenetration by personality and cultural systems. This was sociology on a grand scale again and it has proved to be a significant contribution of macrosociology. One strand in this fabric is the consequence of the development of systematic analysis in economic thought. Not for nothing was Parsons interested in the economist Marshall, for it may be noted he had begun his academic career as an instructor in economics.

Parsons' work, despite the many criticisms that are levelled against it, has one great virtue. It initiated a period in sociological thought when sociological theory was no longer beholden to philosophy; it ushered in an era when social thought was formulated in terms of the ideas of the social sciences, not any longer of physics or biology; this has been recognised by D. Martindale, himself a severe critic of Parsons.[1] Martindale harps on the organismic origins of functionalism, but the fact is that now sociological theory is seen to stand on its own feet. Organisms are but one kind of system, social systems are of a different kind, but there are as many kinds as there are social units. At the macro level we may discern a total social system of social institutions, which is what Parsons is mainly interested in, and in this he is following the British anthropological tradition, but there are systems of roles and social positions which may reasonably be called social organisations; these we shall have more to say about in the next chapter. How far it is fruitful to speak of modern nation-states as systems of institutions is debatable, and especially when it comes to describing their integrative qualities in terms of a common value system. To avoid some of these difficulties Parsons has analysed both personality systems and cultural systems in conjunction with his analysis of social systems. Thus in seeking to describe social action the orientation of the behaving person is seen to be twofold, both *motivational* and in terms of *values*. The former orientation has a number of aspects: *cognitive* (how the person perceives his situation), *cathectic* (the process of investing objects with emotional significance) and *evaluative* (a process of putting things in a preference order). The second orientation similarly has three aspects: *cognitive*, *appreciative* and *moral*. In the process of working out his scheme of thought Parsons,

[1] *The Nature and Types of Sociological Theory* (1961), p. 449.

in conjunction with E. A. Shils,[1] set out a scheme of *pattern variables*. These represent alternative types of choices. They are dichotomies; one side must be chosen before the meaning of a situation is determinate for the actor and before he can act with respect to that situation. Originally, Parsons and Shils indicated the existence of five basic pattern variables. *Universalism* and *particularism* are the names of one. In other words, any individual in a situation requiring choice in his relationship with others will act in terms of either a universally accepted precept or one particular to the situation in which he finds himself. Is he going to act according to rule or in terms of the particular qualities of the person towards whom he is orienting his action? Another set is termed *achievement* and *ascription* (sometimes referred to as *performance* and *quality*). Here a person in deciding how to act focuses his attention on either the achieved aspects of the other person, e.g. his professional status, or else his ascribed qualities, e.g. his sex, age, social class. The third set of pattern variables is called *affectivity* and *affective-neutrality* and represents the difference in choice between a person seeking immediate satisfaction and his postponement or abandonment of it in terms of long range goals, or at least some other goals, perhaps of a moral kind but equally well ones which are merely expediential. Yet another set is known as *specificity* and *diffuseness*, and here the choice takes into account limited and specific factors, e.g. the contrast between a contract entered into, and wider diffuse obligations such as family loyalty. Finally, there is another pattern variable, *self-orientation* and *collectivity-orientation*, i.e. the choice is made either in terms of the individual's own interests or his perception of the needs of the community.

The point of this scheme is to enable the sociologist to identify the typical choices made, especially of an institutionalised kind, to distinguish, as Weber would have said, for example, different types of justice, a rational-legal type from a Kadi-type, or as a modern political scientist has argued, to distinguish different styles of politics.[2] Parsons has applied his analysis to the medical

[1] *Toward a General Theory of Action* (1951); see also T. Parsons, R. F. Bales and E. A. Shils, *Working Papers in The Theory of Action* (1953).

[2] H. V. Wiseman, *Political Systems* (1966).

profession, but it could well be applied to distinguish essential features of high cultures as indeed he indicates. Other writers have endeavoured to elaborate the scheme. Thus S. M. Lipset in *The First New Nation* (1964) has added two more pattern variables: *instrumental* and *consummatory*, indicating a choice between focusing either on means or on ends, and *egalitarian* and *elitist* where the former stresses respect for persons as such and the latter focuses on position, be it achieved or ascribed. Pattern variable analysis may be used to identify similarities and differences between cultures, or it may be used in more restricted manner to refer to aspects of a society, to subsystems of an institutional kind, such as political systems, or even to particular groups and organisations.

The debate about functionalism continues and appears to be resolving itself into a contrast of two major orientations as *functional* theories are contrasted to *conflict* theories. Certainly, there are wide variations in opinion. At one extreme there is the view expressed by Kingsley Davis in his presidential address to the American Sociological Association in 1959, that functionalism is now coterminous with sociological analysis.[1] At the other extreme there are assertions that functionalism is giving sociology a static orientation, that it distorts and misleads. Trenchant criticisms have been made by the English sociologist David Lockwood,[2] by the German sociologist Ralf Dahrendorf,[3] and by many American writers notably Clifford Geertz.[4] Restatements of functionalism have been made by Ernest Nagel[5] and Dorothy Emmet,[6] and the argument that it fails to account for social change has been strongly opposed by Francesca Cancian.[7] Supportive

[1] "The Myth of Functional Analysis as a Special Method in Sociology and Anthropology", *American Sociological Review*, Vol. XXIV, 1959.

[2] "Some remarks on *The Social System*", *British Journal of Sociology*, Vol. 7, 1956.

[3] "Struktur und Function", *Kölner Zeitschrift für Soziologie und Sozialpsychologie*, Vol. 7, 1955, and "Out of Utopia", *American Journal of Sociology*, Vol. LXIV, 1958.

[4] "Ritual and Social Change", *American Anthropologist*, Vol. XIX, 1957.

[5] *Logic without Metaphysics* (1956).

[6] *Function, Purpose and Powers* (1958).

[7] "Functional Analysis of Change", *American Sociological Review*, Vol. XXV, 1960.

contributions to the debate have been made by S. W. Gouldner[1] and by C. G. Hempel.[2]

In contrast to functionalism we may note the development in the past fifteen years of what might be called a neo-Marxist approach to sociological problems. Essentially this is a view that stresses the political commitment of the sociologist, and perhaps its most colourful exponent was C. Wright Mills (1916–1962), but there are today a number of political sociologists who exert considerable influence, among them being S. M. Lipset who is probably the most prominent of the scholars in this field. In Germany, Dahrendorf[3] and Carl Brinkman[4] have argued the case in terms of conflict. In America Lewis Coser has endeavoured to provide a theory of social conflict.[5] In Britain Max Gluckman, from a more social anthropological angle, has contributed to the subject. However, the Marxist inspired approach appears perhaps more strongly in connection with studies of the stratified nature of modern society. Here is a field in which a great deal of sociological research has been carried out since the Second World War. Let us merely mention in passing the work of David Glass and his team at the London School of Economics, which concentrated on studies of social mobility,[6] and the work of S. M. Lipset and R. Bendix[7] in America in analysing the class structure of modern western societies, estimating the degree of social mobility they display, and of course the work of Dahrendorf himself.[8]

We have described this growth of interest in sociological theory as a matter of orientation, and so it is, for it is becoming apparent that a major task of sociology is a discussion as to what its role is. This might be a cause for merriment among some, but the problem is a profound one, profounder than many sociologists

[1] "Reciprocity and Autonomy in Functional Theory", *Symposium on Sociological Theory*, ed. Llewellyn Gross (1959).
[2] "The Logic of Functional Analysis", *Ibid.*
[3] "Toward a Theory of Social Conflict", *The Journal of Conflict Resolution*, Vol. XI, 1958.
[4] *Soziologische Theorie der Revolution* (1948).
[5] *The Functions of Social Conflict* (1956).
[6] *Social Mobility in Britain* (1954).
[7] *Social Mobility in Industrial Society* (1959).
[8] *Soziale Klassen und Klassenkonflikt in der Industrielengesellschaft* (1957), revised, enlarged and translated; *Class and Class Conflicts in Industrial Society*, (1959).

are willing to admit. If for some the issue is between a functionalist type of approach, with consensus as its principal topic of interest, and another which sees conflict and change as central, there are others who perceive the issue to be between a sociology that is purely instrumental and a sociology which is encyclopaedic, encyclopaedic not in the sense of trying to embrace all social sciences, but in the sense that there is a task of understanding our own and other societies arising from comparative studies, in which for this to be successful broad but precise categories of thought have to be forged, in which a scheme whereby comparisons can be made has to be worked out and tested and repeatedly revised. Inherent in all this is a fundamental problem of method, for this process leads to ever more general theories, more or less of the kind Parsons has tried to advance. In reflecting on this problem, the very distinguished French sociologist, Raymond Aron, says "By a curious paradox, it seems that the more such general theories of society try to be scientific, the less they become so. Let us take an example. When we consider an interpretation of societies which begins with the economic system, it may be accepted so far as it claims only to be one among other possible interpretations. It is one way of looking at events. On the other hand, if it tries to reduce everything to economic phenomena, and declares itself scientific on those grounds, it ceases to be scientific because it then imposes on social reality a simplified structure which it does not possess. In so far as such theories are regarded as limited in scope, they are scientific. In so far as they claim to present an exact, authentic and universally valid reproduction of social structures they cease to be scientific."[1] Here is a theoretical problem for the sociologist. It has been brought to our notice again by Aron. Essentially, it is the problem of deciding if sociology is relativistic or capable of providing ultimately a universal system, or perhaps, as Aron believes, if there is a way of avoiding both positions without abandoning the problem. In short, development in sociological theory is not merely a matter of conceptual refinement but a matter of thinking through some fundamental philosophical problems *which the sociological task itself has produced.* Herein is to be found also the locus of that gamut of problems

[1] *Eighteen Lectures on Industrial Society* (1961, trans. 1967), p. 27.

which forms the sociology of knowledge,[1] and which is concerned with the place of values in sociological discussion, a subject of central concern to Weber[2] as it has become for Aron; but to pursue this subject further would be to write another book.

This excursion into sociological theory does not, of course, cover the whole ground; this has not been our intention. Rather it has indicated, we hope, the nature of modern macrosociological discussion at the theoretical level. For surveys of modern sociological theories the reader should turn to a book like *Modern Social Theories* (1961), by C. P. and Z. K. Loomis, or the writings of Sorokin (1966) and Timasheff (1967), already mentioned. Suffice it to say that discussion of sociological theory is increasing, but is being carried on by people who have been deeply involved in empirical social research. To this extent the speculative and empirical traditions have come closer together.

III: SOCIAL INSTITUTIONS

In Chapter III we pointed out that as early as the beginning of the second half of the nineteenth century there was a convergence of thought among a number of sociologists both in Britain and France, noticeably Spencer and Durkheim, that led to their focusing attention on the Great Society, as Graham Wallas was to call it, or in other words there was a tendency to see the task of the sociologist to be less a matter of spelling out the chronology of social evolution than of describing the significant features of the emerging capitalist society, as it was known in England and later in Germany and America: a society that was industrial and urban and complex in both these respects; a society that could be contrasted to the simple, non-literate or primitive society of the Dark Continent or of the Isles of the Pacific. Partly, this was still tied to a propensity to analyse the nature of social change, but increasingly it came to be seen that description and analysis of

[1] For a survey of this field see W. Stark, *The Sociology of Knowledge* (1958). The principal contributions to the subject during this century include K. Mannheim's *Ideology and Utopia* (trans. 1936) and his *Essays on the Sociology of Knowledge* (1952). See also D. G. MacRae, *Ideology and Society* (1962).

[2] *Methodology in the Social Sciences* (articles orginally published in the *Archiv für Sozialwissenschaft und Sozialpolitik*, and translated by E. A. Shils, 1949).

the emerging society was *de rigueur* for the sociologist. Without acknowledgement, it was Comtean statics that began to prevail. If it did so chiefly in the work of Durkheim and Weber, towards the end of the nineteenth century, this is merely to say why these two sociologists held, and still hold, the key to the development of sociological studies. Let us consider how this approach to the subject has been taken up by the post-World War II students of society.

The classical writers, before Weber and Durkheim, to sound the first notes of this theme were Comte, de Tocqueville and Marx, but of these it was Marx's influence which played the leading part. It was his work which chiefly attracted the attention of Max Weber and, of course, it was his writings which helped form the core of the official ideology of the communist powers in Eastern Europe, an ideology which inevitably influenced sociological thought. The modern sociologist, unless he be very parochial in outlook and interests, is inevitably drawn into making comparisons, not so much today between the primitive and the industrial societies, as between the great industrial powers, especially America and Soviet Russia. Moreover, those historians who have the closest affinity to the sociological outlook, namely the economic historians, have naturally emphasised the economic basis of modern society. Hence, in the stream of work that has poured from their pens, from Werner Sombert's *Der Moderne Kapitalismus* (1916–1917) to R. H. Tawney's *Religion and the Rise of Capitalism* (1926), to name but two classics and to say nothing of subsequent works, there have been powerful currents guiding the sociological imagination. If perhaps some writers, on the fringe of sociology proper, have dominated this field, this has not detracted from the propensity of sociologists to see modern society as a capitalist social structure changing into something else which, albeit with qualifications, is perceived to be socialist. Such has been the case with Joseph Schumpeter, whose book, *Capitalism, Socialism and Democracy* (1943, revised 1947) has, of its kind, proved to be one of the important works of this century.

Raymond Aron, however, has pointed out that there has been a recrudescence of an earlier practice in recent years which has tended to replace the dominance of the concept of *capitalism*, and this reflects a willingness to think, both politically and sociologically, of *industrial* societies (a term used by Spencer), before the Marxian thesis gained its hold in this discussion. Aron, himself, rather more influenced by the Saint-Simonians and by de Tocqueville, prefers this approach. This latest fashion is not unconnected with the easing of the international situation and the decline in intensity of the cold war. He warns against certain dangers in using the expression, for no one nation-state is *the* industrial society; rather we should speak of an *industrial type* of society. It is Aron's aim, among other things, to dispel the myth, as he calls it, that capitalism necessarily evolves into socialism on the Soviet model; indeed, he is concerned to discuss the different forms industrial development may take.[1]

A different approach to the study of modern society relies, by contrast, on the study of the kind of society which preceded it; in a way this is the tradition of Max Weber and Edward Westermarck arguing the case for recognising the significance of the past for interpreting the present. Thus Peter Laslett's *The World we have lost* (1965) urges an approach largely through history and demography. Laslett displays an antipathy to monocausal theories and his approach is a nice blend of an appreciation of demographic facts and the coherence of a system of values. His work reflects the growing tradition in Britain for economic and social historical studies, about which Laslett together with D. E. C. Eversley and W. A. Armstrong have written in the book edited by E. A. Wrigley, *An Introduction to English Historical Demography* (1966), which is the first of a number of publications planned by the Cambridge Group for the History of Population and Social Structure. What is of particular interest about this group of writers is their attempt to subject the historical records which are available to us to the methods of statistical analysis. This, until very recently, has been an unexplored avenue of historical research. Here a sociological approach meets the historical interest in a fruitful manner. It should be noted that an implication of Laslett's work is that the comparative study of the social institutions of simple societies need not be restricted to a single time dimension or to the study of those societies which possess no records. We are obtaining

[1] *Op. cit.* (1961, trans. 1967), p. 5.

today a much clearer picture of social life in the relatively undifferentiated and simple society of the past. Indeed, archaeological anthropology has much more to offer than an earlier generation thought possible, and here is an important growing point in macrosociology, especially in the U.S.A.

Among macrosociological studies are those of societies other than the modern West. Karl Wittfogel's monumental work *Oriental Despotism* (1957) takes its point of departure from Weber's work and examines the nature of the social structures in river valley civilisations making use of water power on a large scale for irrigation or communication. It discusses the nature of the social organisation required to control and utilise large numbers of labourers, the institution of slavery often connected with it, and the consequences of such administrative structures for other aspects of the society, especially political structures.

Again, there have also been studies of feudal societies of the kind from which the modern West has emerged. Thus Marc Bloch's two volume study *La société féodale*: Vol. I, *la formation de dépendence* (1939), Vol. II, *les classes et le gouvernement des hommes* (1940), translated *Feudal Society* (1961) may be regarded as a prominent example. Similarly, there have been studies of societies which emerged with the rise of capitalist enterprise, but where the dominant institution was slavery. Thus the southern states of America have provided a rich field for the historical sociologist and among the studies of note we may mention S. M. Elkin's *Slavery: A Problem in American Institutional and Intellectual Life* (1959), and from a different approach W. J. Cash's *The Mind of the South* (1941). These two works do not, of course, exhaust the field, but they may be taken as being roughly representative of it.

The period since the Second World War has been one of unprecedented growth in sociological teaching and research and there has, as might be expected, been a developing division of labour. Thus, whilst it is true that generally interest is concentrated on the nature of the industrial society and its recent development, it is also true that the study of it has been much more piecemeal than hitherto. Emphasis has perhaps been on some aspects rather more than on others, but an examination of a selection among the scores of introductory textbooks on sociology published in the past twenty years immediately shows how the subject is in fact considered. Usually there is a section on social stratification, often somewhat untidy in treatment because it is not very clear where the boundaries lie, whether, for example, ethnic and colour differences should be considered a part of social stratification. There is usually a section on the family and perhaps also the institution of marriage; there is a section on political structures, although much of this is usually left to the political scientist to develop; there is usually a section on religion and on other aspects of the society which are perceived to be related to the problem of social control, e.g. the institution of law, public opinion forming agencies such as the press and radio, and educational institutions. Finally, we should mention that much interest is taken by sociologists in the growth of cities so that urban sociology has also become a major part of the organised activities of academic sociologists, sometimes incorporating rural studies too, but latterly developing a line of thought and activity known as *social area analysis*. In the rest of this chapter we shall briefly outline what seem to us to be the main developments in these various fields, which collectively may be described as the study of social institutions.

Social Stratification

It must not be supposed that interest in this field is new. John Millar, the Scottish professor of Laws, wrote *On the Origin of the Distinction of Ranks* as early as 1771, but the modern inspiration stems largely from Marx and Weber on the one hand and from what one might call the deliberate ignoring of that tradition by some people in the U.S.A. Thus whilst there have been those to point to the importance of economic determinants of social positions, and especially to see and to discuss the barriers between ethnic groups and most particularly between white and coloured people in America and South Africa, more or less in Marxist categories, there have been those who have taken a different approach to the topic; these fall into two groups. Firstly, there is Kingsley Davis, and those who think like him, who have supported a functionalist view of social stratification[1]; a view that has strong support and has initiated fruitful discussion of the subject. Secondly, there are those, notably W. Lloyd Warner, who represent the curious reaction of Americans to the notion of a class-structured society. Warner's work has consisted of analysing the nature of status distribution in America, blandly ignoring the difficult but pertinent problems raised by the Marxist approach. Whilst recognising differences, he has pointed to their outward expression rather than to the society in which such differences are embedded. His is an avowedly anthropological approach of a type which is quite untheoretical and which is concerned only with the task of observation and recording in convenient categories.[2] Davis fired his shots in the mid-1940s and Warner carried out his immense labours about the same time. Yet his *Yankee City Series*, which we referred to in Chapter XII, appears to bear no relationship at all to the work of Marx and Weber on the one hand or to Davis and Moore on the other. In the event, Warner's work, impressive though it be, has not proved to be a growing point, and his work is no longer of much interest to the present generation of sociologists. But between the theorists the battle continues. Yet, having criticised those who fail to appreciate the importance of locating the sources of power, especially economic power, let it be said that there is a growing awareness that *class* as a concept is less useful than the concept of *élite* and that, by the same token, some considerable value attaches to the notion of local status groups. The situation in the advanced industrial society where there are large numbers of people on the margin, both above and below, the middle class renders this kind of analysis less and less useful. In the small community the status group is important, whereas in the large-scale society the study of the élite is of paramount importance for an understanding of the springs of action and the seat of authority.

On the empirical level a number of interesting studies have been carried out in Britain and Germany and some comparisons made between America and Europe. Thus there have been studies

[1] *Op. cit.* (1959). See also K. Davis and W. E. Moore "Some Principles of Stratification", *American Sociological Review*, Vol. X, 1945.
[2] *Social Class in America* (1949).

of social mobility (a term first used by Sorokin)[1] carried out in both Britain and the U.S.A., where the index of mobility has been based on a grading of occupations.[2] Lipset and Ramsøy have pointed out that, contrary to popular opinion, there is no great difference in social mobility between America and European countries;[3] this theme runs through the work of Lipset and Bendix and has already been referred to. Another type of study has shown that the theory of "embourgeoisement" of the working classes, whereby it is thought that with increasing real wages, and the material comforts these bring, the manual workers are adopting middle class views and especially political views, is ill-founded; this is the burden of the work of J. H. Goldthorpe and D. Lockwood in England.[4] There have been many studies of class attitudes and values; to mention a few we may cite those of H. H. Hyman,[5] Ely Chinoy,[6] and S. M. Miller[7] all reproduced in P. I. Rose's *The Study of Society* (1967).

There are many other studies of social stratification but we shall refer to some of them in considering the other main institutional aspects of modern society, for social stratification is generally a pervasive feature of industrial types of society. This will become immediately apparent as we turn to the development of political sociology.

The Sociology of Politics

Immediately after the Second World War the interest that had been stimulated by studies of the stratified character of society led to questions being asked about how people in different social

[1] *Social Mobility* (1927).

[2] J. Hall and D. Caradog Jones "The Social Grading of Occupations", *British Journal of Sociology*, Vol. 1, 1950, and A. Inkeles and P. Rossi "National Comparisons of Occupational Prestige", *American Journal of Sociology*, Vol. 61, 1956.

[3] "Class and Opportunity in Europe and the U.S.", *Commentary*, Vol. 18, 1954.

[4] "Affluence and the British Class Structure", *Sociological Review*, Vol. 2, 1963.

[5] "The Value Systems of Different Classes", *Class, Status and Power* (1953), edd. R. Bendix and S. M. Lipset.

[6] *Automobile Workers and the American Dream* (1955).

[7] "The Outlook of Working-Class Youth", *Blue Collar World: Studies of the American Worker* (1964), edd. A. P. Shostak and W. Goldberg.

classes vote in elections. In Britain this was set off by the landslide Labour victory in the 1944 election, but in America it was stimulated by the loss of power by the Democratic Party after having had many years in office; but in both cases it was the growth of public opinion polls which stimulated interest. Thus in Britain a study was carried out of electoral behaviour in the Borough of Greenwich near London.[1] This followed an examination by J. Bonham of the way in which middle class people vote.[2] There were two aspects of this general development: on the one hand there was an attempt to say something more precise about political values and attitudes, to find out precisely who held what views, and on the other hand there was an interest in the mechanics of voting behaviour. In America great interest was also displayed in the location of power, especially political power. A scheme for this kind of study had already been provided by Goldhamer and Shils[3] but more concrete studies were carried out by C. W. Mills,[4] and by a group of political scientists interested in sociological ideas.[5]

The gradual dissolution of the British Empire and the development of the Commonwealth, entailing the granting of independence to many and varied peoples in the Sub-Continent of India, Africa and the Far East, led to a development of studies of underdeveloped countries. These were not merely political, but extended to studies of urban life and the migration of people from the rural hinterland to cities, the process of incipient industrialisation, the problems which arose as a result of changes from traditional forms of life and social control to new ways. Thus, David Apter, making use of a functionalist orientation, made a study of the old Gold Coast, or the Republic of Ghana as it became.[6] G. Wilson[7]

[1] M. Benney, A. P. Gray and R. H. Pear, *How People Vote: A Study of Electoral Behaviour in Greenwich* (1956).

[2] *The Middle-Class Vote* (1954), Cf. P. K. Hastings, "The Voter and the Non-Voter", *American Journal of Sociology*, Vol. 62, 1956.

[3] "Types of Power and Status", *American Journal of Sociology*, Vol. 45, 1939–40.

[4] *The New Men of Power* (1948). *The Power Elite* (1956).

[5] H. D. Lasswell, D. Lerner and L. E. Rothwell, *The Comparative Study of Elites: An Introduction and a Bibliography* (1952). See also H. D. Lasswell, *Power and Personality* (1948), V. O. Key, *Politics, Parties and Pressure Groups* (1947).

[6] *The Gold Coast in Transition* (1956).

[7] *An Essay on the Economics of Detribalisation in Northern Rhodesia* (Rhodes-Livingstone Paper No. 5, 1941).

and W. F. Wertheim[1] have written on aspects of this subject on the basis of empirical studies in Africa and Indonesia respectively, and there is also the famous work by Margaret Mead, *Cultural Patterns and Technical Change* (1953), published under the auspices of U.N.E.S.C.O. and also Clifford Geertz, *Old Societies and New States* (1963). A fair amount of the interest in under-developed countries centred on fertility and mortality rates and their often surprising changes and implications, but it has been the political developments in these countries which have brought political scientists and sociologists together in a common task. Similarly, there is a current interest in revolutions arising from the question: what are the conditions under which democratic societies collapse, for the parliamentary regimes initially set up in many of the new countries have patently failed.

During the post-war period a number of political events have led to minor studies by sociologists. The McCarthy period in the U.S.A. led to some analyses of the situation giving rise to this aberration, the most notable being E. A. Shils' book *The Torment of Secrecy* (1956). Political extremism has always been a feature of political sociology, but the war-time attempts to cope with this problem, which were mainly psychologically and psycho-analytically oriented, such as *The Authoritarian Personality* (1950) by Adorno *et al.*, and latterly in M. Rokeach and his associates' *Open and Closed Mind* (1960), do not appear to have led to any very important developments; criticism was levelled at the F. scale and indeed few books have had so much attention given to them as *The Authoritarian Personality*, but the deficiencies in this kind of analysis do not appear to have been overcome, despite further work in this field, such as that of H. Eysenck reported in his *Psychology of Politics* (1954).

The most notable development in political sociology has been the take over of functional analysis, especially elements of Parsonian theory. Thus a new orientation has been sought for political science, which suffered from the devastating criticisms of political philosophy in T. D. Weldon's book *The Vocabulary of Politics* (1953). The result has been the work of G. A. Almond and J. S. Coleman, *The Politics of the Developing Areas* (1960), which besides

[1] *Indonesian Society in Transition* (1956).

treating comparatively the "dramatic, social and political changes" that have taken place in Asia, Africa and Latin-America, is primarily an attempt to construct a theoretical framework to assist in the comparative analysis of political systems. This notion of political *systems* is the mainspring of the work of David Easton, whose three books[1] progressively develop the same kind of theme. An English treatment of the subject may be found in the work of H. V. Wiseman.[2]

One further development may be mentioned, that of W. Kornhauser, whose book *The Politics of Mass Society* (1959) is prominent in the literature on Mass Society. Kornhauser argues that a mass society "will be vulnerable to political movements destructive of liberal democratic institutions, whilst in so far as a society is *pluralist*, these institutions will be strong".[3] He maintains that the theory of mass society and the theory of social pluralism employ similar categories of analysis, and that therefore they are two statements of a more general theory. More specifically Kornhauser declares: "A society is a 'mass society' to the extent that both élites and non-élites are directly accessible to one another by virtue of the weakness of groups capable of mediating between them"[4] and he concludes that "the theory of mass society stresses the need for autonomy of certain social units if order with freedom is to be secured".[5] We shall say more about the literature on mass society later. Let us turn now to another institutional complex which is a major field of sociological research.

The Family

The family is not strictly speaking an institution, but an organisation; yet it is what people usually think of when discussing in a general manner matters relating to kinship, marriage, divorce, adoption and all the norms which govern parents in raising their children.

In the pre-war period most sociological studies of family relationships were oriented to what, in some quarters, came to be known as social pathology; i.e. abnormal factors. Thus there was

[1] *The Political System* (1953); *A Framework for Political Analysis* (1965): *A Systematic Analysis of Political Life* (1965).
[2] *Op. cit.* [3] *Op. cit.*, p. 7. [4] *Ibid.*, p. 228. [5] *Ibid.*, p. 229.

an interest in poverty and the effects it had on families. Obviously the great depression and the persistent unemployment of the inter-war period had a lot to do with this outlook. But there was also concern about divorce, for it was thought that the family was breaking down, that its stability was being greatly impaired and that, indeed, its future was bleak; that the strains of modern urban society were telling and that the weak spot was family life. In the post-war period, studies of the family were essentially no less problem-centred, but the specific interest in social pathology has somewhat waned; instead, the kind of question that sociologists ask themselves is: How can one study the family in a general way and not just select families which are obviously abnormal? The first answer was to be found, so it seemed, in an appeal to the social anthropologists. Thus the valuable work done on kinship by Radcliffe-Brown and others[1] and the many monographs on non-literate peoples where kinship and family are such important parts of the social fabric appeared to offer a line of development. Raymond Firth and his colleagues in London were among the first to make the attempt to apply the categories of the social anthropologist to the study of family and kinship in the metropolis, and their *Two Studies of Kinship in London* (1956) was the result. This work was followed shortly afterwards by *Family and Kinship in East London* (1957) by M. Young and P. Willmott. It is perhaps not without significance that this was a study of East London families, for the suggestion that they were considered among the more primitive of their English kind is hard to escape. In the event the anthropological approach was disappointing. Perhaps this is not surprising for the structure and functions of the family in modern industrial society are not the same as for those of the family in a non-literate and under-developed rural society. But one advantage did accrue, for it was seen that if there is a break-down in the family, if there are features of family life that leave something to be desired, or if, in short, there are problems connected with the family which are not merely a matter of insufficient income, then other factors in the environment should be examined. The post-war studies that shed light on the family did indeed point to the vicissitudes of slum clearance, and the

[1] "Introduction" in *African Systems of Kinship and Marriage* (1950).

loneliness in new towns and the problems of relations with kinsfolk and neighbours in new housing estates; a subject we shall explore further in the next chapter.

One of the curious facts about people's attitudes to the family is the persistence decade after decade of the view that in times past the family was a much more stable affair, that marriages were more secure and that high levels of moral behaviour between the sexes obtained. The growth of the divorce rate gave strong support to this prejudice, which as O. R. McGregor[1] in Britain and W. J. Goode[2] in America have both pointed out is quite unrealistic; divorce being easier to obtain today than hitherto, and other courses being open to spouses which are not recorded in detail or quantitatively for the past. The influence of this prejudice on sociologists has been persistent, and thus one feature of post-war studies has been a continuing concern with broken families. It has been thought there has been an increase in their number. To some extent war does increase family disruption as women are widowed and children separated from parents, but the problems of families settling down again in the post-war world also excited attention. Was the high divorce rate an indicator of breakdown? It was thought it was and that perhaps this stemmed in part from the depression of the 1930s which it was supposed produced a generation of children maladjusted to family life in industrial society later themselves to found families of their own. This led to a considerable literature on child care, the practices and attitudes of parents towards their children. Notable studies to be mentioned are the popular work of J. Bowlby in Britain[3] and the comparative studies of J. W. M. Whiting and I. L. Child in America.[4] A more recent British study of considerable interest is that of J. and E. Newson,[5] for their investigation makes an analysis of child care practices by social classes, a theme taken up comparatively by J. Klein's *Samples from English Cultures* (1965), Vol. II. To be sure there were family problems, but the most significant fact to emerge from such reflections was the extraordinarily high rate of employment of women, and especially of

[1] *Divorce in England* (1957). [2] *After Divorce* (1956).
[3] *Child Care and the growth of love* (1953).
[4] *Child Training and Personality: A Cross-cultural Study* (1953).
[5] *Infant Care in an Urban Community* (1963).

married women outside the home. The employment of non-married women was not new, although the pattern was, but now married women were working in increasing numbers in factory, workshop, department store and office. It had grown in the war in many countries of the West, but it was also a persistent post-war feature. This led to questions being asked about the structure of the family in terms of the roles played by its members. This was the subject of a very stimulating study, despite its methodological weaknesses, by Elizabeth Bott: *Family and Social Network* (1957). The major study in this field, however, was the important work by T. Parsons and R. F. Bales, *The Family: Socialisation and Interaction Process* (1955), a study that stands out as distinctive in the literature for being clearly concerned to ask theoretical questions about structure and function in terms of roles, although it should be added that much of the work of W. J. Goode[1] also meets this requirement. Thus the recent history of studies of the family may be regarded as a move from the examination of the internal structure to the investigation of the external one; a move to view the family in its setting. But the main difficulty has always been that of getting away from the abnormal. The problem remains of carrying out an empirical study of normal families and especially over the entire range of social classes. If the middle class family resists investigation, how much more the upper?

In Germany after the war there was a strong sociological interest in the family. In many ways it represented a break with an older tradition. In 1912 F. Müller-Lyer had published *Die Familie* (translated 1931), an evolutionary account tracing the development of the family from prehistory to the present; the author's theme was that a sociological law could be discerned, a movement from the biological to the social in family structure and life. It was a work not unrepresentative of the interests of the time, for Helen Bosanquet in England also brought out a book entitled *The Family* (1906) written in much the same manner. But these new post-war German studies looked at the structure of the family and especially at its attitudes. Authoritarian attitudes, generally attributed to German parents, were examined in

[1] See his "Theory of the Family" in R. K. Merton *et al.* eds. *Sociology Today* (1959), and also his book *Die Struktur der Familie* (1960).

the light of studies of evacuated families, of families whose members had been separated and then reunited, of families in a society which had become disillusioned with politics and politicians. Thus G. Würzbacher produced his *Leitbilder Gegenwärtigen Deutschen Familienlebens* (1954). This was soon to be followed by Helmut Schelsky's work, some of it based on researches in Hamburg and the evacuation district around that city, reported in a book entitled *Wandlungen der Deutschen Familie in der Gegenwart* (1955). A year later R. Fröhmer, M. von Stackelberg and W. Eser brought out *Familie und Ehe. Probleme in der deutschen Familien der Gegenwart*. These were not speculative studies like those of Max Horkheimer[1] and Müller-Lyer of the earlier period, although Horkheimer was also interested in authority in the family. These were in the new tradition of post-war empirical studies of the kind which Hilde Thurnwald had initiated with her study of 498 families in Berlin (*Gegenwartsprobleme Berliner Familien*, 1948), but they were all about the contemporary situation and they were all in greater or less degree related to values and attitudes. The ideology had failed, and its failure was one which concerned the family; this at least had some bearing on the older philosophical, if not ideological, tradition.

The literature on the family is immense but the reader who wants to pursue some of the recent work on the sociology of the family should consult the American *Journal of Family and Marriage* and refer to the various readers published in America, among them being: R. N. Anshen (ed.), *The Family: Its Function and Destiny* (1949 revised 1959), R. F. Winch, R. McGinnis and H. R. Barringer, *Selected Studies in Marriage and the Family* (rev. ed. 1963), H. T. Christensen, *Handbook of Marriage and the Family* (1964) and the standard work of N. W. Bell and E. F. Vogel, *The Family* (1960). For a small and refreshing book which endeavours to dispel much of the nonsense talked and written about the family, *The Family and Marriage in Britain* (rev. ed. 1966) by Ronald Fletcher may be commended. Among the historical studies of the family, A. W. Calhoun has written in three volumes *A Social History of the American Family* (1960), and in England there is Margaret Hewitt's study, *Wives and Mothers in Victorian England* (1958).

[1] *Studien über Autorität und Familie* (1935).

Sociology of Religion

Despite its importance the social institution of religion is relatively neglected; at least this is so when compared with the sociological research carried out into social stratification, social organisation in industry and the study of small groups. Most of the work since the Second World War has been done in France, some in Britain, relatively little in America and almost none in Germany. Let us look first at America and Britain.

The great traditions initiated by Max Weber and Ernst Troeltsch into comparative studies in the sociology of religion and the analysis of primitive religion by Émile Durkheim and Marcel Mauss has not been matched in size and scope by anything comparable in America and Britain. To be sure these writers have influenced sociologists very greatly in all countries, and there have been some important contributions to the former of these two traditions such as H. R. Niebuhr's book *The Social Sources of American Denominationalism* (1929), and the theoretical contributions, sparked off by Durkheim, that have been incorporated into textbooks like that of Kingsley Davis entitled *Human Society* (1950), and M. J. Yinger's *Religion, Society and the Individual* (1957); but there have not been significant developments, nor can it be said that between 1940 and 1960 was there a feeling that more should be done. Possibly this is because with increasing industrialisation it was thought at that time that the secular society, which accompanied it, would entail a diminished role for organised religion, and of course the philosophical temper of the social sciences, still mainly utilitarian and positivist, may also have been responsible. But the fact is that religion has not withered away, and even though church attendance may have declined in places, it should be noted that there is a surprisingly high incidence of church attendance and activity in the U.S.A.[1] What has

[1] Only a few studies, and these spasmodically, have been carried out to assess the extent of the erosion of church membership. In Scotland, J. Highet, published some figures in *The Churches of Scotland Today* (1950) and *The Scottish Churches* (1950). In England M. Argyle has some figures on *Religious Behaviour* (1958), and B. Wilson in *Religion in Secular Society* (1967) has an appendix with a few figures, and so has D. Martin in *A Sociology of English Religion* (1967). More general figures are found in G. Naïdendoff, "Panorama statistique des religions contemporaines", *Lumière et Vie* (1953).

attracted some sociologists to the subject has been less this fact than the extraordinary resilience of some of the sects, particularly Pentecostal sects. This has led to further thought about the distinction made by Troeltsch between sects and churches.

In America, the series of minor studies carried out before the war in Chicago, describing some of the Negro migrant religious groups, has not been developed, but there have been studies of Jehovah's Witnesses,[1] the Doukhobors,[2] the Mennonites[3] and the Mormons.[4] In Britain Bryan Wilson made a comparative study of three sects, published as *Sects and Society: A Sociological Study of Three Religious Groups in Britain* (1961). This and the above-mentioned other studies represent a development of the distinction made by Troeltsch, a discussion continued in Wilson's *Religion in Secular Society* (1966), his *Patterns of Sectarianism* (edited 1967) and in David Martin's *Pacifism* (1965).

One factor in the very recent resurgence of interest in religion in Britain centres on the principal churches; for since the war, when a number of moral and social topics came up for discussion, the churches have been repeatedly referred to. Thus in the discussions on homosexuality, leading to the Wolfenden Report, the Church of England played a major part, but so also did other denominations. Also it has been the case in discussions on abortion and prostitution, and latterly on divorce. The part played by the churches in Britain has been underestimated, but its growing recognition is leading to a reappraisal by sociologists.

In France many descriptive studies have been carried out to provide an estimate of church attendance and the attitudes of the faithful. G. Le Bras[5] has written about religion in rural areas, E. G. Leonard[6] has examined French Protestantism, and S. R. Schram[7] its relationship to politics, but the major sociological product is *Premiers Itinéraires en Sociologie Religieuse* by F.

[1] H. H. Stroup, *The Jehovah's Witnesses* (1945).
[2] H. B. Hawthorn, *The Doukhobors of British Columbia* (1955).
[3] G. F. Hershberger, *The Mennonite Church in the Second World War* (1951).
[4] T. O'Dea, "Mormonism and the Avoidance of Sectarian stagnation: A Study of Church Sect, and Incipient Nationality", *American Journal of Sociology*, Vol. 60, 1954, and *The Mormons* (1957).
[5] "Description de la France catholique", *Nouvelle Revue Théologique*, Vol. 70, 1948.
[6] *Le protestant français* (1953).
[7] *Protestantism and Politics in France* (1952).

Boulard (translated *An Introduction to Religious Sociology*, 1960), a book which comes as a consolidating measure following other studies such as those of Abbé Michonneau,[1] M. R. Loew,[2] and some of Boulard's earlier work.[3] This work is oriented entirely to missionary enterprise by the Roman Catholic Church; perhaps it is for this reason that the work has been largely ignored in America and Britain. Yet it must not be supposed that being evangelistic in aim it is not sociological in content. Boulard's main achievement is twofold. He has constructed what he calls a religion map to show the character of religious practice as it was in 1954. This map compares regular conformity and seasonal conformity; it shows which areas provide recruits for the priesthood, and it considers the spiritual state of a diocese now in relation to the attitudes held by the clergy and people during the Revolution. In short, it is an attempt to discern correlations and to arrive at an understanding of significant relationships. Secondly, Boulard elaborates a concept of natural areas and groupings. His view is best expressed in his own words:

> Take, for example, the Etang de Berre in the diocese of Aix-en-Provence, formerly used by a few fishermen. After the First World War the Etang became an extension of Marseilles. The Shell Petroleum Company built refineries on its shores, while an aircraft factory and Marseilles airport found suitable sites for expansion. An international proletariat came to look for work. Today men of all races, languages and religions are mixed up together. It is clear that all this has combined to produce a special area of its own, which is no longer like the neighbouring Aix country.
>
> Of course there are still marked differences between smaller districts but they are still absorbed in the general tonality of the natural grouping. This profoundly modifies mentality; it has a gradual effect upon religious practice; it may, as at the Etang de Berre, alter the population structure. The cinema, the press and working class movements may take on a special colouring in a natural grouping. A natural grouping develops a characteristic social life, and it is here the Gospel must take root.[4]

Quite obviously Boulard, who is a priest and canon of the Church, has his eye on the nature of church organisation relevant to such

[1] *La Paroisse: Communauté Missionaire?* (1946), trans. *Revolution in a City Parish* (1949).
[2] *En Mission Prolétarienne* (1944), trans. *Mission to the Poorest* (1950).
[3] *Problèmes missionaires de la France rurale* (2 vols. 1945). [4] *Op. cit.*, p. 94.

natural groupings, but whatever his ultimate aims, the method of description and analysis is thoroughly sociological and there are many substantive by-products of his labours which are of general interest, not the least interesting being the comments he has to make about method and technique in researches in the sociology of religion; moreover, the scale on which he has operated, assisted by the disciplined help of a priesthood under authority, is impressive. This aspect of sociology in France is well advanced.

It remains briefly to mention one or two other studies of quality. W. Herberg's *Catholic, Protestant and Jew* (1955) attempts, on a Durkheimian basis, to relate religious observance by the three religious groups in America to their experienced need for identification. A book by N. J. Demerath entitled *Social Class in American Protestantism* (1955) is an attempt to relate, after Weber, the social background of Protestants to particular denominational or sectarian allegiances. A similar work has been carried out in a French parish by Émile Pin, *Pratiques Religieuses et Classes Sociales* (1956). Also in the same category one by G. Lenski, *The Religious Factor* (1961). Finally, a major contribution to macrosociology must be cited. This is Werner Stark's three volume work *The Sociology of Religion: A Study of Christendom* (1966–7) a work that is historical sociology on the grand scale, which endeavours to describe the social forms of the Christian religion in their various manifestations. It is a study of ideological roots, it makes use of some interesting concepts for the comparative study of religious forms, and it speaks to many of the religious and political problems of our times; it bids fair to being one of the major achievements in the sociology of religion. This is a field of research which seldom attracts funds. That it has continued despite a generally antipathetic climate and lack of resources shows the recurrent interest of sociologists in an aspect of their subject which deserves serious attention.

The Institutions of Law and Education

Sociologists have always been interested in the means of social control, which includes law in addition to religion, education, and the means of forming public opinion, as well as being interested in the process of socialisation, which means chiefly being concerned with education in its various forms. The classical writers, Montesquieu, Durkheim and Weber, all wrote on both law and education. Today separate specialisms have been formed for these several pursuits.

In many ways, it has to be admitted, sociologists are not today as well aware as they were of the importance of legal institutions. Certainly, we do not find anyone of the calibre of Sir Henry Maine or Roscoe Pound writing today. Indeed, the development of a sociology of law was left mostly to the Germans, and it has suffered as a result of the decline of the universities in that country since 1933. The academic tradition, which is associated with the names of Georg Jellinek[1] and Rudolf Stammler,[2] and later of Barna Horváth[3] and P. W. Jerusalem,[4] together with the works of Maine and Vinogradoff in Britain, helped to form a literature of some significance. In more recent years, of the many writers on the subject only one name stands out in this tradition, that of Eugen Ehrlich, whose principal work *Grundlegung der Soziologie des Rechts*, published in 1913, has been translated as *Fundamental Principles of the Sociology of Law* (1936). This work essentially tries to relate the law as a body of norms to the groups and associations which make up society; the law of the land for him was but a higher order of law and was related to a governing group, but there are other laws relating to other groups, and social control in society depends on these bodies of law as well. In this view he was accompanied by others. Thus later the Russian emigrés, Georges Gurvitch and Nicholas Timasheff, both wrote on the subject; the former contributed greatly to the continuance of the study of the sociology of law in France. Karl Renner, the former Austrian President, wrote from a different angle and provided a Marxist treatment of the subject. But all this was pre-war. Since then the relevant part of Weber's work has been translated into English and so has Renner's.[5] Post-war writings

[1] *Die sozialethische Bedeutung von Recht, Unrecht, und Strafe* (1878).
[2] *Wirtschaft und Recht* (1895).
[3] *Rechtssoziologie* (1934).
[4] *Soziologie des Rechts* (1925).
[5] *The Institutions of Private Law and their Social Functions* (1949), edited by O. Kahn-Freund.

have been spasmodic and various in content. Two works of W. Friedmann[1] provide descriptions of how the law in Britain has changed with changing circumstances, and the growth of administrative law is especially noted. John N. Hazard[2] has done much the same for the Soviet Union. In the U.S.A. a strong interest in jurisprudence has led to discussion on the borders of law and sociology, and it may be suggested that the more active role of the Supreme Court in that country in the legislative process, especially with regard to outstanding social problems like segregation, will give rise to much more interest in the sociology of law.

In the general field of the relationship of law and society much of the work has been carried out by jurists who have drawn on sociological insights to illustrate some particular points in comparative legal studies. It is doubtful if the trained sociologist without a legal education can in fact contribute much at this level. This appears to be the conclusion to be drawn from the thoughtful essay written by Philip Selznick.[3] On the other hand there is room for collaboration, as is seen in the attention given by lawyers and sociologists to legal organisations. In this connection a recent and useful work is *Society and the Law: New Meanings for an Old Profession* (1962) edited by F. J. Davis and others.

Two further aspects of the subject may be mentioned. One lies in the field of international law, where there is a task of locating the sources of power and of discerning the political forces which have led to developments in international law. In this field Charles de Visscher has written an influential book entitled *Théories et Réalités en Droit International Public* (3rd edn. 1960) and W. G. Friedmann one entitled *Law in a Changing Society* (1959). The other aspect of the subject is quite different and relates to the interest taken by some social anthropologists in the legal institutions of primitive people. Outstanding in this field is the work of Max Gluckman, South African born lawyer and anthropologist, who has written *The Judicial Process among*

[1] *Law and Social Change in Contemporary Britain* (1951), *Law in a Changing Society* (1959).

[2] *Law and Social Change in the U.S.S.R.* (1953).

[3] "The Sociology of Law", *Sociology Today* (1959) eds. R. K. Merton, L. Broom and L. S. Cottrell.

the Barotse (1955) and *Politics, Law and Ritual in Tribal Society* (1965), but reference should also be made to E. A. Hoebel's *The Law of Primitive Man* (1954). Of course, some sociological writings on social control and disorder and on organisations connected with control, such as the police, may be said to have some bearing on the sociology of law, but to place them under the same rubric is stretching the meaning of the term too far.

The sociology of education is a topic which has come to the fore greatly since the war. The reasons for this are not always very clear. In Britain there has been an official sponsorship of research in this field related to the great expansion in secondary and higher education since 1944, but it is not quite clear as to why there should be such a vogue for it in America. Perhaps it may be seen in relation to teacher training, for the part played by psychology after the First World War in shaping education policy and pedagogical techniques seems to have been augmented, indeed partly replaced, by sociological studies of the class-room, the school in the community and the values and aims of educators in relation to social aspirations. Egalitarianism is rife, and education is seen to be the linch-pin of policies designed to promote it. This is certainly the case in Britain where the first shots were fired by a small book[1] reporting on educational opportunity and relating it, or the lack of it, to social class. In a book published in 1959, Neal Gross[2] laments that so few good sociologists choose to research in this field, but he admits there is a large literature of somewhat dubious value passing under this title, and he suggests that the two are not unrelated. But since then American sociologists have produced some very interesting work. Thus James Coleman's *The Adolescent Society* (1961) has shed new light on the values of American teenagers, and Talcott Parsons has examined the socialisation process in terms of a theory of action and pointed also to the nature of the teaching process, seeing it as selective as well as socialising.[3] Thus much of the recent work in this field is related to matters broader than the task of instruction. A very

[1] J. E. Floud, A. H. Halsey and F. M. Martin, *Social Class and Educational Opportunity* (1956).

[2] "Sociology of Education" in R. K. Merton *et al.* (1959) *op. cit.*

[3] *Op. cit.* (1955) and "The School Class as a Social System", *Harvard International Review*, Vol. 29, 1959.

great deal of the research recently carried out, or in progress, is about the connection between education and social class or ethnic background. For this reason the sociology of education is being brought into the mainstream of sociological thought and investigation in both Britain and America. But the focus of interest is far removed from that of Durkheim. It is not what is taught or done in schools that is primary in this interest so much as who is educated and to what level. It is not a case of discovering what system will select equitably and efficiently, or what kind of syllabus will meet the requirements of society for occupational provision, but how best may egalitarianism be advanced; at least this seems to be the case in Britain. It may be suggested that when the present fashion changes, sociologists may be more willing to study the relationship of education to other institutions such as religion and the family with more interest in the types of values that are inculcated, and that consideration will be given to the demands of the economy for a supply of labour of different qualities and capabilities; but for the present it is mostly the class background of the child or the organisation of the school that claims the sociologist's attention. This may be seen in a number of recent works, among the best being *Education, Economy and Society* (1961) edited by A. H. Halsey, J. Floud and C. A. Anderson.

Urban Sociology

The study of American cities has never ceased to fascinate sociologists in that country, especially since the rise of the Chicago School under Park and Burgess, but the great monographs of the two Weber's are a convenient point of departure in a short description of the way urban sociology has grown. Max Weber's classic *The City* (trans. 1960) was part of his great work on economy and society and we have already referred to it in Chapter VII. Adna F. Weber's *The Growth of Cities in the Nineteenth Century* (1899, reprinted 1963) represents one of the earliest and best of the contributions to urban history. Both books are careful and scholarly works in the comparative tradition; moreover, they are urbane works, catholic in outlook and interest. Few of the many recent contributions to urban sociology can be so described. Of the many studies carried out by American scholars few have any reference to cities outside the U.S.A., and, indeed, some theoretical contributions appear to be based almost entirely on studies of American cities alone. It is not difficult to see why there has been this parochial tendency, for many of the social problems of the U.S.A. are connected closely with the great metropolitan areas, and the Chicago School grew up on the basis that its members would have something to contribute of use, something relevant to the dominant concerns of those times, such as unemployment, internal migration, immigration and ethnic group adjustment, crime and especially gang warfare; all these clearly conditioned the nature of the Chicago outlook. The main approaches to the subject in the inter-war period were the descriptive tradition of Park's students, the ecological approach of Burgess and others, and the natural environmental outlook of Lewis Mumford as seen in his book *The Culture of Cities* (1938) and his other works. The post-war period has been one in which many have been influenced by the ecological approach, but there has also been a general awareness that what was being studied was not so much a physical structure, within which people live, so much as a way of life. *Urbanisation* has come to be a word that represents the changes taking place in social organisation and outlook not only by those living in cities but even rural denizens, for the way life is altering is producing more and more homogeneity in modern society. This view, which owes much to European writers like Simmel, Durkheim and Tönnies, was developed in the U.S.A. by Louis Wirth,[1] who was impressed by the process of secularisation, the segmentation of roles and the growth of associations rather than community. This outlook has been very influential in American sociology and the term *urbanism* occurs in the titles of many articles in the journals. The outcome of this has been to direct the attention of some sociologists away from the physical structures of town and city toward an analysis of modern culture, and toward the social psychology of modern man, whilst others who adhere rather more closely to the original notion of urbanisation have leaned heavily on demographic studies and some of those who have followed this

[1] "Urbanism as a Way of Life", *American Journal of Sociology,* Vol. 44, 1938.

course have developed the analysis of census tracts for metropolitan areas.

Thus a great many American sociologists are moving away from the study of cities as such, although a mass of data is available for cities all over the world. In Europe there have been a number of valuable studies: H. Pirenne's *Medieval Cities* (trans. 1925), and R. E. Dickinson's *The West European City* (1951) are just two such works, more historical and geographical respectively perhaps than sociological, but none the less useful sources for sociologists. Having said this, however, we should note that there is a growing awareness of the importance of making comparative studies and on this topic an essay by Gideon Sjoberg is instructive.[1]

In Britain, very little study has been made of cities as such, although Ruth Glass edited a book relevant to the upsurge of interest in town planning immediately after the war.[2] Much of the work has been in the microsociological tradition and centres on small scale studies of neighbourhoods, and this we shall refer to in the next chapter. In Germany there were similar small scale studies, but also some larger ones; especially noteworthy is the Darmstadt Social Survey. In France too there have been studies, more of areas than of cities, statistical, demographic, but with some sociological observations. A number of books have been published in America containing sometimes lengthy articles on various aspects of urban sociology. One of the best is *The Study of Urbanization* (1965) edited by P. M. Hauser and L. F. Schnore, which contains several interesting articles, including two by Sjoberg. Another, which aims to assess the work that has flowed from the Chicago School, is edited by E. W. Burgess and D. J. Bogue entitled *Contributions to Urban Sociology* (1964).

An important development in urban sociology is what has come to be known as *social area analysis*. It may be said to have begun with a study by E. Shevsky and M. Williams in the late 1940s in Los Angeles.[3] It both arose out of, and made use of, detailed ecological maps of a number of cities (Columbus, Chicago, St Louis,

[1] "Comparative Urban Sociology" in R. K. Merton *et al., op. cit.*

[2] *Social Background of a Plan. A Study of Middlesborough* (1948).

[3] *The Social Areas of Los Angeles: Analysis and Typology* (1949).

Minneapolis, St Paul and Seattle), and work done by McKenzie and others at Chicago. This study in Los Angeles proceeded on the assumption that urban phenomena are regional manifestations of changes in a total society and that the facts of economic differentiation, of status and power have a significance transcending in importance that of the relationships occurring within the boundaries of the local community.

In their book *Social Area Analysis: Theory, Illustrative Application and Computational Procedures* (1955) Eshref Shevsky and Wendell Bell say that the urban typology of the social area analysis of Los Angeles is "a classificatory schema designed to categorise census tract populations in terms of three basic factors —social rank, urbanisation and segregation. Each census tract population was given three scores, one for each of the indexes of the factors; and then the tract populations with similar configurations of scores on the three indexes were grouped together into larger units called social areas." And they go on to say: "We conceive of the city as a product of the complex whole of modern society; thus the social forms of urban life are to be understood within the context of the changing character of the larger containing society".[1] The method employed is the categorisation and statistical analysis of large quantities of data, and the consideration of a large number of variables suitably weighted. Among these factors are the changing distribution of skills, changes in the arrangements of occupations and the consequences for social ranking, the analysis of family patterns, the changing composition of the population, its distribution and how far it is given to being segregated or isolated with consequences for ethnic status, and so forth. In their concluding statements the authors make powerful claims. Let them speak in their own words:

> . . . . the formulation of social trends in relation to current differentiating factors, including the typology based on these factors, in its present form has sufficient coherence, internal consistency, and specificity for us to make these further claims for it: (a) it is simple in statement, (b) it serves as an organising principle, (c) it is theory-linked; it permits the derivation of testable propositions, (d) it is precise in its specifications: it permits

[1] *Op. cit.*, p. 3.

observer agreement, (e) it represents a continuity with similar formulations which it aims to replace.[1]

The Mass Society

Before leaving the subject of macrosociology it is necessary to refer to the more recent attempts of social scientists to analyse the nature of modern urban and industrial culture. This usually entails making an appeal to ideas culled from the social psychologists. Notable among such attempts is that of David Riesman and his colleagues, who in 1950 published what became a widely read book, *The Lonely Crowd*, whose sub-title is *A Study of the Changing American Character*. Riesman determines a number of character types, the *tradition-directed*, the *inner-directed* and the *other-directed*. The first of these is typical of a custom-oriented society which demands conformity, the second is governed by drives implanted in childhood which remorselessly carry him towards predestined goals, whilst the behaviour of the third type is manipulated by other people through words and images. Riesman argues that these are all found in society today but that the proportions shift and so does the influence of any one type in response to various social and cultural changes inherent in the growth of a capitalist economy, the greater extension of urbanisation and even various kinds of demographic trends.

The concept of *Mass Society* is a recent one and it may be said to have been inspired, if not guided, by Riesman's work. Some would say that Riesman is not really writing sociology, that his work is impressionistic and suggestive rather than scientific, and that it belongs more with good journalism or even with popular books like Vance Packard's *The Status Seekers* (1959). But there are sociologists, mainly with a strong political interest, who aim to describe and analyse the nature of modern movements, especially political ones, who endeavour to show how public opinion is formed, and who wish to discern the structural factors giving rise to mass feelings. They are, indeed, like Riesman, serious critics of modern culture. Sometimes the literature which is produced stems from the work of social psychologists like Adorno and others on author-

[1] *Ibid.*, p. 59.

itarian attitudes, sometimes it is a consideration of the mass media of communication and its effects on attitude formation, sometimes it is an analysis of specific social movements. A good review of this field is to be found in *Collective Behaviour* (1957) by R. H. Turner and L. M. Killian. Much of this work lies in the field of social psychology and consequently will not be treated here, but it is a field which borders on both sociology and political science.

Writers on mass society are often concerned about the relationship of the individual to his society, the degree of freedom an individual enjoys in modern urban industrial society, how the individual perceives his social environment and how he evaluates it. Broadly speaking, there are two diametrically opposed views. One regards the development of human dignity, and points to evidence of increasing conformity, mediocrity, disillusionment and alienation. The other view denies there is a loss of liberties and stresses the advantages accruing from a weakening of traditional features holding up new developments, and points to a broad and fundamental consensus that contributes to solidarity. There is agreement that on the whole mass society relies on ideological movements, that such movements produce more or less creative and culture-sustaining élites, and that through these élites *mass man*, although unqualified in many respects, is able to participate in important decision-making processes, either by means of party machines, or simply through plebiscites and referenda. Kornhauser, who is prominent in this kind of sociological investigation, has been interested to describe and analyse the role of mediating institutions.[1] This work is very much an American product as may be seen from a perusal of the essays edited by P. Olsen in *America as a Mass Society* (1963).

[1] *Op. cit.*

CHAPTER XVII

MICROSOCIOLOGY

The distinction drawn between macro- and micro-sociology, a distinction made popular by Georges Gurvitch,[1] is not a very clear-cut one. Nevertheless it is convenient to divide the subject up into studies of total societies and major institutional complexes on the one hand, and studies which are concerned with limited, small-scale, aspects of social life on the other. If we are to seek a theoretical justification for the distinction it may perhaps be found in the nature of the units which make up social systems. Thus at a fairly abstract level some sociologists study normative orders, complexes of which constitute a total social system or society, whilst others are more interested in particular norms as they bear upon human interaction either in face-to-face relationships or in those which are proximate to them. Hence it is possible to distinguish between social institutions on the one hand and social organisations and social groups on the other. Herein lies our division of the subject of sociology, capable of being discussed at *macro-* and *micro*-levels. In this chapter we shall be surveying the development of studies of social organisation and small groups, but we shall also look briefly at the work of sociologists who have investigated small communities. To look at it another way, we might say that we shall be concentrating on social groups, i.e. groups of persons, and on groupings of such groups, whether they are found in business, government, school, church, or community.

Formal organisation

When we speak of an organisation we are referring to some arrangement of people where there is a purposive design, the arrangement being the result of specific aims of specific people, of *Gesellschaft* rather than *Gemeinschaft*, to use Tönnies' distinction, or association rather than community. Modern society has

[1] *Traité de sociologie* (1958) Ch. 2.

developed largely in terms of the growth of such associations, or what P. Blau and W. R. Scott call formal organisation.[1] The subject is of interest to various kinds of people besides sociologists. Thus some people specialise in the study of administration, others approach it from the angle of the political scientist, others as applied economists or business consultants. Here we shall limit ourselves to a reference to sociological research and discussion, otherwise we would soon find ourselves discussing the gamut of matters that is included under the rubric *industrial relations* and this is not intended.[2] The sociological approach to the study of organisation may be said to stem mainly from the work of Max Weber, but it is referred to implicitly by Karl Marx,[3] who of course was interested in the business enterprise as well as the political party. But Weber perceived administrative organisation to be the key to an understanding of the nature of modern society. His treatment of the subject was very general. He was concerned to elaborate an *ideal type* of bureaucracy resting on rational legal legitimacy for its authoritative basis.[4] Much of the analysis of modern forms of administration has been modelled on Weber's classic article.[5] Weber specified the characteristics of bureaucratic administration to be a division of labour with regard to positions which form a hierarchy, a set of norms governing the behaviour of the incumbents of those positions, norms providing for the application of general rules to particular cases, norms which provide for uniformity and continuity of operation, a state of impersonality in official relationships between people in the organisation and between members and others outside it, in so far as those outside it are related to the organisation for some purpose, and the members of the administrative organisation to pursue careers, with specified terms of tenure of employment and remuneration, their appointment and promotion to be on the basis of their possession of technical qualifications. It was Weber's view that this

[1] *Formal Organisations: A Comparative Approach* (1963).

[2] For a popular introduction to this subject see R. F. Tredgold, *Human Relations in Modern Industry* (1963).

[3] *Capital* (trans. 1930 from the 4th German edition published in 1890), Ch. 13 "Machinery and large-scale Industry".

[4] See Ch. VII.

[5] "Bureaucracy" *From Max Weber: Essays in Sociology* (trans. by H. Gerth and C. W. Mills, 1947).

type of organisation was the most efficient. Indeed, in the opinion of Blau and Scott it is a matter of criticism that Weber is somewhat ambivalent about bureaucratic administration, defining it sometimes in terms of efficiency of operation, at other times in terms of authority of a rational legal nature, with the drawback, as they point out, that he fails to mention the disadvantages that may be present in such an administrative organisation, the *dysfunctions*, the factors which detract from efficiency as a result of the authority structure, and also that he does not draw attention to informal relationships, which abound in concrete instances of organisation everywhere and which bear both upon efficiency and the absence of it.[1]

Other writers have preferred different approaches to the study of administrative organisation. Some have been guided less by formal sociological considerations than by experience and reflection. Such is the case with Mary Parker Follett (1868–1933) who achieved a high reputation in America for writing about administrative matters. Her collected papers, published posthumously as *Dynamic Administration* (1941), contain many insights into organisational processes. A similar case is C. I. Barnard (1886–1961), an American businessman who reflected deeply on his experience but also read widely in sociology, whose famous book, *The Functions of the Executive* (1948), has been influential among sociologists as well as businessmen. In this, and a number of his papers, he provided a different way of looking at the formal organisation. Barnard considered that the basis of interaction is co-operation. To get things done people combine to pursue their common aims. Hence an organisation is a system of consciously co-ordinated activities of a plurality of persons. This depends for its success chiefly on the nature of the system of communication between people, and hence he saw organisation mainly as a system of communication channels and the status system as part of it. In order for people to co-operate they must be rewarded, not only in sharing the common purpose and achieving it, but each must be rewarded individually and so satisfactions have to be built into the system; the status system, therefore, is part of this.[2]

[1] See Ch. VII.
[2] "Functions and Pathology of Status Systems in Formal Organisations" *Industry and Society* (ed. W. F. Whyte, 1946).

H. A. Simon is another writer on the subject.[1] For him, administration is a matter of making decisions; accordingly in analysing such processes he discerned three stages: firstly, there are the occasions calling for decisions and this is a matter of obtaining information relevant to the purpose of the organisation and using it; secondly, there is a process of inventiveness, of developing and analysing different possible courses of action; and thirdly, there is the selection of a course of action. The stages are, therefore, those of intelligence (in the military sense), design and choice. Each of these stages may be broken down; their sequence may not in fact be simple. He analysed what he called programmed and non-programmed decisions. Here he pointed to the differences between routine decision-making and decision-making which depends upon human judgement. He argued that the latter kind is increasingly susceptible to modern techniques like operational research, electronic data-processing, and computer simulation.[2]

Yet another American contributor is Talcott Parsons, whose general theoretical work in sociology lends itself to the study of organisations. Parsons has provided a framework for studying social systems of all kinds; that is to say his framework is relevant to a consideration of any system of relationships designed to enable a number of people to attain a common end. For such a system to exist and persist it must solve a number of problems; these are the well-known functional prerequisites: the first is *adaptation*, i.e. the social system must exist in an environment and that means coming to terms with it by altering its own structure as well as the environment; the second is *goal-achievement*, i.e. there must be a formulation of its goals and decisions about how to achieve them; the third is *integration*, which implies establishing the pattern of relationships between the members of the organisation such that collaboration will ensue to achieve the ends prescribed; and the fourth, *pattern maintenance*, which means that there has to be a means of enabling the motivation of members to persist over time, and indeed not merely the motivation of members but also other

[1] *Administrative Behaviour, a study of decision-making processes in administrative organisation* (1951).

[2] *The New Science of Managerial Decision* (1960).

features of the social life of the members as they have developed collectively.[1] These are basic problems, common to all organisations but the means of meeting them will vary according to the aims of the organisation and of other considerations which thus render organisations different in type.

A different kind of theoretical development, stemming originally from the writings of Simmel and latterly from the ideas of G. C. Homans expressed in his book *Social Behaviour: Its Elementary Forms* (1961), is elaborated by P. M. Blau in his *Exchange and Power in Social Life* (1964). Homans in this later work of his has tried to establish the principles of inter-personal processes. Blau, however, has endeavoured to derive from such simpler processes the principles of social processes of a higher order, namely those which obtain in social organisations and in the more intricate institutionalised relationships of, say, a professional nature; or in other words his is a study of the principles of social structures. In his analysis exchange is a fundamental category, for he argues that a service done by one person to another gives rise to gratitude, which is expressed in some reciprocal service. In this process a bond is established between the parties. Social exchange can, he says, be considered to underlie the relations between groups as well as between individuals. His analysis goes beyond what might be strictly called an economic analysis, for there are unspecified obligations and social life depends upon trust. If such reciprocated exchanges create and maintain ties between people, imbalances in exchange create status and power differences. Blau also discusses the nature of opposition and more particularly he points to the interaction of social groupings, less in terms of adjusted equilibrium states than in terms of periodic reorganisations that display dialectical features.

The problems of administrators have led to a widespread interest in sociology in the hope that in this social science they may obtain assistance. The sociology of organisation has thus come to be a popular branch of the subject, capable of drawing research funds. Nowhere is it more advanced than in the U.S.A., where the sociological contributions to the study of administration and

[1] *The Social System* (1952) and Parsons and Shils (1951), *op. cit.*

management have grown exceedingly during the past two decades, but there have been notable contributions in Britain, France and Germany. The literature is vast and varied. It is a mixture of the prejudices and reflections of practitioners based on their experience, of studies by psychologists and especially social psychologists, and also those of sociologists. An early collection of articles, much used by sociologists, is *Reader in Bureaucracy* (1952) edited by R. K. Merton *et al.* The relevant U.N.E.S.C.O. Trend Report (1958) has an article by S. N. Eisenstadt, and Blau and Scott have a good bibliography at the end of their book.[1] U.N.E.S.C.O. has also published a collection of articles on the social aspects and implications of technical and economic change which has much that bears on organisation in its wider meaning,[2] whilst A. Etzioni has edited a collection of articles on complex types of organisation;[3] a useful collection of articles is to be found in the large work edited by J. G. Marsh, *Handbook of Organisations* (1965).

Connected with the study of social organisation is the investigation into occupations, including professional associations and trade unions. This entails a study of both the roles that people play, and the norms that govern and in fact define the roles. Much of this work is purely descriptive, covering the nature of the work, the remuneration received for it, the patterns of recruitment and training, including career patterns, and so forth. But some studies analyse the nature of role conflict, the relationship between occupation and personality traits, the distribution of power and prestige in an occupation and the general body of norms connected with it. To mention a few British studies, David Lockwood has written about clerical workers,[4] Asher Tropp about schoolteachers,[5] and K. Prandy about scientists and engineers.[6] In the U.S.A. there have been a number of studies centring on particular problem areas in certain occupations. Thus W. Kornhauser and W. D. Hagstrom have discussed the difficulties of scientists in

[1] *Op. cit.*
[2] B. F. Hoselitz and W. E. Moore (eds.), *Industrialisation and Society* (1963).
[3] *Complex Organisations: A Sociological Reader* (1961).
[4] *The Blackcoated Worker: A Study in Class Consciousness* (1958).
[5] *The School Teachers* (1957).
[6] *Professional Employee: A Study of Scientists and Engineers* (1965).

industry,[1] R. Blauner[2] has examined the worker in industry and his attitudes, whilst in France and Belgium many have written about the attitude of the worker to technical change,[3] a theme which is much in evidence in recent studies both in Europe and America. Georges Friedmann has written extensively on the subject of occupations, and among his works his *Le Travail en Miettes* (1956) has been translated into English.[4] There is an extensive literature developing in Germany, for example several items are to be found among the publications of the Frankfurt Institute's *Beiträge zur Soziologie* and a number of books have been published since the war on various aspects of industrial sociology, notable among them being those by H. Schelsky,[5] and R. Dahrendorf.[6] Generally good surveys of this field may be obtained from *Work and Society* (1958) by E. Gross and *The Sociology of Work* (1954) by T. Caplow.

The development of this subject seems to be moving in the direction of improving the explanatory models used, and especially the introduction of mathematical models.[7] Meanwhile, although it remains to be seen first how successful this approach will be, it seems likely that sociologists will want to continue to test Weberian ideas or those arising from the tradition he inaugurated. Lastly, there is likely to be a continuation of the work on professional roles and associations, and especially the role of the professional in industry and government, where obvious areas of conflict of interest exist, but where the problem grows with the more widespread use of professional people. In any case the changes in industrial organisation particularly those arising from technical innovations will necessitate changes in occupational roles, so that it is likely to be a continuing concern of the sociologist to examine and comment on the implications for status, well being, and efficiency. This reference to roles should make us pause to consider the valuable contribution which role theory has made to general sociological studies.

[1] *Scientists in Industry* (1962).
[2] *Alienation and Freedom: The Manual Worker in Industry* (1964).
[3] See publications of the Institut de Sociologie Solvay.
[4] *The Anatomy of Work* (1961).
[5] *Ausgaben und Grenzen der Betriebssoziologie* (1954).
[6] *Industrie und Betriebssoziologie* (1956).
[7] See H. A. Simon, *Models of Man, Social and Rational* (1957).

Role Theory

The growth of role theory has proved to be a prominent feature in the development of sociology. Its advance has been favoured because it is an orientation which both sociologists and social psychologists may share. It is an attempt to provide a conceptual framework suitable for the discussion of personal interaction in organisations and in institutionalised relationships, such as professional, familial and class-room relationships.

The formal use of role theory is relatively recent in origin. In 1933 Katherine Lumpkin wrote a book entitled *The Family: a study of Member Roles*, whilst a year later G. H. Mead, the outstanding American social psychologist and historian of ideas, wrote his famous work, *Mind, Self and Society*, in which the task of explaining just how man becomes human is attempted. It is interesting to note that Mead found it necessary to make use of the concept of *self* and to argue that the self is a product of communication, that is an aspect of interaction. His argument, that man becomes a self in the process of role taking, of taking the role of the other in an interaction situation, is now well known; this is one intellectual line of development of role theory. It contributed to the general development of what is now known as symbolic interaction theory, as exemplified by E. Goffman's popular book *The Presentation of the Self in Everyday Life* (1959), and in the collection of essays edited by A. M. Rose as *Human Behavior and Social Processes: An Interactionist Approach* (1962). Another line of development, pointed out by M. Banton in his book *Roles: an Introduction to the Study of Social Relations* (1965), is derived from social anthropology. This may be seen, for instance, in the work of Ralph Linton, whose textbook *The Study of Man* (1936) enjoyed a great vogue just before and just after the war. Linton was less interested to say something about inter-personal relationships than he was to discuss the relationship between person and culture, with the implication that there is consensus regarding the expected patterns of conduct in any one society.

The development of role theory since the war has been considerable. It has mainly been the preserve of social psychologists and sociologists, for the social anthropologists, with the exception of S. F. Nadel[1] and M. Banton,[2] have not taken it up in any noticeable degree. Social psychologists, however, have explored the possibilities through studying role in relation to perception, to behaviour, and to conflict, and, of course, its contribution to the major task of establishing a theory of personality, or of the self. For a full account of this work see the article "Role Theory" by T. R. Sarbin in *Handbook of Social Psychology* (1954) edited by G. Lindzey. Sociologists have contributed to the study of roles by identifying some general features, as may be seen in the use of such terms as *role-set,* which R. K. Merton[3] introduced to discuss the complex of relationships with a plurality of people or groups that a person, such as a school-teacher, may have, all making demands on him, some of which may be incompatible with others. Other concepts such as *role-taking* and *role-standpoint* have been elaborated by R. Turner,[4] whilst *role-handicap* figures in a study of adoptive parenthood by H. D. Kirk,[5] and *role-conflict* in numerous studies, of which a good example is to be found in *Explorations in Role Analysis* (1958) by N. Gross, W. Mason and A. W. McEachern.

Finally, philosophical consideration has been given to this subject. Thus, Dorothy Emmet, who has already contributed to the literature on functional theory, has recently examined problems of concern to both sociologists and moral philosophers. "What people think they ought to do," she says, "depends largely on how they see their roles, and (most importantly) the conflicts between their roles." The concept of role for her is "a bridge notion between myself as an individual, with my proper name and my personal responsibility, and 'my station and its duties' in the institutional world of the society in which I have to live".[6] Role theory in sociology thus touches fundamental theoretical aspects of the subject; it is related to the relationship of personality and culture, it is used in the analysis of institutionalised relationships,

[1] *Social Structure* (1957).

[2] *Roles: An Introduction to the Study of Social Relations* (1965).

[3] "The Role-set: Problems in Sociological Theory", *British Journal of Sociology,* Vol. VIII, 1957.

[4] "Role Talking, Role Standpoint and Reference Group Behaviour", *American Journal of Sociology,* Vol. LXVI, 1956.

[5] *Shared Fate: A Theory of Adoption and Mental Health* (1964).

[6] *Rules, Roles and Relations* (1966), p. 15.

and in interaction systems of an organisational kind, as well as in small groups. For a brief summary see the entry on "Role" by D. J. A. Woodland in *A Dictionary of Sociology* (1968) edited by G. D. Mitchell.

Social Groups in Industry

Many of the investigations connected with industrial relations focus on the small group of people employed on a work bench, or the group of people selected to make up a works council, or a committee of one kind or another. Famous among such studies is the series of investigations called the Hawthorne studies, carried out in the Western Electric Company's plant and recorded by F. J. Roethlisberger and W. J. Dickson.[1] These studies of work groups were briefly described towards the end of Chapter XIII and need not be referred to here further, except to say that they set the stage for many other studies oriented to human relations in industry. They were begun in 1927, but it was not until the late 1930s that further developments occurred. These were largely the result of the work of Kurt Lewin and his collaborators who were interested to compare democratic and authoritarian leadership in groups of boys,[2] but later went on to take up studies, suggested by war-time needs, in the use of small groups for the changing of attitudes. Thus groups of housewives were observed under different conditions designed to encourage them to change the food habits of their families by using offal instead of prime cuts of beef. These studies centred around the comparison of the lecture and the discussion group as vehicles for effecting lasting changes in belief in the desirability of using the substitute foods.[3] Lewin is important, not so much for this kind of study as for his theoretical formulation. He put forward a *field* theory of group behaviour which has been widely used by some investigators to explain the behaviour of people in groups. Thus L. Coch and J. R.

[1] *Management and the Worker* (1939).

[2] K. Lewin, R. Lippitt and R. K. White, "Patterns of Aggressive Behaviour in Experimentally Created 'Social Climates'," *Journal of Social Psychology*, Vol. 10, 1939.

[3] "Forces behind food habits and methods of change", *Bulletin of the National Research Council*, No. 108, 1943.

P. French,[1] in their study of changes in methods of production in a factory making pyjamas, employ the conceptual apparatus of a field of forces in order to compare and contrast the different methods of securing the support of the workers, whose attitudes to their work were proved to be so big a factor in the success or failure of the technical change-over. Essentially, Lewin argued that the behaviour of members of a group can be described in terms of a field, analogous to the magnetic field that the physicist speaks of, where there is a distribution of forces, and where any item of behaviour can be analysed in terms of a balance of such forces, so that the force in the direction of a further item of such behaviour is exactly matched by a force in the opposite direction of equal strength. When behaviour varies from its initial level it moves in a force-field where the forces are unequal and does so in such a way that the stronger force tends to return the behaviour to what it was originally; of course it may not do so if the forces are so distributed that an initial imbalance is created requiring a new equilibrium to be achieved, but this represents a change. It will be seen that with a set of concepts of this kind it is possible to discuss behaviour in groups in terms of group dynamics, equilibrium states, and the like. The kinds of topics which lend themselves to this sort of analysis include discussion of levels of worker productivity, levels of labour turnover, the effects of training and the inputs of managerial skills. Applications of field theory to social situations was the subject of a book by Lewin, entitled *Resolving Social Conflicts* (1948); his premature death prevented the full development of his ideas and their application, but he succeeded in establishing at the Massachusetts Institute of Technology a research group, whose members have since added much to the development of studies in small groups. His Research Center for Group Dynamics has since moved to Ann Arbor, Michigan.

Experimental Group Studies

The literature on small groups is now very great; it is chiefly an American literature. It began during the war years and rapidly

[1] "Overcoming Resistance to Change", *Human Relations*, Vol. 1, No. 1, 1948.

increased. F. L. Strodtbeck[1] claimed that there were 31 publications between 1940 and 1944, that the number had risen to 55 for the five years from 1945 to 1949, and that there were 152 publications between 1950 and 1953. Since then a spate of articles and books has appeared, many items being published in the *Journal of Abnormal and Social Psychology*, as it used to be called, now in the *Journal of Social Psychology*; output of research reports is now running at about 200 per annum. Of these reports, many are studies carried out in laboratory conditions. The studies of Lewin, Lippett and White, referred to above, may be regarded as among the early ones, but by about 1950 a number of American scholars were settling down to carry through programmes of research on experimental groups. Notable among these studies were those on communication.

There are various ways of defining a group. It may be quite concretely defined in terms of the members, but some investigators have found it profitable to see a group as a communication network. This was how H. J. Leavitt[2] perceived his experimental groups, which consisted of several five-member groups with different communication structures: a star shaped one, a 'Y' shaped one, a chain and a circle. To the members he presented a problem involving the assembly of information differentially distributed throughout each group. The expected results, namely that there would be a sequence of achievement in the above order, were confirmed as regards speed of performance. However, Christie and his colleagues decided to replicate the studies,[3] albeit with slight differences, for they changed the tasks, and found that the nature of the task has a bearing on the question of which communication structure is most efficient. Sometimes the star is most efficient, but change the task and it fails compared with the circle. Here we have studies which isolate the variables and display the relationships between them. Given size, and assuming equality of ability among the members of a group, the variation in

[1] "The Case for the Study of Small Groups", *American Sociological Review*, Vol. XIX, No. 6, 1954.

[2] "Some effects of certain communication patterns on group performance", *Journal of Abnormal and Social Psychology*, Vol. 46, 1951.

[3] L. S. Christie, R. B. Luce and J. Macy, "Communication and Learning in Task-oriented Groups", Research Laboratory of Electronics, Technical Report No. 231, Massachusetts Institute of Technology, 1952.

communication structure is seen to account for different degrees of efficiency, but only if task is held constant; change the nature of the task and that too in addition to communication network affects performance. Here was a contribution to the formal analysis of group behaviour. But what is significant in all this, and the reason for selecting these particular experiments for inclusion in this account, is that here we have some cumulative development in sociological studies.

Another similar contribution was that of R. F. Bales who elaborated a method for recording the behaviour of members of a group engaged in performing a task.[1] Bales defined a group as "A number of persons engaged in interaction with one another in a single face-to-face meeting or a series of such meetings, in which each member receives some impression or perception of each other member distinct enough so that he can, either at the time or in later questioning, give some reaction to each of the others as an individual person, even though it be only to recall that the other was present."[2] Every action is treated as an interaction, and for the purpose of recording the behaviour of a group such interactions have to be classified. Bales provided for three major classes of behaviour; two social-emotional areas, one positive and the other negative, and a task area which is neutral. In the positive social-emotional area, he says, a person's behaviour either shows solidarity, or tension release, or agreement. Thus, helpful remarks or compliments show solidarity; criticism would be in the negative social-emotional area. In the neutral task area would be included suggestions, requests for information and so forth. Bales succeeds in isolating twelve categories in all, implying that they are both exhaustive and distinctive, into which items of behaviour may be placed. Later, in conjunction with Talcott Parsons and E. A. Shils,[3] he modified them, but essentially he has urged the use of schedules for recording what happens in groups. In this way he provides not only a means of recording observations, but a set of categories, the interrelationships of which may be the basis for advancing hypotheses which may be verified. Hence, his contribution to small group studies lies in the clear understanding which we obtain

[1] *Interaction Process Analysis* (1950) [2] *Ibid.*, Ch. 2.
[3] *Working Papers in the Theory of Action* (1953).

of the relationships between communication, evaluation, control, decision, tension-reduction and reintegration. All this represents a step towards a general theory of group behaviour.

Among the topics that interest students of small groups is the question of how norms develop in a group, the evolution of likes and dislikes and the part played by sentiment; topics which have been examined by Josephine Klein.[1] Other writers, such as Morton Deutsch, have taken up the subject of the pursuit of goals and the effects of competitive or co-operative processes;[2] these researches are oriented mainly to decision-making studies, and following from them are studies of leadership such as those by Helen Jennings.[3] This last author is particularly noteworthy, for she helped to popularise the method of sociometry, first used by J. Moreno, as a way of establishing the pattern of choices amongst members of a group for social participation; it is now a widely used technique. This was the kind of development that small group studies showed in the decade from 1950 to 1960. It is represented by the collection of articles by D. Cartwright and A. Zander;[4] a review of the work done from the end of the war until 1956 is provided by R. F. Bales *et al.*[5] Perhaps the most influential contribution of this period was that of G. C. Homans, exemplified in his book *The Human Group* (1950), which provided a framework for comparing groups of different kinds within a single conceptual framework. This was an exercise which analysed group behaviour in terms of an *internal* and an *external system*, each consisting of the following elements: actions, interactions and sentiments. The external system is that combination of the elements which solves the problem of adaptation, i.e. survival in an environment; the internal system is that combination of elements which develops over and above the external system, which gives a group its distinctive qualities, and which represents the elaboration of interaction and sentiment to the point where one can say the group has its own culture. In his book, Homans referred to five studies

[1] *The Study of Groups* (1956).

[2] Morton Deutsch, "The Effects of Cooperation and Competition upon Group Process", *Human Relations*, Vol. 2, 1949.

[3] *Leadership and Isolation* (2nd edn. 1950).

[4] *Group Dynamics: Research and Theory* (1953).

[5] "Structure and Dynamics of Small Groups", *Review of Sociology* (edited by J. B. Gittler, 1957).

by other sociologists and anthropologists, including the Hawthorne studies, a study of an island in the Pacific, and a rural community. It is open to question how far such diverse social phenomena can be usefully compared within such a simple framework as he used, but the interesting feature is the attempt to provide such a framework, to do so holistically, and to derive a series of deductive propositions of a general character. The most famous proposition to emerge from the study is that "persons who interact frequently with one another tend to like one another",[1] a proposition which he failed to qualify sufficiently, but which had a bearing on the work of some urban sociologists interested in neighbourhood groups. To this we shall now turn.

Small Community Studies

Small group studies were not responsible for small community studies, but the two did come together about 1950, a notable case being a study of the married students housed on a special estate by the Massachusetts Institute of Technology in Boston.[2] The study of the small community has a long history, and one source lay in the work of the Chicago School, especially as influenced by anthropologists, which led to work on both rural communities and small urban areas, both slum districts and suburbia. The post-war interest in urban and rural planning had a bearing on its development, especially in Britain, and the tasks of reconstruction in Germany stimulated it there as well but, in the main, the study of the small community is a British rather than an American development.

In Britain a variety of small communities were the objects of investigation including some rural parishes in Devon,[3] a Cumberland village[4] and a Welsh one;[5] other enquiries focused on parts of the big cities. The movement took place in circumstances of

[1] *Op. cit.*, p. 111.

[2] L. Festinger, S. Schachter and K. Back, *Social Pressures through Informal Groups* (1950).

[3] G. D. Mitchell, "Social Disintegration in a Rural Community", *Human Relations*, Vol. III, 1950, W. M. Williams, *A West Country Village, Ashworthy: Family, Kinship and Land* (1963).

[4] W. M. Williams, *The Sociology of an English Village: Gosforth* (1956).

[5] R. Frankenberg, *Village on the Border* (1957).

limited research funds which proscribed any large-scale studies, but it also arose out of the renewed interest in observing what people do, how they live, and how they perceive their social environment. Perhaps, in Britain, Mass-Observation had some influence in this direction, but it was also quite markedly an anthropological kind of interest. Not many sociologists were being produced at that time and geographers, social anthropologists and psychologists turned their attention towards the small community. Partly, as we observed in the last chapter, there was a belief that family life might be illuminated by the application of the anthropological interest in kinship, but it was also the holistic treatment of the social anthropologist which provided the attraction. At any rate, studies of housing estates were undertaken at Liverpool and Sheffield,[1] Birmingham and Coventry,[2] Oxford[3] and elsewhere, as well as studies of small towns like that of Banbury.[4] Here was microsociological investigation springing up spontaneously in various places, at first without any connection between the investigators. It represented an attempt to find out how people did live, what were the problems attendant upon urban development and especially the post-war housing estate development. Empirical social science was emphasised and the working class areas in rural and urban settings proved most amenable to investigations of this kind.

On the whole these small community studies emphasised the interaction of neighbours, and it was here that Homans' hypothesis came in for criticism. It was abundantly plain that relationships on new housing estates left much to be desired. The procedure for the selection of people for municipal housing favoured the young couple with several children. Housing estates therefore were noted for high densities of children. As time passed this became more noticeable, for the children grew from infancy to adolescence and in the process aggravated the problems of neighbours, many of whom found themselves in strange surroundings, facing a variety of contrary standards of life, often isolated from kinsfolk, and obliged to spend money on fares for travelling to

[1] G. D. Mitchell *et al.*, *Neighbourhood and Community* (1954).
[2] L. Kuper, *Living in Towns* (1953).
[3] J. Mogey, *Family and Neighbourhood* (1956).
[4] M. Stacey, *Tradition and Change* (1961).

work and to visit kin, to which they were unaccustomed, and in other ways which were novel and contrary to the family tradition in which they were brought up. The confusion of many of these socially and geographically mobile people has been documented in these studies both in Britain and America, for the examination of housing estates was also paralleled by the study carried out by H. H. Kelley in New England.[1] They show how predispositions have a bearing on attitude formation, on the nature of neighbourly relationships, and on the problems of adjustment. In this connection the work of Elizabeth Bott,[2] although on a small scale, is very suggestive of the kinds of factors which have contributed to the varying responses of people to the environment they have found themselves in; environments which were different not only geographically but socially.

One contribution to emerge from this post-war tradition of small community studies was Josephine Klein's two-volume work, *Samples from English Cultures* (1965), one of the most impressive attempts to draw general conclusions from a comparative study of community studies. Klein was keen to compare and contrast some of the different ways of life in England in order to see if there was a pattern (in the sense in which Ruth Benedict used the term), or at least, perhaps, to see if the data that had been assembled in various research reports did fall into place in an orderly fashion. Here is a study, cast in general categories, of the traditional working class pattern of family and neighbourly life, how it changed in the course of urban development and a growing economy, taking on a new shape, and the nature of the middle class culture to which it approximated. In this work she described the changing face of Britain, no longer a simple two-class structured society, but one displaying variety of adaptation. In telling her story, Klein also has much to say (especially in her second volume) of the determinants of personality development; hence, in this work justice is done to both the sociological and psychological aspects of a study of cultures.

An attempt to do something of the same sort, but on the

[1] *Changing Attitudes through Social Contact* (1951).
[2] *Family and Social Network: Roles, Norms and External Relationships in Ordinary Urban Families* (1957).

basis of one urban and one rural study in Australia, had already taken place in 1954, when O. A. Oeser and S. B. Hammond[1] carried out a study in Melbourne, and at this same time Oeser and F. E. Emery[2] did one of a small township in Victoria. These authors were much influenced by Lewin's field theory. Theirs is mainly a study of tensions in a community where there are immigrants. They were interested to see how the personality of people was affected by structural factors in the community. They show reason to believe that all situations which curtail freedom of movement, such as the roles of employee or school-child, give rise to frustrations. They predict from their conceptual scheme the kinds of differences that may exist between rural and urban school-children and then verify their inferences. Like Klein's work, these Australian social scientists have shed light on the culture of a people. Thus, the study of the small community has proved to be not just a series of descriptive studies of varying interest, but a tradition within sociology that has led to some theoretical formulations. In this respect the work has a cumulative quality; in short it has proved an advance in the subject. It has also shown how sociology and social psychology have been brought together. In this respect the study of the small group, the small community and the field theory of personality have coalesced. At the same time, the work of social anthropologists and urban sociologists has converged, for R. Frankenberg has in addition to his study of a Welsh village endeavoured to relate a number of rural and urban studies within a framework of thought of a more general nature, as may be seen in his *Communities in Britain* (1966), whilst P. H. Mann has taken up the theme of neighbourhood studies in his book *An Approach to Urban Sociology* (1965). In short, urban studies in Britain in the microsociological tradition have contributed to the theoretical development of sociology just as the studies of small groups in the U.S.A. have advanced the cause of general sociology.

[1] *Social Structure and Personality in a City* (1954).
[2] *Social Structure and Personality in a Rural Community* (1954).

CHAPTER XVIII

CURRENT TRENDS

In this account of the growth of sociology during the past hundred years little has been said about some subjects which are closely allied to it. Demography, for example, has developed during our period. This has grown very largely *pari passu* with the development of statistical analysis which has itself grown since the founding of the Royal Statistical Society in the 1830s. Malthusian ideas have repeatedly claimed the attention of sociologists. Thus D. V. Glass edited an *Introduction to Malthus* in 1953 and, in the U.S.A., Kingsley Davis has commented on the theory too.[1] Glass has also pursued the subject *via* the Population Investigation Committee, located at the London School of Economics. Such a subject bears directly on sociological investigation and quite clearly it has great application. Moreover, it is interesting to see the increasingly close connection between demography, social history and sociology, as we indicated in Chapter XVI.

Again, we have said little about the application of sociology, and yet this is becoming widespread. The work of Sutherland[2] in the U.S.A. and especially his theory of differential association has helped to advance criminology very greatly. So also has the work of R. K. Merton[3] on the analysis of the relationship between means and goals. Furthermore, there is the study by Cohen[4] of groups of juvenile delinquents, and that of Cloward and Ohlin[5] in the application of microsociological insights to the investigation of this category of deviant behaviour. In Britain, Wilkins[6] also contributed to criminological discussion from a sociological point

[1] *The Population of India and Pakistan* (1951), and *Human Society* (1948), Chaps. 20 and 21.

[2] E. H. Sutherland, *White Collar Crime* (1961) and *Principles of Criminology* (with D. R. Cressey, 6th edn. 1960).

[3] *Social Theory and Social Structure* (1949).

[4] A. K. Cohen, *Delinquent Boys: The Culture of the Gang* (1956).

[5] R. A. Cloward and L. E. Ohlin, *Delinquency and Opportunity, a Theory of delinquent gangs* (1960).

[6] L. T. Wilkins, *Social Deviance: Social Policy, Action and Research* (1964).

of view, whilst Hermann Mannheim[1] has endeavoured to bring together sociological and other approaches to the subject. But to describe this development and also the applications of sociology to other fields, such as that of public and social administration, where the study of social organisations has so much relevance, would be to extend this book to an intolerable length. Similarly, we might have mentioned such applied branches as medical sociology, industrial sociology, and the application of sociology to the study and improvement of the effectiveness of mass media of communication.

With the improvement in techniques of investigation such as questionnaire construction, interviewing and data processing, especially the use of computers, so there has been a growing demand for sociologists in government, industry, market research agencies, and the like. Governments do not hesitate to spend large sums where they believe sociology may help, especially is this so in the U.S.A. The establishment of the Government Social Survey in Britain, the financing of the Institute of Criminology in Cambridge and the research carried out, or sponsored, by Ministries into delinquency, housing, educational provision, and so forth, testifies to the value of applying sociology. This may be expected to grow, and the future is likely to hold much in store for those interested to apply sociology to social problems and to the task of obtaining greater social control in modern large-scale organisations, in public opinion formation and in the processes of attitude change. But, it may well be asked: will this lead to more fundamental contributions to the subject? Will it help sociological research to acquire a cumulative character? One may be forgiven for being pessimistic. Doubtless, there will be a growth in the amount of work done, the degree of influence exerted, and the practitioners of the subject may increase in number, but unless resources are devoted to the study of fundamental problems progress will be slow.

The situation today is that most of the theoretical underpinning of current research has its origins in the work of fifty years ago, largely in the seminal work of Durkheim and Weber. To be sure there have been some remarkable developments since then,

[1] *Comparative Criminology* (1965).

but it is a matter for conjecture as to how far sociologists of tomorrow will be able to produce anything of the same calibre as the giants of yesterday. And this is not a doubt that arises merely because of the current strong desire to apply social science and the vogue of operational research. After all, both Durkheim and Weber had contemporary social problems too which they wanted to resolve. The difficulty we envisage arises from the development of the modern University in Europe and America, where the emphasis is on professional scholarship. By "professional scholarship" we mean the modern academic career pattern, whereby promotion depends upon published research reports. Of course it is necessary to research and to publish, and rightly promotion should *inter alia* depend on success in this respect, but the system at present discourages long term research planning and emphasises individual researches of a highly specialised nature. The University system which allows this, a system based for the most part on a group of scholars with private means that gives them leisure, and which obtained *par excellence* in Imperial Germany, is an institution of the past. Moreover, although secondary schooling has improved it has been extended to more children, it has become standardised and specialised. If today there are attempts to reduce the specialisation there are also tendencies to reduce selectivity and the few very able pupils will have far less opportunity to come into contact with the very good teachers, nor will such teachers have the opportunity to devote a large proportion of their time to the able few. Democratic processes are egalitarian ones, and egalitarian society is not geared to producing excellence. It is doubtful if the modern educational systems of America and Britain, or indeed those of France and Germany, could today produce a Weber, a Hobhouse, or a Sorokin. Therefore, it is unlikely that many will appear capable of carrying on the great tradition of comparative studies, which essentially does depend on a single mind surveying the great mass of data, with insight and industry, with time to engage in the laborious task of sifting, classifying and comparing. For even supposing some great mind and energy is devoted to such a task in congenial circumstances, it is unlikely that there will be academic support for him if his colleagues are working to shorter time schedules. How many

Universities are prepared to deliberately foster such long term scholarship? Our answer cannot be optimistic. Therefore, we may expect to see two kinds of work done: more trivial researches undertaken by candidates for the Ph.D. degree and also some collaborative undertakings, mainly of an applied or policy-oriented nature. What kind of enterprise is group or team research? It is quantifiable, empirical and usually cautious, limited in duration and on the whole it is seldom cumulative but rather inter-disciplinary, broad in scope as various social sciences are brought to bear on a subject, rarely a study in depth, and nearly always practical. These arguments are pessimistic ones. However, let us turn from speculation to examine the discernible current trends in research.

Firstly, there has been a development of urban studies, they have been outlined in Chapter XVI. Planning of cities and the industrial development of new countries will very likely stimulate further research in this field. Educational changes in Britain have fostered sociological enquiry, and more may be expected. Moreover, sociology is now being introduced into colleges of education, it is likely therefore to lead to research oriented to pedagogical purposes. Studies of organisations and of small groups are coming closer together, and there is an immense increase in the resources devoted to this development; it is likely to continue. But if we are to examine some of the very recent trends in research students' interests we may suggest that there is a growing desire to investigate religious and political behaviour. We have referred to this already: it seems to reflect an awakened interest in the sociology of knowledge. Much of the current vogue for Weber's writings lies in this aspect of his work, and it may well be that sociologists will turn to other writers of the past, to the writings of Edward Westermarck, for instance, for *The Origin and Development of Moral Ideas* (1906) may have some leads for the researcher into the relationship of social forms and social ideas and outlook.

Sociology has grown on the back of the natural sciences. Its practitioners call themselves scientists and pay their deep respects to quantification, rigorous use of methodological techniques, propositional statements, use of technical jargon and the like. All these are necessary and the aspiration is to be commended.

But we may hope that the signs of an undue piety in this respect will not become exaggerated. We may hope too that the traditional world of scholarship, from which sociology emerged, will not be without its continuing effect; for sociology is a human study, it has its roots in social events, which are historical events; it depends on selection of subject matter and on guiding passion, and these flow from philosophical concerns. It is not always possible to be exact and much of what is valuable in the tradition has been concerned with phenomena incapable of measurement, but this has not meant that the work has been unscholarly. The warnings of Sorokin[1] about "fads" and "foibles" should be taken seriously, and those of Gurvitch[2] on "quantofrenia" and "testomania" are not frivolous. Piety has much to commend it, but it can be narrow and bigoted in science, and social science no less than in other spheres of life; a catholic outlook in sociology has the possibility to promote sanity, balance and liberality, and it may be added that such a catholicity in outlook will be fostered if sociologists overcome their present national insularity; too frequently there is a failure to discuss what sociologists have written in languages other than their own.

If the sociologist acquires a place in society as prophet and preacher, and it would seem there are some signs of his role being so cast, then it would be well that he should develop the independence and detachment of the scholar, rather than the activism of the administrator, that he find in sociology an intellectual task with its own rewards and its own demands, for his professional role is primarily not that of practitioner, but of observer.

[1] P. A. Sorokin, *Fads and Foibles in Modern Sociology* (1955).
[2] G. Gurvitch, "La crise de l'explication en sociologie", *Cahiers Internationals de Sociologie*, Vol. 21, 1956.

INDEX OF NAMES

Index of Names

Index of Names

Index of Names

Index of Names

INDEX OF CHAPTERS AND SUB-TITLES